THE HOLY EUCHARIST
BY
St. Alphonsus de Liguori

THE HOLY EUCHARIST

Published by Magisterium Press

New York City, NY

First published 1850

Copyright © Magisterium Press, 2015

All rights reserved

Except in the United States of America, this book is sold subject to the condition that it shall not, by way of trade or otherwise, be lent, re-sold, hired out, or otherwise circulated without the publisher's prior consent in any form of binding or cover other than that in which it is published and without a similar condition including this condition being imposed on the subsequent purchaser.

ABOUT MAGISTERIUM PRESS

Magisterium Press is a Catholic publishing house that loves to spread the word and love of Jesus Christ to everyone, Christians and non-Christians alike.

I

The Sacrifices of the Old Law were Figures of the Sacrifice of Jesus Christ

All the sacrifices of the old law were figures of the sacrifice of our divine Redeemer, and there were four kinds of these sacrifices; namely, the sacrifices of peace, of thanksgiving, of expiation, and of impetration.

1. The sacrifices of peace was instituted to render to God the worship of adoration that is due to him as the sovereign master of all things. Of this kind were the holocausts.

2. The sacrifices of thanksgiving were destined to give thanks to the Lord for all his benefits.

3. The sacrifices of expiation were established to obtain the pardon of sin. This kind of sacrifice was specially represented in the Feast of the Expiation by the emissary-goat, which, having been laden with all the sins of the people, was led forth out of the camp of the Hebrews, and afterwards abandoned in the desert to be there devoured by ferocious beasts. This sacrifice was the most expressive figure of the sacrifice of the cross. Jesus Christ was laden with all the sins of men, as Isaias had foretold: The Lord hath laid on him the iniquity of us all? He was afterwards ignominiously led forth from Jerusalem, whither the Apostle invites us to follow him by sharing in his opprobrium: Let us go forth therefore to him without the camp, bearing his reproach. He was abandoned to ferocious beasts; that is to say, to the Gentiles, who crucified him.

4. Finally, the sacrifices of impetration had for their object to obtain from God his aid and his grace.

Now, all these sacrifices were abolished by the coming of the Redeemer, because only the sacrifice of Jesus Christ, which was a perfect sacrifice, while all the ancient sacrifices were imperfect, was sufficient to expiate all the sins, and merit for man every grace. This is the reason why the Son of God on entering the world said to his Father: Sacrifice and oblation Thou wouldst not; but a body Thou hast fitted to me. Holocausts for sin did not please Thee. Then said: Behold, I come; in the head of the book it is written of me, that I should do Thy will, O God? Hence, by offering to God the sacrifice of Jesus Christ we can fulfil all our duties towards his supreme majesty, and provide for all our wants; and by this means we succeed in maintaining a holy intercourse between God and ourselves.

We must also know that the Old Law exacted five conditions in regard to the victims which were to be offered to God so as to be agreeable to him; namely, sanctification, oblation, immolation, consumption, and participation.

1. The victim had to be sanctified, or consecrated to God, so that there might not be offered to him anything that was not holy nor unworthy of his majesty. Hence, the animal destined for sacrifice had to be without stain, without defect; it was not to be blind, lame, weak, nor deformed, according to what was prescribed in the Book of Deuteronomy. This condition indicated that such would be the Lamb of God, the victim promised for the salvation of the

world; that is to say, that he would be holy, and exempt from every defect. We are thereby instructed that our prayers and our other good works are not worthy of being offered to God, or at least can never be fully agreeable to him, if they are in any way defective. Moreover, the animal thus sanctified could no longer be employed for any profane usage, and was regarded as a thing consecrated to God in such a manner that only a priest was permitted to touch it. This shows us how displeasing it is to God if persons consecrated to him busy themselves without real necessity with the things of the world, and thus live in distraction and in neglect of what concerns the glory of God.

2. The victim had to be offered to God; this was done by certain words that the Lord himself had prescribed.

3. It had to be immolated, or put to death; but this immolation was not always brought about by death, properly so called; for the sacrifice of the loaves of proposition, or show-bread, was accomplished, for example, without using iron or fire, but only by means of the natural heat of those who ate of them.

4. The victim had to be consumed. This was done by fire. The sacrifice in which the victim was entirely consumed by fire was called holocaust. The latter was thus entirely annihilated in order to indicate by this destruction the unlimited power that God has over all his creatures, and that as he created them out of nothing, so he can reduce them to the nothingness from which they came. In fact, the principal end of the sacrifice is to acknowledge God as a sovereign being, so superior to all things that everything before him is purely nothing; for all things are nothing in presence of him who possesses all things in himself. The smoke that came from this sacrifice and arose in the air signified that God received it as a sweet odor, that is to say, with pleasure, as is written of the sacrifice of Noe: Noe offered holocausts upon the altar; and the Lord smelled a sweet savor?

5. All the people, together with the priest, had to be partakers of the victim. Hence, in the sacrifices, excepting the holocaust, the victim was divided into three parts, one part of which was destined for the priest, one for the people, and one for the fire. This last part was regarded as belonging to God, who by this means communicated in some manner with those who were partakers of the victim.

These five conditions are found reunited in the sacrifice of the Paschal Lamb. The Lord had commanded Moses that, on the tenth day of the month on which the Jews had been delivered from the slavery of Egypt, a lamb of one year and without blemish should be taken and separated from the flock; and thus were verified the conditions enumerated above, namely: 1. The separation of the lamb signified that it was a victim consecrated to God; 2. This consecration was succeeded by the oblation, which took place in the Temple, where the lamb was presented; 3. On the fourteenth day of the month the immolation took place, or the lamb was killed; 4. Then the lamb was roasted and divided among those present; and this was the partaking of it, or communion; 5. Finally, the lamb having been eaten, what remained of it was consumed by fire, and thus was the sacrifice consummated.

II

Fulfillment of the Prophetic Figures

The Sacrifice of our Lord, as we have said, was a perfect sacrifice, of which those sacrifices of the Old Law were but signs, imperfect figures, and what the Apostle calls weak and needy elements. The sacrifice offered by Jesus Christ really fulfilled all the conditions mentioned above. The first condition, which is the sanctification, or the consecration of the victim, was accomplished in the Incarnation of the Word by God the Father himself, as is mentioned in the Gospel of St. John: Whom the Father hath sanctified? Likewise, when announcing to the Blessed Virgin that she was chosen to be the Mother of the Son of God, the Angel said: The Holy which shall be born of thee shall be called the Son of God. Thus this divine victim, who was to be sacrificed for the salvation of the world, had already been sanctified by God, when he was born of Mary. From the first moment in which the Eternal Word took a human body, he was consecrated to God to be the victim of the great sacrifice that was to be accomplished on the Cross for the salvation of men. In regard to this our Lord said to his Father: But a body Thou hast fitted to me that I should do Thy will, O God?

The second condition, or the oblation, was also fulfilled at the moment of the Incarnation, when Jesus Christ voluntarily offered himself to atone for the sins of men. Knowing that divine justice could not be satisfied by all the ancient sacrifices, nor by all the works of men, he offered himself to atone for all the sins of men, and hence he said to God, Sacrifices, and oblations, and holocausts for sin, Thou wouldst not. Then said, Behold, I come to do Thy will, O God. Then the Apostle adds immediately, which will we are sanctified by the oblation of the body of Jesus Christ once. This last text is remarkable. Sin had rendered all men unworthy of being offered to God and of being accepted by him, and, therefore, it was necessary that Jesus Christ should offer himself for us in order to sanctify us by his grace, and to make us worthy of being accepted by God. And this offering which our Lord then made of himself did not limit itself to that moment, but it only then began; it always has continued since, and it will continue forever. It is true it will cease on earth at the time of Antichrist: the Sacrifice of the Mass is to be suspended for twelve hundred and ninety days; that is, for three years six months and a half, according to the prophecy of Daniel and from the time when the continual sacrifice shall be taken away and the abomination unto desolation shall be set up, there shall be a thousand two hundred ninety days?

The third condition of the sacrifice namely, the immolation of the victim was evidently accomplished by the death of our Lord on the Cross.

There remains for us yet to verify, in the Sacrifice of Jesus Christ, the two other conditions requisite to render a sacrifice perfect that is, the consumption of the victim and i\it partaking of it.

It is then asked, What was this consumption of the victim in the Sacrifice of Jesus Christ for although his body was by death separated from his holy soul, yet it was not consumed, nor destroyed.

The anonymous author of whom I spoke in the beginning, says that this fourth condition was fulfilled by the resurrection of our Lord; for, then, his adorable body was divested of all that is terrestrial and mortal, and was clothed in divine glory. He adds that it is this glory that Jesus Christ asked of his Father before his death: And now glorify Thou me, O Father, with Thyself, with the glory which I had, before the world was, with Thee? Our Lord did not ask this glory for his divinity, since he possessed it from all eternity as being the Word equal to the Father; but he asked it for his humanity, and he obtained it at his resurrection, by which he entered in a certain manner into his divine glory.

In speaking of the fifth condition, which is, the partaking of the victim, or Communion, the same author says that it is also fulfilled in heaven, where all the blessed are partakers of the victim of the Sacrifice that Jesus Christ continues to offer to God while offering himself.

These two reflections, made by the author to explain the two last conditions of the Sacrifice of Jesus Christ, are wise and ingenious; but for myself I think that the two conditions of which there is question, namely, the consumption and Communion, are manifestly fulfilled in the Sacrifice of the Altar, which, as has been declared by the Council of Trent, is the same as that of the Cross. In fact, the Sacrifice of the Mass, instituted by our Lord before his death, is a continuation of the Sacrifice of the Cross. Jesus Christ wished that the price of his blood, shed for the salvation of men, should be applied to us by the Sacrifice of the Altar; in which the victim offered is the same, though it is there offered differently from what it is on the Cross, that is, without the shedding of blood. These are the words of the Council of Trent: "Although Christ our Lord was to offer himself once to his Eternal Father on the altar of the Cross by actually dying to obtain for us eternal redemption, yet as his priesthood was not to become extinct by his death, in order to leave his Church a visible sacrifice suited to the present condition of men, a sacrifice which might at the same time represent to us the bloody sacrifice consummated on the Cross, preserve the memory of it to the end of the world, and apply the salutary fruits of it for the remission of the sins which we daily commit; at his last supper, on the very night on which he was betrayed, giving proof that he was established a priest forever according to the order of Melchisedech, he offered to God the Father his body and blood, under the appearances of bread and wine, and, under the same symbols, gave them to the apostles, whom he constituted at the same time priests of the New Law. By these words, Do ye this in remembrance of me he commissioned them and their successors in the priesthood to consecrate and offer his body and blood, as the Catholic Church has always understood and taught." And further on the Council declares that the Lord, appeased by the oblation of the Sacrifice of Mass, grants us his graces and the remission of sins. It says: "It is one and the same victim; the one that offers sacrifice is the same one who, after having sacrificed himself on the Cross, offers himself now by the ministry of the priest; there is no difference except in the manner of offering."

Jesus Christ has, then, paid the price of our redemption in the Sacrifice of the Cross. But he wishes that the fruit of the ransom given should be applied to us in the Sacrifice of Altar, being himself in both the chief sacrificer, who offers the same victim, namely, his own body and his own blood; with this difference only, that on the Cross his blood was shed, while it is not shed at the altar. Hence the Roman catechism teaches that the Sacrifice of the Mass does not serve only to praise God and to thank him for the gifts that he has granted us, but it is a true propitiatory sacrifice, by which we obtain from the Lord pardon for our sins and the graces of which we stand in need. Because the fruit of the death of Jesus Christ is applied to us by the Sacrifice of the

Altar, the Church expresses herself thus in her prayers: "As often as the memory of the Sacrifice of the Cross is celebrated, so often is accomplished the work of our redemption."

Now, in the Mass we find not only the three essential parts of the Sacrifice of the Cross, that is, the sanctification and oblation of the victim, as also the immolation, which is here done mystically, the consecration of the body and that of the blood taking place separately, but we also find the two other parts of the sacrifice; namely, the destruction or consumption, communion or partaking, of the victim. The destruction or consumption is accomplished by the natural heat of those who receive the consecrated Host. Communion or partaking of the victim consists in the distribution of the Holy Eucharist to the faithful who approach the altar for this purpose.

In this manner we clearly see realized in the Sacrifice of the Altar the five conditions required in the ancient sacrifices, all of which were signs and figures of the great Sacrifice of our Lord.

SHORT EXPLANATION OF THE PRAYERS OF MASS

Mass is rightly divided into six parts. The first part is the preparation for the sacrifice; and this is made at the foot of the altar. The second part extends from the Introit to the Credo, inclusively and was formerly called the Mass of the Catechumens, who had to leave the church after the Credo. The third part contains the Offertory and the Preface. The fourth part comprises the Canon with the Pater Noster ; for the Canon in olden times finished with the Pater Noster, as a learned author concludes from a passage in the writings of St. Gregory the Great. The fifth part begins with the prayer Liberanos, qucesumus, Domine ("Deliver us, O Lord, we beseech Thee"), which is a preparation for Communion, and includes Communion. The sixth and last part comprises under the form of thanksgiving the rest of the Mass.

FIRST PART

The Preparation that is made at the Foot of the Altar

In nomine Patris et Fili et Spiritus Sancti. Amen ("In the name of the Father, and of the Son, and of the Holy Ghost. Amen").

In order to sacrifice a victim one must have the power over its life and death; but as God only has the power over the life of his incarnate Son, who is the victim of the Sacrifice of the Mass, the priest needs divine authority in order to be able to offer Jesus Christ to his heavenly Father. Yet as he is invested with the authority that belongs to the priesthood, he says, in union with Jesus Christ, who is the principal one that offers that sacrifice, In the name of the Father, and of the Son, and of the Holy Ghost; thus declaring that he offers the sacrifice by the authority of the three Persons.

The priest afterwards recites the antiphon Introibo adaltare Dei ("I will go unto the altar of God") and the psalm Judica me Deus ("Judge me, O God"). He implores the help of God against the enemies who are laying snares for him. Then expressing the pain that he feels of seeing himself, as it were, rejected by the Lord, he begs him to assist him with his light, and to console him with the graces that he promised by leading him into his tabernacle. Finally, he reproaches himself for indulging in fear, for why should he be troubled when he has with him his God in whom he should confide?

Innocent III attests that the recitation before Mass of the psalm Judica me was the custom of his time, that is, in the twelfth century; and Cardinal Lambertini, afterwards Benedict XIV, assures us that it was recited before the eighth century. The psalm is concluded with the Gloria Patri. It was Pope St. Damasus who ordained that each psalm should be concluded in this manner. It is, however, believed that the Gloria Patri was introduced by the Council of Nice, or, as we are told by Baronius and St. Basil, even by the Apostles, the Council of Nice having added only these words, Sicut erat, etc.

Before leaving the people to go up to the altar, the priest says to them, Dominus vobisenm

("The Lord be with you"). By these words he wishes and asks that Jesus Christ may grant to the people as well as to himself the effects of the prayers that he has said; and the server expresses to him the same wish when answering for all the people: Et cum spiritu tuo ("And with Thy spirit"). These reciprocal wishes indicate the union of faith in Jesus Christ that exists between the priest and the people.

Thee, O Lord, by the merits of Thy saints, etc. Having reached the altar, he kisses it, to unite himself to Jesus Christ, represented by the altar; and, through the merits of the holy martyrs whose relics are therein enclosed, he conjures our Lord to deign to pardon him all his sins.

From the first ages the Church was accustomed to offer up the Eucharistic sacrifice on the tombs of the martyrs who had sacrificed their lives for God, and who for this reason have always been particularly honored in the Church. During the first period of the Church there were no other festivals than those of the mysteries of Jesus Christ, those of the Blessed Virgin, and the anniversaries of the martyrs. However, it is not to the saints, but only to God that altars are erected, "and," as St. Augustine says, "we have not erected an altar to the martyr, Stephen, but with the relics of the martyr Stephen we have erected an altar to God."

SECOND PART
From the Introit to the Credo

It is usually in the Introit that the Church proposes the subject of the feast that is celebrated. Mention is therein made of some divine mystery, of the Blessed Virgin, or of some other saint whom the Church honors on that day, so that we simply render this honor to the saint, since the sacrifice, as we have said, is offered only to God. It is asserted that the author of the Introit is St. Gregory the Great, as may be seen in the works of Benedict XIV.

Kyrie, eleison; Christe, eleison. These are Greek words that mean "Lord, or Christ, have mercy." This prayer is addressed three times to the Father, three times to the Son, and three times to the Holy Ghost. Durand says that Mass was begun to be said in Greek in the Oriental Church at the time of the Emperor Adrian I, about the year 140. Pope St. Sylvester ordered that, after the example of the Greeks, the Kyrie eleison should be said in the Latin Church. According to Cardinal Bellarmine this custom was introduced into Italy about a hundred and fifty years before St. Gregory. Thereby is shown the union that exists between the Greek and the Latin Church.

Gloria in excelsis Deo, etc. ("Glory be to God on high, etc."). This canticle or prayer is formed of the words that the celestial choirs used when the Angel came to announce to the shepherds the birth of the Savior; "Glory to God in the highest and on earth peace to men of good will." The remaining words were added by the Church. In it God is thanked for his glory, because God has used our salvation for his glory by saving us through Jesus Christ, who, in offering himself as a sacrifice to his Father, has procured salvation for men, and has given, at the same time, infinite glory to God. Then the Church, addressing herself to Jesus Christ, asks him by the merits of his sacrifice to have pity on us; and she concludes by proclaiming him: Quoniam tu solus Sanctus, tu solus Dominus, tu solus Altissimus, Jesu Christe, cum Sancto Spiritu in gloria Dei Patris. Amen ("For Thou only art holy; Thou only art Lord; Thou only, O Jesus Christ, art Most High in the glory of God the Father. Amen"). For our Savior, who sacrifices himself as a victim, is at the same time God, equal to Him to whom the sacrifice is offered.

Here follow the Epistle and the Gospel. While listening to the reading of the Epistle, we must hear it as if it is God himself who speaks by the mouth of his prophets and apostles.

The Epistle is followed by the Gradual, which, according to Bellarmin, was sung in former times while the deacon ascended the steps of the ambo an elevated pulpit to read the Gospel. The Gradual was followed by the Alleluia, a Hebrew word that signifies Praise the Lord. But in Lent the Alleluia, which expresses joy, is replaced by the Tract, which Abbot Rupert calls the lamentation of penitents.

The priest then leaving the left side of the altar, which represents the Jewish people, passes to the right side, which represents the Gentiles, who accepted the Gospel that was rejected by the Jews. We should listen to the Gospel as if we heard the words of our divine Savior instructing us himself, and we should at the same time ask him for the necessary help to put in practice what he teaches. It is an ancient custom to stand during the reading of the Gospel, to show that we are ready to follow the precepts and counsels that our Lord points out to us.

Credo ("I believe"). While the priest is reciting the symbol, we should renew our faith in all the mysteries and all the dogmas that the Church teaches. By the symbol was formerly understood a military sign, a mark by which many recognize one another, and are distinguished from one another this at present distinguishes believers from unbelievers. Benedict XIV tells us that at Rome the recitation of the symbol during Mass was begun only in the eleventh century.

THIRD PART
The Offertory and the Preface

The Offertory embraces everything from the Dominus vobiscum till the Preface. In offering the bread and wine the priest calls them the immaculate Host, the Chalice of salvation. We should not be astonished at this; for all the prayers and all the ceremonies before and after the consecration have reference to the divine Victim. It is at the moment of consecration that the Victim presents himself to God, that he offers himself to him, and that the sacrifice is offered; but as these different acts cannot be explained at the same time, they are explained one after the other. The priest then offers by anticipation the bread prepared for the sacrifice, and while saying, Suscipe, sancte Pater, hanc immaculatam Hostiam, etc.

A little water is mixed with the wine to represent the mixture or the union that takes place in the Incarnation of the Word between the divinity and the humanity, and also to represent the intimate union that is effected in the sacramental Communion between Jesus Christ and the person who communicates a union which St. Augustine calls Mixtura Dei et hominis ("A mixture of God and of man"). Hence the priest, in the prayer which he recites while mixing the water with the wine, beseeches God to grant that, as his divine Son became partaker of our humanity, we may be made partakers of his divinity. The Council of Trent declares that this mingling of water and of wine in the chalice is prescribed: "The holy Synod admonishes that it is enjoined on the priests by the Church that they should mix water with the wine that is to be offered in the chalice, as it is believed that the Lord has done the same thing." However, this is only an ecclesiastical, not a divine precept.

Offerimus tibi, Domine, Calicem salutaris, etc. ("We offer unto Thee, O Lord, the Chalice of salvation, etc."). The chalice of salvation is offered to the Lord, so that it –may arise in his divine presence as an agreeable odor, for our salvation and for the salvation of the whole world. Cardinal Bona, in his Liturgy, assures us that neither in the Sacramentarium of St. Gregory, nor in other authors, is any prayer found for the offering of the bread and of the wine; however, the same Cardinal says that in the ancient Liturgy which he caused to be published we find the prayers that were recited by the clergy as well as by the faithful when the latter presented to the priest their offerings. Moreover, our French author says that the prayers recited at present by the priest at the oblation of the bread and of the wine have reference to the offerings which the faithful formerly made, not at the altar, but at the balustrade of the choir.

Orate, fratres, etc. ("Brethren, pray, etc."). By these words the priest exhorts the people to supplicate the Lord to receive this sacrifice for the glory of his name and the good of the faithful. The server then answers in the name of the people by praying to God to accept this sacrifice: Suscipiat Dominus Sacrificium de minibus tuis, etc. ("May the Lord receive this sacrifice from thy hands, etc.").

Then follows the Secret, a prayer that refers to the offerings made by the people, namely, of the bread and wine that are to be changed into the body and the blood of Jesus Christ. The Church asks the Lord to bless them and to render them profitable, not only to those who present them, but to all the faithful, just as may be seen in the Secret of the fifth Sunday after Pentecost: "Mercifully receive, O Lord, these offerings of thy servants; that what each hath offered to the honor of thy name, may avail to the salvation of all." Thus the Offertory is concluded.

Before passing to the Canon, the priest reads the Preface, in which he exhorts the faithful to raise their hearts to God: Sursum corda ("Lift up your hearts"). The people answer that they have already done so; Habemus ad Doininum ("We have lifted them to the Lord"), And the priest continues by inviting them to unite with him in thanking the Lord: Gratias agamus Domino Deo nostro ("Let us give thanks to our Lord God"). He afterwards says that it is just and salutary to render thanks through Jesus Christ, who alone can worthily give thanks for the eternal salvation and for so many benefits granted to men and also to angels, who also give thanks to God through Jesus Christ for all the gifts that they have received. The priest entreats the Lord to accept our prayers united with those of the angels, who celebrate his glory by repeating without ceasing the canticle, Sanctus, Sanctus, Sanctus, Dominus Dens Sabbath! ("Holy, Holy, Holy, Lord God of Hosts!"); and he concludes by repeating the words used by the Jewish people in their acclamations at the triumphant entry of Jesus into Jerusalem: Benedictus, qui venit in nomine Domini! Hosanna in eoccelsis ("Blessed is he that cometh in the name of the Lord! Hosanna in the highest!")

FOURTH PART
The Canon

Te igitur, clementissime Pater, etc. ("We therefore humbly pray and beseech Thee, most merciful Father, etc."). Here begins what we call the Canon of the Mass, which the Council of Trent declares to be free from every error, since it is composed of the very words of our Lord, of the traditions of the apostles, and of pious regulations of the Holy See. The Canon is very ancient it was already in use in the fourth century, according to the testimony of St. Ambrose. The priest first prays to his heavenly Father in the name of the whole Church, and through the merits of Jesus Christ, to accept and to bless the offerings that are made to him, and that are called gifts without spot. ("These gifts, these presents, these holy unspotted sacrifices"). These words apply not only to the bread and the wine that have been offered, but refer by anticipation to the body and the blood of Jesus Christ, into which the bread and the wine are soon to be changed; hence they are called unspotted sacrifices. Innocent III refers these last words to the purity of the heart and of the body with which the priest should celebrate Mass: "We call them by this name because of the purity of heart and of body with which the priest should offer them." But this is rather a spiritual and mystical reflection, the proper explanation is that which precedes it above.

The Holy Sacrifice is, before all, offered for the Catholic Church by praying to God that he may preserve her in peace, may defend her, maintain her in unity, and govern her through the ministry of the pastors, by communicating to them his Holy Spirit. It must be observed that the prayers of the Church, during the Holy Sacrifice, should be addressed to God the Father, as was ordained by the Third Council of Carthage: "During the August Function the prayer should be addressed to God the Father." It does not follow that the other divine Persons should be excluded from these prayers; but they are considered together in the Person of the Father, their first principle, and this is the reason why the Church is accustomed to pray to the Father, with the Son, in the Holy Ghost.

Communicantes et memoriam venerantes, etc. ("Communicating with the saints and honoring the memory, etc."). This prayer is said in order to enter into communion with the Church triumphant. Thereby we honor, in the first place, the memory of the Mother of God, then that of the apostles, then that of the martyrs and of all the other saints, through the merits and the intercession of whom we beg our Lord's protection in all our necessities. We who are travelers upon earth form only-one body with the saints who are in heaven, and united with them in the same spirit, we offer to God the same sacrifice.

Quam oblationem tu, Deus in omnibus, qucesumus, benedtctam, adscriptam, ratam, rationabilem, acceptabilemque factre digneris; ut nobis corpus et sanguis fiat dilectissimi Filii tui Domini uostri Jesu Christi ("Which oblation do Thou, O God, vouchsafe in all respects to make blessed, approved, ratified, reasonable, and acceptable, that it may become to us the body and blood of Thy most beloved Son, Jesus Christ our Lord"). In this prayer the priest asks God to cause this oblation to be blessed (benedictaui), that by this blessing the bread and the wine may be changed into the body and the blood of Jesus Christ; that it may be admitted (adseriptam), that is, subtracted from all profane usage and wholly consecrated to the divine Majesty; ratified (ratam), that is, approved as a perfect sacrifice; reasonable or rational (rationabtlem), this includes an allusion to a passage in the Epistle to the Romans, in which St. Paul says: "I beseech you that you present your bodies a living sacrifice, holy, pleasing unto God, your reasonable

service;" acceptable (acceptabileni), that is, altogether agreeable and worthy of being received, differently from the victims and the oblations of the Hebrew people, which were not sufficient to appease the divine justice incensed against sinners; and, finally, Ut nobis corpus et sanguis fiat dilectissimi Fili tui ("That it may become to us the body and blood of Thy most beloved Son"). The priest, according to St. Thomas, does not thereby ask that the consecration, be accomplished, but that it be profitable to us.

Qui pridie quam pateretur, etc. ("Who the day before he suffered," etc.). Here the priest, renewing the memory of the Passion of Jesus Christ, relates what the Lord did on the evening before his death, when he instituted the Sacrament and the sacrifice of his body and blood. Then the priest does the same thing, and consecrates by pronouncing the very words used by Jesus

Christ, as St. Ambrose remarks: "He uses not his own words, but the very words of Jesus Christ."

The form of the consecration is taken from St. Matthew: Hoc est corpus meum ("This is my body"). These words need no explanation, since they themselves declare what mystery is accomplished, namely, the change of the bread into the body of Jesus Christ.

The form of the consecration of the chalice is as follows: Hie est enim calix Sanguinis mei, novi et ceterni Testamenti, mysteruttn fidei, qui pro vobis et pro multis effnndetur in remissionein peccatorum ("For this is the chalice of my blood of the new and eternal testament, the mystery of faith, which shall be shed for you, and for many, to the remission of sins"). These words the Church has taken from different texts of the Gospel, partly from St. Luke, partly from St. Matthew. St. Luke says: This is the chalice, the new testament in my blood, which shall be shed for you. St. Matthew: For this is my blood of the new testament which shall be shed for many unto remission of sins? The word cetenri, "everlasting," is found in St. Paul: In the blood of the everlasting testament. The other words, Mystery of faith, the Roman catechism declares are taught by sacred tradition, which is the guardian of Catholic truths. This divine mystery is called Mystery of faith, not to exclude the reality of the blood of Jesus Christ, but to show that in it the faith shines forth in a wonderful manner, and triumphs over all the difficulties that may be raised by human reason, since it is here, says Innocent III, that we see one thing and believe another. We believe, he adds, that the form that we read in the Canon was received from Jesus Christ by the Apostles, and that they transmitted it to their successors.

The consecration is followed by the elevation of the host and of the chalice: this is done, writes Sassi, in order to prove the truth of the Eucharist which was attacked by Berengarius at the beginning of the twelfth century. The same truth is again professed at the second elevation shortly before the Pater Noster, when the priest says, Omnis honor et gloria ("All honor and glory"). It was also at the time of the heresy of Berengarius that the custom was introduced of ringing the bell at the elevation of the Host and of the chalice.

Heze quotiescunique feceritis, inmei memoriam facietis ("As often as ye do these things, ye shall do them in remembrance of me"). After the two consecrations the priest repeats the words of Jesus Christ, by which our Savior commanded his Apostles and their successors to do, in memory of his Passion, what he had just done himself in their presence.

Undeet memores.Domine, etc. ("Wherefore, O Lord, calling to mind," etc.). Here the priest calls to mind the Passion of our Lord, his resurrection, and ascension. He offers to the divine majesty in the name of the Church the consecrated victim, which he calls a pure Host, exempt from every sin; holy, being united with the divinity in the person of the Word; immaculate, without any stain; and then, "The holy bread of eternal life, and the chalice of everlasting salvation." While pronouncing these words he blesses the bread and the chalice with the sign of the cross. On this subject Luther turns to ridicule the Roman Church by asking how the priest blesses Jesus Christ how the creature blesses the Creator. We answer here that the priest blesses the Host, not by his own authority, nor in his own name, but in the name and by the authority of the Eternal Father, who alone can bless Jesus Christ as man and as victim. Such is the answer given on this point by Innocent III. St. Thomas answers differently by saying that after the consecration the priest does not make the sign of the cross to bless, but only to remind us of the power of the cross and of the death of our Lord.

Per quern hec omnia semper bona creas, etc. ("By whom, O Lord, Thou dost always create," etc.). By the Word Thou hast created this bread and wine, and now, by the same Word, Thou hast sanctified them by reserving them for the sacrifice. Thou hast quickened them by changing them into the body and the blood of Jesus Christ; Thou hast blessed (benedicts) them and transformed them into a source of benediction for the Church of Christ; and, finally, Thou hast given us all these good things (et prcestas nobis) by distributing them to the faithful in Holy Communion. And all these favors the Church asks through the merits of Jesus Christ: Per ipsum, that is, through him; cum ipso, in union with our Savior; in ipso, in him as the members are in the body, since God recognizes as his own only those who are united with Jesus Christ.

THE PATER NOSTER

Oremus. Prœceptis salutaribus moniti, etc. ("Instructed by Thy saving precepts, etc."). The Church militant regards herself as entirely composed of sinners; she thinks herself unworthy to call God her Father, and to address to him the seven petitions, which in the name of the faithful she is going to address to him by reciting the Pater Noster, ("Our Father"). Hence she protests that she only dares to address to God this prayer because God himself has commanded her to do so. She then teaches us that we may venture to present to God the seven petitions which contain the whole economy of our salvation, because it is pleasing to him and he himself gives us the command. We are so miserable, and our mind is so limited, that we do not even know what graces we should ask of God in behalf of our own salvation. Regarding our poverty and our insufficiency, Jesus Christ himself deigned to compose our prayer or to indicate the subjects on which we should address Almighty God. He instructs us to say:

Pater noster, qui es in coelis ("Our Father, who art in heaven, etc."). The Apostle St. John says: Behold what manner of charity the Father hath bestowed upon us that we should be called, and should be the sons of God. It is assuredly only by the effect of extreme love that we worms of the earth have been enabled to become the children of God, not by nature, but by adoption; and such is the immense grace that the Son of God has obtained for us by becoming man; for St. Paul says: You have received the spirit of adoption of sons, whereby we cry, Abba (Father) Can a subject wish for greater happiness than to be adopted by his king or a creature to be adopted by its Creator? This is what God has done for us; and he wishes that we should address to him with filial confidence the following prayer:

1. Sanctificetur nomem tuum ("Hallowed be Thy name"). God cannot possess a greater sanctity than that which he possesses from all eternity, because he is infinite; hence what we ask in this prayer is merely that God may make known in every place his holy name, and that he may make himself loved by all men: by unbelievers, who know him not; by heretics, who do not know him in the right manner; and by sinners, who know him but do not love him.

2. Adveniat regnum tuum ("Thy kingdom come"). Two kinds of dominion God exercises over our souls the do minion of grace and the dominion of glory. By these words we ask for both, namely, that the grace of God may reign among us in this life, that it may direct and govern us, so that one day we may be judged worthy of glory, and may have the happiness to possess God and be possessed by him for all eternity.

3. Fiat voluntas tua, sicut in celo, et in terra ("Thy will be done on earth, as it is in heaven"). The whole perfection of a soul consists in the perfect accomplishment of the will of God, as is done by the blessed in heaven. Hence Jesus Christ wishes us to ask the grace to accomplish the will of God upon earth, as the angels and saints accomplish it in heaven.

4. Panem nostrum quoiidianum da nobis hodie ("Give us this day our daily bread"). Such is the text as we find it in St. Luke. By this prayer we ask God for the temporal goods of which we stand in need to sustain our present life. The words "Our daily bread" teach us that we should ask

for this kind of goods with moderation, after the example of Solomon, who asked only what was necessary: Give me only the necessaries of life. It is to be remarked that in the Gospel of St. Matthew, instead of the daily bread, we read, Give us this day our super substantial bread. By this super substantial bread we must understand, according to the explanation given by the Roman catechism, Jesus Christ himself in the Sacrament of the Altar, that is, in Holy Communion. We ask this heavenly bread every day, Give us this day, because every good Christian should communicate every day, if not really at least spiritually, as we are exhorted by the Council of Trent.

5. Et dimitte nobis debita nostra, sicut et nos dimittimus debitoribus nostris ("And forgive us our trespasses, as we forgive them that trespass against us"). To eat worthily of this heavenly bread, we must be free from mortal sin, or at least be washed of it by the blood of the Lamb in the sacrament of penance. We say, free from mortal sin; but it must be observed that if anyone should communicate with an actual affection for some venial sin, he could not be said to communicate without offering some indignity to our Lord at least if he communicates often.

6. Et ne nos inducas in tentationem ("And lead us not into temptation"). How are these words to be understood? Does God sometimes tempt us does he lead us into temptation? No; for St. James says: God is not a tempter of evils, and He tempteth no man. This text we must understand as we do that of Isaias: Blind the heart of this people lest they see? God never blinds any sinner, but he often refuses to grant to some, in punishment for their ingratitude, the light that he would have given them had they remained faithful and grateful. Hence when it is said that God makes any one blind, it is meant that he withholds the light of his grace. This, therefore is the sense of the prayer, and lead us not into temptation; we ask God not to permit us to have the misfortune of being in those occasions of sin in which we might fall. Hence we should always watch and pray as the Lord exhorts us to do, in order not to fall into, temptation: Watch ye, and pray that ye enter not into temptation? To enter into temptation means the same as to find one's self in the danger of falling into sin; we should therefore often say to God, Lord, lead us not into temptation.

7. Sed libera nos a malo ("But deliver us from evil"). There are three kinds of evils from which we should ask the Lord to deliver us the temporal evils of the body, the spiritual evils of the soul, and the eternal evils of the next life. As for the temporal evils of this life, we ought always to be disposed to receive with resignation those that God sends us for the good of our souls, such as poverty, sickness, and desolation; and when we ask God to deliver us from temporal evils we should always do so on condition that they are not necessary nor useful for our salvation. But the true evils from which we should absolutely pray to be delivered are spiritual evils, sins, which are the cause of eternal evils. Moreover, let us be convinced of this infallible truth, that in the present state of corrupt nature we cannot be saved unless we pass through the many tribulations with which this life is filled: Through many tribulations we must enter into the kingdom of God.

The priest finishes the Lord s prayer with the word Amen, which he pronounces in a low voice, because he represents the person of Jesus Christ, who is the foundation of all the divine promises. This word is a summary of all the petitions that have been made petitions the repetition of which pleases the Lord, for the more we pray to God the more he will hear our prayers. The great people of this world are not pleased when they are importuned by petitions; but this importunity is pleasing to God, says St. Jerome. Cornelius a Lapide even assures us that God wishes that we should persevere in this importunity in our prayers.

FIFTH PART
From the Prayer "Libera nos" till the Communion

Immediately after the Pater Noster the priest recites the prayer Libera nos, qucesumus, Domine ("Deliver us, O Lord"), by which he asks the Lord for himself and for all the faithful to grant, through the intercession of the Blessed Virgin, of the apostles and of all the saints, a continual peace during the days of the present life, so that his divine mercy may preserve them from every sin and from all confusion.

He then says, Pax Domini sit semper vobiscum ("May the peace of the Lord be always with you"). He wishes the peace of the Lord for all his brethren, who answer him with the same wish: Et cum spiritu tno ("And with thy spirit"). He makes at the same time upon the chalice, with the particle of the Host which he holds in his hand, three signs of the cross, which indicates, according to St. Thomas, the three days that Jesus Christ spent in the tomb.

The priest then drops the sacred particle into the chalice and says these words: Hamp let commixtio et consccratio Corporis et Sanguinis Domini nostri Jesit Christi fiat accipientibus nobis in vitam ceternam! ("May this mixture and consecration of the body and blood of our Lord Jesus Christ be to us that receive it effectual to eternal life"). Explaining these words, Consccratiofiat, Bellarmin says that we do not here ask that the consecration should take place, but that it be profitable for eternal life to those who are about to receive Jesus Christ in Holy Communion. This mixture of the holy species represents the union of the divinity with the humanity which was at first effected in the womb of Mary through the Incarnation of the Word, and which is renewed in the souls of the faithful when they receive him in the Eucharistic Communion.

Agnus Dei, qui tollis peccata mundi ("Lamb of God, who takest away the sins of the world"). Before Communion the Lamb of God, Jesus Christ, as the victim of the sacrifice, is invoked, and is invoked three times, to point out the need that we have of his grace, in order to be reconciled with God and to receive his peace.

Here follow the three prayers that precede Communion.

In the first prayer Domine Jesu Christe, qui dixisti Apostolis tuis, Pacem relinquo iwbis ("Lord Jesus Christ, who said to Thy Apostles, I leave you peace") prayer is offered to God that he may vouchsafe to grant peace to the Church in consideration of her faith, and keep her in union, according to his will, by delivering her from the division produced by false doctrines, and from all that is contrary to the divine will. And here the Church has introduced the custom that the faithful should give one another the kiss of peace, to remind them that their hearts should be united in charity. Before giving the kiss of peace, the priest kisses the altar, to show that he cannot give the peace unless he has first received it from Jesus Christ, who is represented by the altar.

In the second prayer, Domine Jesu Christe, Fili Dei vivi, the priest asks Jesus Christ, by virtue of his adorable body and blood, to deliver him from all evils, and to keep him always united with him.

In the third prayer he beseeches the Lord that this Communion may not turn to his condemnation, but may be for the salvation of his soul and body. The Holy Eucharist protects the soul against temptations and passions; it extinguishes the fire of concupiscence that burns in our bodies, and is a powerful remedy against the death of the soul.

SIXTH PART
Thanksgiving

Quid retribuam Domino pro omnibus quce retribuit mihi? ("What shall I render to the Lord for all he hath rendered unto me?") The priest says, For all, etc., because he who receives Jesus Christ in Communion receives all the gifts and all the goods that one can desire, according to the words of St. Paul: How hath He not also, with Him, given us all things. He says, What shall I render? because man is not capable of thanking God as he should thank him. Jesus Christ only can worthily thank the Eternal Father for the gifts that he bestowed upon men. The priest therefore adds: Califem salutaris accipiam, et nomen Domini invocabo ("I will take the chalice of salvation, and call upon the name of the Lord"). He supplicates the Divine Redeemer to thank the heavenly Father for himself and for all men.

After having taken the precious blood he renews his thanks to God in the following words: Quod ore sumpsimus, Domine, pura mente capiamus, et de munere temporall fiat nobis remedium sempiternum ("Grant, O Lord, that what we have taken with our mouth we may receive with a pure mind, that of a temporal gift it may become to us an eternal remedy"). By this prayer the Church makes us ask God that, as our mouth has received this divine food and drink, our hearts may also receive them, so that they may be for us an eternal remedy that may forever heal us of all our infirmities.

Finally the priest says, Corpus tuum, Domine, quod sumpsi, et Sanguts quem potavi, adhcereat visceribus meis ("May Thy body, O Lord, which I have received, and the blood which I have drunk, cleave to my bowels"). In this prayer, and in the last prayer called Post-communion, he asks, through the merits of Jesus Christ in this mystery, and through the intercession of the saint whose memory is celebrated, that this divine Savior may always preserve him in this intimate union with him, and that no stain may rest on his soul, which has been nourished by a sacrament so holy and so pure.

Ite, Missa est ("Go, the Mass is ended"); or, Benedicamus Domino ("Let us bless the Lord"). It is with these words that the priest dismisses the people, just as if he said, The Sacrifice is accomplished; and those who are present while thanking God by the mouth of the server, say, Deo Gratias ("Thanks be to God"). "To give thanks to God," says St. Augustine, "is to acknowledge that all good things come from God, and to thank him for them."

This explanation of the prayers of Mass may be serviceable to all to the faithful as well as to priests.

HEARING MASS

In order to hear Mass with devotion, it is necessary to know that the sacrifice of the altar is the same as that which was once offered on Calvary, with this difference, that on Calvary the blood of Jesus Christ was really shed, but on the altar it is shed only in a mystical manner. Had you been present on Calvary, with what devotion and tenderness would you have attended that great sacrifice! Enliven your faith, then, and consider that the same action is performed on the altar, and that the same sacrifice is offered not only by the priest, but also by all who attend Mass. Thus, all perform, in a certain manner, the office of priests during the celebration of the Mass, in which the merits of the Passion of our Savior are applied to us in a particular manner.

It is, moreover, necessary to know that the sacrifice of the Mass has been instituted for four ends. 1. To honor God. 2. To satisfy for our sins. 3. To thank God for his benefits. 4. To obtain the divine graces. Thence arise the following considerations which may aid us to hear Mass with great fruit:

1. By the oblation of the person of Jesus Christ, God and man, to the Eternal Father, we give to God infinite honor; we give him greater honor than he would receive from the oblation of the lives of all men and all angels.

2. By the oblation of Jesus Christ in the Mass, we offer to God a complete satisfaction for all the sins of men, and especially for the sins of those who are present at Mass; to whom is applied the same divine blood, by which the human race was redeemed on Calvary. Thus, by each Mass more satisfaction is made to God than by any other expiatory work. But although the Mass is of infinite value, God accepts it only in a finite manner, according to the dispositions of those who attend the holy sacrifice, and, therefore, it is useful to hear several Masses.

3. In the Mass we render to God an adequate thanksgiving for all the benefits that he has bestowed upon us.

4. During the Mass we can obtain all the graces that we desire for ourselves and for others. We are unworthy of receiving any grace from God, but Jesus Christ has given us the means of obtaining all graces, if, while we offer him to God in the Mass, we ask them of the Eternal Father in his name, for then Jesus himself unites with us in prayer. If you knew that while you pray to the Lord, the divine Mother, along with the whole of paradise, united with you, with what confidence would you pray? Now when you ask of God any grace during the Mass, Jesus (whose prayers are more efficacious than the prayers of all who are in heaven) prays for you, and offers in your behalf the merits of his Passion.

You will do well, then, to divide the Mass into four parts, as follows:

1. From the Beginning to the Gospel

Offer the sacrifice of the Mass to honor God, saying: My God, I adore Thy majesty. I would wish to honor Thee as much as Thou deservest; but what honor can I, a miserable sinner, give Thee? I offer Thee the honor which Jesus renders to Thee on this altar. I have given Thee: I am sorry for them above all things, and in satisfaction for them I offer Thy Son, who sacrifices himself again for us on this altar, and through his merits I pray Thee to pardon me, and to give me holy perseverance.

2. From the Elevation to the Communion.

Offer Jesus to the Eternal Father in thanksgiving for all the graces that he has bestowed upon you, saying:

Lord, I am unable to thank Thee; I offer Thee the blood of Jesus Christ in this Mass, and in all the Masses that are at this moment celebrated throughout the world.

3. From the Communion to the End

You will ask with confidence the graces that you need, and particularly sorrow for your sins, the gift of perseverance, and of the divine love; and you will recommend to God, in a special manner, the persons with whom you live, your relatives, poor sinners, and the souls in purgatory. I do not find it amiss if you recite vocal prayers during Mass, but I desire that you should not fail at the same time to fulfil the four duties to God that I have pointed out to you; namely, honor, expiation, thanksgiving, and prayer. I desire you to hear as many Masses as possible. Every Mass heard in this manner will obtain for you a treasure of merits.

DIONS EXERCISE TO ACQUIRE THE PROPER DISPOSITION FOR MAKING A GOOD CONFESSION

Act of Adoration

Supreme and adorable Majesty, God of heaven and earth, I firmly believe that Thou art present, and that Thou seest me and knowesj; the dispositions of my heart. I adore Thee and render Thee my humble homage, acknowledging Thee for my God, my Creator, and my Sovereign Redeemer. In testimony of this my faith, I prostrate my soul and body before the throne of Thy Infinite Majesty, and offer Thee the adoration which is due to Thee alone.

Examination of Conscience

We ought to represent confession to ourselves as the last one of our life, and dispose ourselves to make it as one would do who is at the point of death. We should ask God for the grace to make well the examination of conscience, and for the necessary light to know well our sins. Hence let us recite the Vent Creator Spiritus.

O Father of lights! who enlightenest every man that comes into the world, send into my heart a ray of light, of love, and of sorrow, that I may know, detest, and confess the sins which I have committed against Thee.

Prayer before the Examination of Conscience

Mother of my God, who art so charitable to sinners that desire to repent, assist me by thy intercession. My guardian angel, who hast been a spectator of all my crimes, help me to discover the sins which I have committed against my God. All ye saints of heaven, pray for me, that I may bring forth fruits of penance. Amen.

Offering of the Examination

Jesus, my God and Savior, I offer Thee the examination which I am going to make, that Thy divine justice may be glorified in it. I look to Thee with confidence for the grace to do it well. Thus, therefore, in the spirit of charity, in order to please Thee, and to accomplish Thy holy will, together with every intention that can procure Thee the greatest honor and glory, I under take it.

Motives of Contrition

I

The Greatness and Sanctity of God

Reflect, that sin, however trifling it may be, greatly offends Almighty God, and is an insult to the infinite perfections of him whose greatness knows no limits and who is consequently deserving of infinite love. By sin you displease one who loves you most tenderly. Oh! reflect well on this, and you will discover how base, how cruel, how unreasonable it is to offend him. But, alas! we shall never, during this life, be able fully to comprehend the entire malice even of a venial sin, or know what punishment he deserves who commits it.

An Act of Contrition

O my infinitely amiable God! I acknowledge that my sins are multiplied beyond the number of the hairs of my head, or the grains of sand on the sea-shore. But, if I had committed only one, in committing it I have offended Thy infinite perfections. Oh! why then is not my heart penetrated with infinite grief and regret? I have sinned against Thy goodness, which I ought ever to have loved. I have preferred a vile creature, a petty honor, a miserable pleasure, some vain interest, to Thy sovereign majesty, which I ought to have adored, served, and honored. Ah! my God, pardon my sins. O infinite beauty, infinite goodness! how could I have the audacity to insult and despise Thee? But I now heartily repent of my ingratitude and disloyalty; I wish sincerely that I had never offended Thee, and resolve never to offend Thee again. Yes, I had rather sacrifice all that I possess, and forfeit my honor and my life, than ever more offend so good a God.

II

The Benefits of God

Reflect that God is our sovereign benefactor, who has bestowed upon us innumerable benefits, both general and particular. He has drawn us out of nothing, and formed us to his own image and likeness, without having any need at all of us we are continually dependent upon him for our preservation. He has redeemed us with the price of the blood of his Son; he has made us Christians in preference to thousands of others whom he has left in the darkness of infidelity; he has borne with us in our sins until the present time; he has given us many and easy means of saving our souls; and still we repay all his mercies with ingratitude. He has created all creatures for our benefit, and the only use which we make of them is to offend him.

An Act of Contrition

Oh! how great has been my ingratitude there is, there can be, none equal to it. O my amiable Savior! Is this the recompense that I have made Thee, for having drawn me out of the abyss of nothing, in which I should still be, were it not for Thee is this the value that I set upon the precious blood of Thy veins spilt with so much pain and so much love for me? Ungrateful creature that I am! who will give sighs to my heart and tears to my eyes, that I may bewail, as I ought, the insults which I have offered to my God, my sovereign benefactor? O God of goodness! have mercy on me. I greatly desire, and firmly resolve, never to offend Thee more. Ah! why was I born to receive so many benefits from my God, and still to offend him so often and so grievously as I have done? How could I employ in offending him the hands, the feet, the tongue, the ears, the heart which he gave me to use in his service? O unhappy eyes! O criminal hands! O unfaithful heart! you, by your sins, have been the cause of the pains, the torments, and the cruel death which the Son of God suffered upon the cross.

III
The Presence of God

Reflect that the Most Blessed Trinity, Father, Son, and Holy Ghost, the only and almighty God, is everywhere present, that he sees all things, knows all things, and penetrates the inmost and most secret thoughts of our heart. He is that divine and infinite Majesty before whom the highest seraphim tremble with a holy fear, and veil their faces through respect; and we have the audacity to sin in his presence; to say, to do, and to think what, if known, would cover us with confusion before the meanest of men. Reflect, moreover, that this God, before whom we sin, is our sovereign Judge, who at the moment of our death will inevitably pass sentence upon the thoughts, the words, the actions, of which we may be found guilty.

An Act of Contrition

Supreme and just Judge of the living and the dead, Thou who seest and knowest all things, even those very secrets that pass in the interior of my heart, and which I would not have known to any creature upon earth, is it possible that I should dare to appear in Thy presence, after having been so unfaithful to Thee? Alas! I cannot fly from Thee, because Thou art present everywhere: I cannot hide myself from Thy view, because Thou seest all things. Ah! has not my insolence been insupportable in having dared, in the presence of Thy exalted majesty, before whom the purest angels cover their faces, to do what I would not have done before the meanest and the last of men? O my God! have mercy on me: I detest, with my whole heart, all my sins for the love of Thee.

Another Act of Contrition

O my God! I am covered with shame and confusion, when I reflect that I have lived in Thy presence with so little regard and respect, and that I have so often broken the protestations that I have made never to offend Thee more. O God! if I had made so many promises to any creature upon earth, how much should I feel ashamed at having broken my word! But, where Thou art concerned, I pay little regard to my resolutions, since I daily insult Thee before Thy eyes. Oh! how great is Thy goodness in having borne with me so long! O God of my heart! since Thou hast dealt mercifully with me in the course of my most heinous crimes, do not withdraw Thy mercy, now that I repent of all my dis loyalties.

Offering of the Holy Mass to obtain Remission of Sins

Heavenly Father, Father of mercy and God of consolation, who does comfort us in all our pains, accept, I beseech Thee, this sacrifice of the body and blood of Thy only Son, which I offer Thee to-day in union with the Church militant and the Church triumphant, in memory of the Passion, the resurrection, and the ascension of my Savior, and in honor of the Blessed Virgin and of ail the heavenly court, in order to satisfy for my sins and those of all men. Behold, O my God, on this altar Thy well-beloved Son, the one object of Thy complacency; listen to the voice of his wounds; consider the precious tears which from his cross he shed, whilst he prayed so humbly for me, his faithless murderer, but now a penitent sinner. Behold his heart burning with so pure, so ardent a love; and in consideration of his merits, deliver us from all the evils that we have deserved on account of our sins. Yes, O merciful Father! pardon us for the love of Jesus Christ who is our advocate and mediator, and who makes satisfaction for us, whilst together with the Holy Ghost he renders Thee all glory and all honor forever and ever. Amen.

ACTS FOR HOLY COMMUNION

I
PREPARATION FOR COMMUNION

St. Francis de Sales says, that our Savior can never be seen more amiable and more tender, in all that he has done for us, than in the Holy Communion, in which he, so to say, annihilates himself and becomes food, that he may unite himself to the hearts and bodies of his faithful. Therefore the learned Gerson used also to say, that there was no means more efficacious than the Holy Communion whereby to enkindle devotion and the holy love of God in our souls.

And, indeed, if we speak of doing something agreeable to God, what can a soul do more agreeable to him than to receive Communion? St. Denis teaches us that love always tends towards perfect union; but how can a soul be more perfectly united with Jesus than in the manner of which he speaks himself, saying: He that eateth My flesh and drinketh My blood abideth in Me and I in him? St. Augustine says, that if every day you receive this sacrament, Jesus will be always with you, and you will always advance in divine love.

Again, if there is question of healing our spiritual infirmities, what mo-re certain remedy can we have than the Holy Communion, which is called by the sacred Council of Trent "a remedy whereby we may be freed from daily faults, and be preserved from mortal sins."

Whence does it come, asks Cardinal Bona, that in so many souls we see so little fruit with so frequent Communions, and that they constantly relapse into the same faults? He replies: "The fault is not in the food, but in the disposition of him who receives." Can a man, says Solomon, hide fire in his bosom, and his garments not burn? God is a consuming fire. He comes himself in the Holy Communion to enkindle this divine fire; how is it, then, says William of Paris, that we see so diabolical a miracle as that souls should remain cold in divine love in the midst of such flames?

All comes from the want of proper dispositions, and especially from want of preparation. Fire immediately inflames dry but not green wood; for this latter is not disposed to burn. The saints derived great benefit from their Communions, because they prepared themselves with very great care. St. Aloysius Gonzaga devoted three days to his preparation for Holy Communion, and three days he spent in thanksgiving to his Lord.

To prepare well for Holy Communion, a soul should be disposed on two main points it should be detached from creatures, and have a great desire to advance in divine love.

1. In the first place, then, a soul should detach itself from all things, and drive everything from its heart which is not God. He that is washed, saith Jesus, needeth not but to wash his feet, but is clean wholly; which signifies, as St. Bernard explains it, that in order to receive this sacrament with great fruit, we should not only be cleansed from mortal sins, but our feet also should be washed, that is, free from earthly affections; for being in contact with the earth, they excite a sort of repugnance in God, and soiling the soul, prevent the effects of the Holy Communion.

St. Gertrude asked our Lord what preparation he required of her for the Holy Communion; and he replied: "I only ask that thou should come empty of thyself, to receive me."

2. In the second place, it is necessary, in the Holy Communion, to have a great desire to receive Jesus Christ and his holy love. In this sacred banquet, says Gerson, only those who are famishing receive their fill; and the most blessed Virgin Mary had already said the same thing: He hath filled the hungry with good things? As Jesus, writes the Venerable Father Avila, only came into this world after he had been much and long desired, so does he only enter a soul that desires him; for it is not becoming that such food should be given to him who has a loathing for it. Our Lord one day said to St. Matilda: "No bee flies with such impetuosity to flowers, to suck their honey, as I fly to souls in the Holy Communion, driven by the violence of my love." Since then, Jesus Christ has so great a desire to come into our souls, it is right that we also should have a great desire to receive him and his divine love by the Holy Communion. St. Francis de Sales teaches us that the principal object which a soul should have in view in communicating should be, to advance in the love of God; since he who for love alone gives himself to us should be received for love.

Acts before Communion
I. An Act of Faith

Behold, He cometh leaping upon the mountains, skipping over the hills. Ah, my most amiable Savior, over how many, what rough and craggy mountains, hast Thou had to pass in order to come and unite Thyself to me by means of this most holy sacrament! Thou, from being God, had to become man; from being immense, to become a babe; from being Lord, to become a servant. Thou hadst to pass from the bosom of Thy Eternal Father to the womb of a Virgin; from heaven into a stable; from a throne of glory to the gibbet of a criminal. And on this very morning Thou Wilt come from Thy seat in heaven to dwell in my bosom.

Behold He standeth behind our wall, looking through the windows, looking through the lattices? Behold, O my soul, thy loving Jesus, burning with the same love with which he loved thee when dying for thee on the Cross, is now concealed in the Most Blessed Sacrament under the sacred species; and what is he doing? Looking through the lattices. As an ardent lover, desirous to see you correspond to his love, from the Host, as from within closed lattices, whence he sees without being seen, he is looking at you, who are this morning about to feed upon his divine flesh; he observes your thoughts, what it is that you love, what you desire, what you seek for, and what offerings you are about to make him.

Awake, then, my soul, and prepare to receive thy Jesus; and, in the first place, by faith, say to him: So, then, my beloved Redeemer, in a few moments Thou art coming to me? O hidden God, unknown to the greater part of men, I believe, I confess, I adore Thee in the Most Holy Sacrament as my Lord and Savior! And in acknowledgment of this truth I would willingly lay down my life. Thou comest to enrich me with Thy graces and to unite Thyself entirely to me; how great, then, should be my confidence in this Thy so loving visit!

II. An Act of Confidence

My soul, expand thy heart. Thy Jesus can do Thee every good, and, indeed, loves thee. Hope thou for great things from this thy Lord, who, urged by love, comes all love to thee.

Yes, my dear Jesus, my hope, I trust in Thy goodness, that, in giving Thyself to me this morning, Thou wilt enkindle in my poor heart the beautiful flame of Thy pure love, and a real desire to please Thee; so that, from this day forward, I may never will anything but what Thou wiliest.

III. An Act of Love

Ah, my God, my God, true and only love of my soul, and what more couldst Thou have done to be loved by me? To die for me was not enough for Thee, my Lord; Thou wast pleased to institute this great sacrament in order to give Thyself all to me, and thus bind and unite Thyself heart to heart with so loathsome and ungrateful a creature as I am. And what is more, Thou Thyself invitest me to receive Thee, and desirest so much that I should do so! O boundless love ! incomprehensible love! infinite love! a God would give himself all to me! My soul, believest thou this? And what doest thou? what sayest thou? O God, O God, O infinite amiability, only worthy object of all love, I love Thee with my whole heart, I love Thee above all things, I love Thee more than myself, more than my life! Oh, could I but see Thee loved by all! Oh, could I but cause Thee to be loved by all hearts as much as Thou deservest! I love Thee, O most amiable God, and I unite my miserable heart in loving Thee to the hearts of the Seraphim, to the heart of the most blessed Virgin Mary, to the Heart of Jesus, thy most loving and beloved Son. So that, O Infinite Good, I love Thee with the love with which the saints, with which Mary, with which Jesus love Thee. And I love Thee only because Thou art worthy of it, and to give Thee pleasure. Depart, all earthly affections, that are not for God, depart from my heart. Mother of fair love, most holy Virgin Mary, help me to love that God whom Thou dost so ardently desire to see loved!

IV. An Act of Humility

Then, my soul, thou art even now about to feed on the most sacred flesh of Jesus ! And art thou worthy? My God, and who am I, and who art Thou? I indeed know and confess who Thou art that givest Thyself to me; but dost Thou know what I am who am about to receive Thee? And is it possible, O my Jesus, that Thou who art infinite purity desirest to come and reside in this soul of mine, which has been so many times the dwelling of Thy enemy, and soiled with so many sins? I know, O my Lord, Thy great Majesty and my misery; I am ashamed to appear before Thee. Reverence would induce me to keep at a distance from Thee; but if I depart from Thee, O my life, whither shall I go to whom shall I have recourse and what will become of me? No, never will I depart from Thee; nay, even I will ever draw nearer and nearer to Thee. Thou art satisfied that I should receive Thee as food, Thou even invitest me to this. I come then, O my amiable Savior, I come to receive Thee this morning, all humbled and confused at the sight of my defects; but full of confidence in Thy tender mercy, and in the love which Thou bearest me.

V. An Act of Contrition

I am indeed grieved, O God of my soul, for not having loved Thee during the time past; what is still worse, so far from loving Thee, and to gratify my own inclinations, I have greatly offended and outraged Thy infinite goodness I have turned my back upon Thee, I have despised Thy grace and friendship ; in a word, O my God, I was deliberate in my will to lose Thee. Lord, I am sorry, and grieve for it with my whole heart. I detest the sins which I have committed, be they great or small, as the greatest of all my misfortunes, because I have thereby offended Thee, O Infinite Goodness. I trust that Thou hast already forgiven me; but if Thou hast not yet pardoned me, oh, do so before I receive Thee wash with Thy blood this soul of mine, in which Thou art so soon about to dwell.

VI. An Act of Desire

And now, my soul, the blessed hour has arrived in which Jesus will come and take up his dwelling in thy poor heart. Behold the King of Heaven, behold thy Redeemer and God, who is even now coming; prepare thyself to receive him with love, invite him with the ardor of thy desire.

Come, O my Jesus, come to my soul, which desires Thee. Before Thou givest Thyself to me, I desire to give Thee, and I now give Thee, my miserable heart; do Thou accept it, and come quickly to take possession of it. Come, my God! hasten; delay no longer. My only and Infinite Good, my treasure, my life, my Paradise, my love, my all, my wish is to receive Thee with the love with which the most holy and loving souls have received Thee; with that with which the most blessed Virgin Mary received Thee ; to their Communions I unite this Communion of mine.

Most holy Virgin and my Mother Mary, behold, I already approach to receive thy Son. Would that I had the heart and love with which thou didst communicate! Give me this morning thy Jesus, as thou didst give him to the shepherds and to the kings. I intend to receive him from thy most pure hands. Tell him that I am thy servant and thy client; for he will thus look upon me with a more loving eye, and now that he is coming, will press me more closely to himself.

II
Thanksgiving After Communion

There is no prayer more agreeable to God, or more profitable to the soul, than that which is made during the thanksgiving after Communion. It is the opinion of many grave writers (Suarez, Cajetan, Valentia, De Lugo, and others), that the Holy Communion, so long as the sacramental species lasts, constantly produces greater and greater graces in the soul, provided the soul is then constant in disposing itself by new acts of virtue. The Council of Florence, in the decree of Eugenius IV to the Armenians, teaches that the Blessed Sacrament produces the same effect in the soul as material food, which, when it enters the body, takes effect according to the state in which it finds it.

For this reason, holy souls endeavor to remain as long as possible in prayer after Communion. The Venerable Father Avila, even when he was given his missions, used day on which you have communicated to keep yourself united by affections and prayers with Jesus, whom you have received.

Acts after Communion
1. An Act of Faith

Behold, my God is even now come to visit me; my Savior to dwell in my soul. My Jesus is even now within me. He is come to make himself mine, and at the same time to make me his. So that Jesus is mine, and I belong to Jesus: Jesus is all mine, and I am all his.

O Infinite Goodness! O Infinite Mercy! O Infinite Love that a God should come to unite himself to me, and to make himself all mine! My soul, now that thou art thus closely bound to Jesus, that thou art thus one with him, what doest thou? Hast thou nothing to say to him; dost thou not converse with thy God, who is with thee? Ah, yes, renew thy faith; remember that the angels now surround thee adoring their God, who is within thy breast ; do thou also adore thy Lord within thyself. Enter into thyself, and banish thence every other thought. Unite all thy affections, and, clinging closely to thy God.

2. An Act of Welcome

Ah, my Jesus, my love, my infinite good, my all, be ever welcome in the poor dwelling of my soul! Ah, my Lord, where art thou to what a place art Thou come! Thou hast entered my heart, which is far worse than the stable in which Thou wast born; it is full of earthly affections, of self-love, and of inordinate desires. And how couldst Thou come to dwell there? I would address Thee with St. Peter: Depart from me, for I am a sinful man. Yes, depart from me, O Lord, for I am indeed unworthy to receive a God of infinite goodness; go and find repose in those pure souls who serve Thee with so much love. But no, my Redeemer; what do I say? Leave me not; for if Thou departest, I am lost. I embrace Thee, my life; I cling to Thee. Mad indeed have I been in having separated myself from Thee for the love of creatures; and in my ingratitude I drove Thee from me. But now I will never more separate myself from Thee, my treasure; I desire to live and die ever united to Thee. Most blessed Virgin Mary, Seraphim, and all souls, do ye who love God with pure love lend me your affections, that I may worthily attend on my beloved Lord.

3. An Act of Thanksgiving

My God and Lord, I thank Thee for the grace which Thou hast this morning bestowed upon me, of coming to dwell in my soul; but I would wish to thank Thee in a manner worthy of Thee and of the great favor which Thou hast done me. But what do I say how can so miserable a creature as I am ever worthily thank Thee?

Father Segneri says, that the feeling most becoming a soul that communicates is that of wondering astonishment at the thought, and to repeat, "A God is united to me; a God is mine!" David said, What shall I render to the Lord for all the things that He hath rendered to me? But what return shall I make to Thee, my Jesus, who, after having given me so many of Thy good things, hast this morning, moreover, given me Thyself ? My soul, bless, then, and thank thy God as best thou canst.

4. An Act of Oblation

My Beloved to me, and I to Him? Should a king go to visit a poor shepherd in his hut, what can the shepherd offer him other than his whole hut, such as it is? Since, then, O Jesus, my divine king, Thou hast come to visit the poor house of my soul, I offer and give Thee this house and my entire self, together with my liberty and will: My Beloved to me, and I to Him. Thou hast given Thyself all to me; I give myself all to Thee. "My Jesus, from this day forward I will be no longer mine; I will be Thine, and all Thine, May my senses be Thine, that they may only serve me to please Thee. And what greater pleasure, says St. Peter of Alcantara, can be found, than that of pleasing Thee, most amiable, most loving, most gracious God? I at the same time give Thee all the powers of my soul, and I will that they shall be all Thine; my memory I will only use to recall to mind Thy benefits and Thy love; my understanding I will only use to think of Thee, who always thinkest of my good; my will I will only use to love Thee, my God, my all, and to will only that which Thou wiliest."

My most sweet Lord, I offer, then, and consecrate to Thee this morning all that I am and have my senses, my thoughts, my affections, my desires, my pleasures, my inclinations, my liberty; in a word, I place my whole body and soul in Thy hands.

5. An Act of Petition

O my soul, what art thou doing? The present is no time to be lost: it is a precious time, in which thou canst receive all the graces that thou askest. Seest thou not the Eternal Father, who is lovingly beholding thee for within thee he sees his beloved Son, the dearest object of his love. Drive, then, far from thee all other thoughts; rekindle thy faith, enlarge thy heart, and ask for whatever thou wiliest.

Hearest thou not Jesus himself who thus addresses thee: What wilt thou that I should do to thee? O soul, tell me, what dost thou desire of me? I am come for the express purpose of enriching and gratifying thee; ask with confidence, and thou wilt receive all.

Ah! my most sweet Savior, since Thou hast come into my heart in order to grant me graces, and desirest that I should ask Thee for them, I ask Thee not for the goods of the earth riches, honors, or pleasures; but grant me, I beseech Thee, intense sorrow for the displeasure that I have caused Thee ; impart to me so clear a light, that I may know the vanity of this world, and how deserving Thou art of love. Change this heart of mine, detach it from all earthly affections; give me a heart conformable in all things to Thy holy will, that it may seek only that which is more pleasing to Thee, and have no other desire than Thy holy love: Create a clean heart in me, O God.

I deserve not this; but Thou, my Jesus, deservest it, since Thou art come to dwell in my soul I ask it of Thee through Thy merits, and those of Thy most holy Mother, and by the love which Thou bearest to Thy Eternal Father.

LOVING ASPIRATIONS TO JESUS IN THE BLESSED SACRAMENT

BEFORE COMMUNION
I

"Go forth, ye daughters of Sion, and see king Solomon in the diadem wherewith his mother crowned him in the day of his espousals."

O daughters of grace, O ye souls who love God quit the darkness of earth, and behold Jesus, your king, crowned with a crown of thorns; the crown of contempt and suffering with which the impious synagogue, his mother crowned him on the day of his espousals, that is to say, on the day of his death, by means of which he espoused himself on the Cross to our souls. Go forth again, and behold him all full of compassion and love, now that he comes to unite himself to thee in this sacrament of love.

Has it indeed, then, cost Thee so much, my beloved Jesus, before Thou couldst come and unite Thyself to souls in this most sweet Sacrament? Wert Thou indeed obliged to suffer so bitter and ignominious a death? Oh, come, then, without delay, and unite Thyself to my soul also. It was at one time Thy enemy by sin; but now Thou desirest to espouse it by Thy grace. Come, Jesus, my spouse, for never more will I betray Thee; I am determined to be ever faithful to Thee. As a loving spouse, my whole thought shall be to find out Thy pleasure. I am determined to love Thee without reserve; I desire to be all Thine, my Jesus, all, all, all.

II

"A bundle of myrrh is my Beloved to me; he shall abide between my breasts."

The myrrh plant, when pricked, sends forth tears, and a healthful liquor from the wounds. Before his Passion, our Jesus determined to pour forth his divine blood from his wounds in so painful a way, to give it afterwards all to us for our salvation in this bread of life.

Come, then, O my beloved bundle of myrrh, O my enamored Jesus; Thou art indeed a subject of grief and pity to me when I consider Thee all wounded for me on the Cross but then, when I receive Thee in this most sweet Sacrament, Thou becomest indeed to me more sweet and delicious than a bunch of the choicest grapes can be to one who is parched with thirst: A cluster of cypress my Love is to me, in the vineyards of Engaddi? Come, then, to my soul, and revive and satiate me with Thy holy love Ah, what sweetness do I feel in my soul at the thought, that I have to receive within myself that same Savior of mine who for my salvation was pleased to be drained of all his blood, and sacrificed on a cross! He shall abide between my breasts. No, my Jesus, never more will I drive Thee hence; and Thou shalt never more have to leave me. I am determined ever to love Thee, and to be always united and closely bound up with Thee.

III

"While the King was at His repose my spike nard sent forth the odor thereof."

When Jesus comes to dwell in a soul in the Holy Communion, oh, how clearly does she see and know her own nothingness by the bright light which the king of heaven brings with him! As the spikenard is the most lowly amongst plants, so does the soul confess itself the most vile of all creatures; and when thus humbled, oh, how sweet is the odor which she breathes forth to her beloved king and for this reason he invites her to unite herself to him in closer and closer bonds.

If, then, my soul, thou desirest that thy Jesus should repose in thee, consider thy own nothingness. Who art thou what dost thou deserve? Humble thyself as thou shouldst do, by casting away from thyself all self-esteem which may keep Jesus at a distance from thee, or prevent him from coming to repose in thee.

Come to me, my dear Redeemer, come; and by thy divine light make me to see my own lowliness, my misery, my nothingness, that Thou mayest be enabled to repose in me with satisfaction to Thyself, to separate Thyself no more from me.

IV

"Think of the Lord in goodness."

My soul, why art thou so timid and fearful at the sight of the goodness and infinite love of thy Lord why such distrust? Now that thou art made worthy to receive within thee Jesus Christ, let thy sentiments correspond to this grace, by confiding in that goodness of God, who gives thee all himself. Truly his judgments are terrible, but they are terrible only to the proud and to the obstinate; but to the humble and penitent, who desire to love and please him, his judgments are all mercy and love, emanating from a heart full of compassion and kindness. So that David, considering these judgments of God, super abounds with hope have more than hoped in Thy judgments. These judgments made him happy and consoled him: Thy judgments are delightful; I remembered Thy judgments, and was comforted? Ah! our great God is only too loving and generous to those who seek him with love: The Lord is good to the soul that seeketh Him? How good is God to those who seek to unite their will to the divine will: How good is God to Israel, to those that are of a right heart?

My God, my love, my hope, my all, I desire Thee, and Thee alone, to love Thee, to please Thee, and to do Thy will in all things. Let me always find Thee; make me agreeable to Thee; and never let me leave Thee again. So be it. Amen, amen.

V

"The voice of my Beloved knocking: Open to Me, My sister, My love, My dove, My undefiled."

Such are the words which Jesus in the Blessed Sacrament speaks to those who love and desire him. Open to me, he says, O soul, thy heart, and there I will come to unite myself to thee; so that, being one with me, thou mayest become my sister by resemblance, my friend by participation in my riches, my dove by the gift of simplicity, my undefiled by the gift of purity, which I shall communicate to thee. And then he goes on to say, Open to me, or my head is full of dew and my locks of the drops of the night. As if he said: Consider, my beloved, that I have waited for thee all the night of the bad life thou hast led in the midst of darkness and error. Behold, now, instead of bringing scourges to chastise thee, I come in the Blessed Sacrament, with my hair full of heavenly dew, to extinguish in thee all impure desires towards creatures, and to kindle in Thee the happy fire of my love. Come, then, O my beloved Jesus, and work in me what Thou wilt. I renounce the love of all things, in order to be all Thine, and that Thou mayest make me as Thou wouldst have me, entirely united to Thy will.

VI

"Let my beloved come into His garden, and eat the fruit of His apple-trees."

Cornelius a Lapide says that this is precisely the invitation that a soul desirous of the Holy Communion makes to Jesus in the Blessed Sacrament. Come, my beloved, she says, into my poor heart, which at one unhappy time did not belong to Thee; but which now, by the help of Thy grace, has returned to Thee: Come and eat the fruit of Thy apple-trees. Come and taste in me those virtues which Thou dost bring with Thyself when Thou comest to me. O my Lord, at least for the honor of Thy majesty, purify my heart, adorn it, inflame it with Thy love, and make it beautiful in Thy sight, that it may be a worthy dwelling-place for.

VII

"You shall be carried at the breasts."

It is thus that Jesus from the sacred altars invites our souls. Come, he says, and suck my divine milk, which I give you in this Sacrament, wherein I offer you my own blood to drink. But what shepherd, says St. John Chrysostom, ever feeds his sheep with his own blood? Even mothers give their children to nurses to be fed. But Thou, O divine Pastor, art so enamored of our souls as to wish to nourish them with Thine own blood. St. Catharine of Sienna, then, did well in approaching the Holy Communion as if panting to suck the divine milk, in the same way as an infant presses anxiously to suck the milk from its mother's breast. And well might the Sacred Spouse say to her Beloved, Thy breasts are better than wine, signifying that she esteemed the milk of this sacrament, as the sacred interpreters explain it, above all the pleasures of the world, which are transitory and vain, as are transitory and vain also the joys and pleasures of wine.

VIII

"Eat, O friends, and drink, and be inebriated, my dearly beloved."

The "friends," that is beginners, who scarcely enjoy the divine friendship, when they receive the Holy Communion, feed indeed on the flesh of Jesus Christ, but they eat with labor; while those who are on the way to perfection eat with less difficulty. But by the "dearly beloved" are meant the perfect, who, inebriated with holy love, live almost out of the world, forget ting all things, even themselves, and think only how they may love and please their God.

My beloved Jesus, I am not yet perfect; but Thou canst make me perfect. I am not dear to Thee, and it is my own fault, because I have been ungrateful and unfaithful; but Thou canst make me become so, by inebriating me this morning with Thy love. Thy kingdom come? Come, my beloved Lord, and take possession of my whole soul. Establish Thy kingdom in me; so that Thou alone mayest reign in me, that Thy love alone may command me, and that Thy love only may I obey. Inebriate me, inebriate me entirely; make me forget all creatures, myself, my interests, and all, that I may love nothing but Thee, my God, my treasure, all my good, my all; may I sigh for Thee alone, seek Thee alone, think of Thee alone, and please Thee alone. Do this by the merits of Thy Passion. This only do I ask of Thee; this I hope.

IX

"Stay me up with flowers, compass me about with apples because I languish with love."

The languor of the soul is when, forgetful of herself and her affairs, she thinks only of seeking refreshment for her languishing love by holy desires, which are the flowers, and by good works, which are the fruits of divine love.

O my God, O Blessed Sacrament, since Thou wilt have me to be all Thine, make me what Thou wouldst have me. Make me forget everything that does not belong to Thy love. Increase in me always more and more the desire of pleasing Thee. Grant that these flowers may not always remain flowers; make them also become fruits, by my doing and suffering something for Thee, who hast done and suffered only too much for me. O God, O God of my soul, make Thyself loved, but really loved, by me, not only in word, but indeed, before death comes upon me.

X

"My Beloved is white and ruddy, chosen out of thousands."

Our beloved Jesus is all white by his purity, and all red by the flames of his divine love.

My spotless Lamb, all burning with love for me, when shall I make myself like to Thee, pure as Thou art, O lily; burning with love of Thee as Thou dost burn with love of me? Yes, I do renounce all other love, and choose for myself Thy sweet love, my God, my all. Begone, ye creatures! what do you want with me? Go and enjoy the love of those who seek you. I wish only for my God; for God alone will I keep all my heart and

XI

"The goodness and kindness of God our Savior appeared."

St. Paul says that God, by making himself man, showed the world how far his goodness towards us went. But by giving himself in this sacrament, he makes us know the depth of the tenderness of his love towards our souls. "Does it not seem madness to say, Eat my flesh, and drink my blood?" St. Augustine says, does it not seem a madness, Jesus Christ saying to us, as he said in that blessed night, Take and eat, this is My body? O men, he says, to make you understand how much I love you, I will that you should come and feed on my very flesh. O holy faith! And who among us would have been able to demand so much? Who could have even thought of it, if Jesus had not thought it and done it? Some of the followers of Jesus Christ, when they heard that from his mouth, that is, that he wished to give them his body to eat, said that this was too hard a thing, and that they could neither believe nor hear it: This saying is hard, and who can hear it? And they went so far as to leave him, because they would not believe it but yet it is of faith that so it is.

XII

"Do not consider me, that I am brown; for the sun has discolored me."

The heat of my passions, said the Sacred Spouse (and still more ought I to say it, O my dear Jesus), has deformed and blackened me I am black, but beautiful? But I am black by my own works; I am beautiful by Thy merits, O my Redeemer. I was black at one time, when I was alone and separated from Thee; but now that I am united to Thee, Thy grace, Thy beauty, Thy love has made me beautiful.

AFTER COMMUNION

I

"Draw me; we will run after Thee to the odor of Thy ointments."

Since, then, O my dear Jesus, I cannot, while in this life, ascend to Thee, Thou hast willed to descend to me, to unite Thyself to me in this sacrament of love. Draw me, my Lord, all to Thee. I do not wish to draw Thee to me, that Thou shouldst do my pleasure; but I desire that thou shouldst draw me so entirely to Thee by Thy sweet attractions, that I may not be able to desire or do anything else but Thy most holy will. It is just that my inclinations should yield to Thy disposition. Take me up wholly to Thyself; and so united, I shall be free from earthly affections, and shall run with Thee in the path of virtue, and be able to repose peacefully in Thy divine will both in this life and in the next: In peace, in the self-same I will sleep, and I will rest?

II

"The King brought me into the cellar of wine, and set in order charity in me."

It is precisely by this cellar of wine that St. Bonaventure understands the Holy Communion which introduces and then unites the soul to its divine king, and gives it to taste that wine of love which destroys the desire of created things; infuses a well-regulated love, that is just towards itself, charitable towards its neighbor, supreme towards God, loving him above all things, who above all things deserves to be loved.

O Jesus, my king, only Lord of my heart, Thou hast already brought me into the beautiful cellar of Thy love, that is, into Thyself, uniting me to Thee by means of this sacrament of love. Yes, my Lord, I already feel my heart changed. I feel a holy desire, which gives me peace, and makes me loathe all impure affections, and enkindles in me the pure love of Thee. O my Jesus, since Thou hast given me an entrance to this beautiful cellar, let me no more depart from it. Since Thou hast united Thyself to me, do not leave me again. Detach me from the love of all creatures. Unite me to Thee continually more and more on this earth, that I may one day come to be perfectly united to Thee in heaven; where I shall love Thee face to face with all my strength, without interruption and without imperfection throughout all eternity.

III

"My Beloved is gone down into His garden to feed in the gardens, and to gather lilies."

My sweet Savior, since Thou dost descend from heaven to come into my soul, by Thy grace do Thou make it become Thy garden, that Thou mayest gather in it lilies and fruits which are agreeable to Thee. Pardon me, if I have offended Thee. Receive me, if I have left Thee, now that I return penitent to Thee. Give me that purity which Thou dost desire to see in me. Give me strength to do what Thou desirest. Grant me Thy true love, and then shall I become pleasing to Thee. I sacrifice to Thee all my inclinations, and I desire and wish for nothing but to please Thee.

IV

"He is all lovely; such is my Beloved."

Jesus, to those souls who love him as spouses, makes himself altogether desirable, whether he chastises or consoles them, whether he appears near or distant, because he does it all for love, and that he may be loved.

Treat me, then, O my Jesus, as Thou wilt, I will always love Thee ; whether Thou dost give me sweet nesses or tribulations, I know that all will come to me from Thy loving heart, and that all will be for my greater good. My heart is ready, O God, my heart is ready. Behold, my will is ready, O Lord, to accept all that Thou shalt ordain. I will bless the Lord at all times? At all times, whether prosperous or adverse, I will bless Thee, and love Thee, O my Creator. I neither seek nor merit any consolation from Thee; for I have given Thee nothing but bitterness by my sins I seek only Thy good pleasure. Provided Thou art satisfied, I shall be content with any punishment. My Jesus, my Jesus, whether far off or near, Thou shalt always be desirable to me, always dear; whether Thou dost console or afflict me, I will always love Thee, always thank Thee.

V

"Who is this that cometh up from the desert flowing with delights, leaning upon her Beloved?"

Who, then, are those souls who, living on the earth, esteem it a desert? So that, detached from visible things, they live only to God; as if there was no one else but God, whom alone they love and desire to please. And in this way they almost go out of the world, and raise themselves above it; enjoying the delights which are experienced by those who wish for God alone, and who place in God all their hopes. Who, then, are these faithful souls, if not those who often and with pure love unite themselves to Jesus in the Blessed Sacrament?

Yes, my God, such do I also desire to be by the means of Thy grace, detached from all things, and to be all Thine. Henceforth the world shall be to me a desert, where, flying from all attachment to creatures, I will think of nothing but Thee; as if Thou and I were the only persons there. In Thee alone will I put all my confidence, all my love, O God, O beloved God, my hope, my love, my all.

VI

"If she be a wall, let us build upon it bulwarks of silver; if she be a door, let us join it together with boards of cedar."

This is precisely what Jesus does when he comes to a soul in the Holy Communion. He sees that she is a wall too weak to be able to resist the assaults of hell; therefore, by the virtue of the sacrament, he fortifies her with bulwarks of silver, that is, with his divine light. He sees that she is a door inclined easily to be corrupted, and he renews it, adjusting her with planks of strength and perseverance, as is signified by cedar, which is a strong and incorruptible wood; that is, with the gifts of holy fear, with detachment from creatures, with the love of prayer, with supplications, with holy desires, and still more with the gift of divine love, which are the support of holy perseverance: Bread strengthens man's heart. Jesus teaches us, that as earthly bread preserves the life of the body, so the heavenly bread of the Holy Communion preserves the life of the soul: He that eateth Me, the same shall live by Me? He that eateth my flesh and drinketh my blood abideth in Me and I in him. Such are the gracious promises which Jesus makes to him who receives him in the Blessed Sacrament.

Ah, my Jesus ! who is weaker and more unfaithful than I? Thou knowest well how many times I have yielded to my enemies, and how many times they have seized the gate, that is, my will, by which they have entered to ruin me by causing me to lose Thy friendship. Oh, fortify me with Thy light and strength, that I may no more lose Thee or drive Thee from me! My Lord and my dear Redeemer, if I am to turn back and offend Thee again, oh, let me die now, while I hope that I am in Thy grace and united to Thee! I trust not myself; no, nor will I ever, my dear Jesus, live without Thee. But as long as I live, I am in danger of changing my will and betraying Thee, as I have done before: do Thou help me. Help me also, most holy Mary; have pity on me thou who art the Mother of perseverance, obtain for me this gift from thy Jesus. Of thee I seek it, of thee I hope it, of thee I ask it.

VII

"I found Him whom my soul loveth: I held Him, and I will not let Him go."

So ought every soul to say who is united with Jesus in the Blessed Sacrament: Creatures, depart from me; go out altogether from my heart. I loved you once, because I was blind; now I love you not, nor can I ever love you again. I have found another good, infinitely more delightful than you I have found in myself my Jesus, who has enamored me by his beauty; to this love I have given myself entirely. He has already accepted me, so that I am no longer my own. Creatures, farewell: I am not, nor shall I ever again be yours; but I am and shall be always Christ's. He, too, is mine, and will always be mine held Him, and I will not let Him go? Now I have pressed him to my heart, receiving him in the Holy Communion; for the future I will hold him with my love, and will not let him leave me anymore.

VIII

"Arise, O north wind, and come, O south wind, blow through my garden, and let the aromatical spices thereof flow."

Fly from me, O north wind hurtful and cold wind of earthly affections; and come, thou soft, warm breeze of the sacred love of the Holy Spirit, which comes from the Heart of my Jesus in the Blessed Sacrament. Do thou alone breathe through my soul, which has been chosen by Jesus for his garden of delights. Blow; for by thy breath how many fresh and sweet odors of holy virtues shalt thou draw forth from me! My Jesus, my Jesus, Thou canst do this; and this do I hope from Thee.

IX

"I have gathered my myrrh, with my aromatical spices: I have eaten the honeycomb with my honey."

A soul which has received Jesus must be careful to gather myrrh, that it may always offer the sweet odor of those virtues which arise from mortification. I have eaten honeycomb with my honey. In like manner, the soul that loves God alone is not satisfied with the honey, but will also have the honeycomb; therefore it says to Jesus: O Lord, Thy consolations are not sufficient for me, unless Thou givest me Thyself, who art the fountain of consolation; the fruits of love are not enough for me, if Thou dost not give me also Thyself, who art the object of my love. Truly Thou alone will suffice for me; I am ready to renounce all Thy delights, provided I possess Thee alone, my God, and my only good. I love Thee, not to please myself, but to please Thee; for Thou dost desire to be loved by me, and Thou art worthy of all our love, whether Thou dost console or try us.

X

"He hath set me in a place of pasture, and I shall want nothing."

Ah, my beloved Jesus since Thou dost invite me in this feast of love to feed on Thy divine flesh, what more can I ever want? The Lord is my light and my salvation, whom shall I fear? Whom shall I fear, if Thou, O God omnipotent, art my light and my salvation? I give myself all to Thee. Accept me, and then do with me what Thou wilt; chastise me, show Thine

indignation towards me when Thou wilt; kill me, destroy me, and I will say always, with Job: Although He should kill me, I will trust in Him? Whilst I am Thine, and Thou lovest me, I am content to be treated by Thee with every hardship; to be even annihilated, if it so pleases Thee.

XI

"I have graven thee in My hands; thy walls are always before My eyes."

See the loving care that God takes of a soul that he wishes to have to himself. He carries it written in his hands, so that he may never forget it, and says, that sooner would a mother forget her own son than he a soul in grace : And if she should forget, yet will I not forget to. And thy walls are always before My eyes. His eyes are always open, to watch over that soul, so that its enemies do it not harm: Thou hast crowned us, as with a shield of Thy good-will? Our good

God surrounds us with the protection of his good-will, wholly solicitous for our good; and so he delivers us from all dangers. Ah, my God! infinite goodness, who more than any other lovest me and desirest my good, I abandon myself entirely to Thee. Should every other hope fall me, Thou wilt never fail me. I know that I also must co-operate by obeying Thy holy will. Lord, what wilt Thou have me to do? Nothing else can I say; behold me ready and determined, my sweet Savior, to do what Thou pleasest: Thy will be done. Nothing else do I desire but to accomplish Thy will. But do Thou help me, otherwise I shall do no good at all. Teach me not only to know, but also to do, all that pleases Thee: teach me to do Thy will? Eternal Father, grant that I may be able to say with truth, as Thy Jesus did whilst he was on earth always do the things that are pleasing to Him My God! this I desire, this I pray for, and this I hope, through the merits of Thy Son and the most holy Mary.

XII

"My son, give Me thy heart."

O my soul, behold this is all that thy Lord asks of thee; when he comes to visit thee, he would have thy heart and thy will. He gives himself to thee without reserve; it is but reasonable that thou shouldst also give him all thyself without reserve, taking care to follow his will in all things: For the Lord will return to rejoice over thee in all good things? Act in such a manner as that Jesus, when he comes to thee again, may find that thou hast executed all his designs. My Jesus! I wish to please Thee; help Thou my desire. Give me strength, and do with me whatsoever Thou pleasest.

XIII

"What is there that I ought to do to my vineyard that I have not done to it?"

My soul, hear what thy God says to thee; What ought I to do more for thee than I have done? For love of thee I became man I am the Word made flesh? Instead of Lord, I have become servant taking the form of a servant. I went so far as to be born in a stable, like a worm for worms are born in stables: I am a worm, and no man. I died for thee, I died upon the tree of shame was made obedient to death, even the death of the Cross. What remained more for me to do, but to give my life for thee? Greater love than this no man hath, that he should lay down his life for his friends? But my love has in vented and done more for thee. After my death, I have chosen to leave myself in the Most Blessed Sacrament, to give my whole self as food. Tell me what more could I have done to gain thy love?

XIV

"Put Me as a seal upon thy heart."

Yes, my beloved Jesus, since I have consecrated to Thee my whole heart, it is but just that I should put Thee as a seal of love upon it, to close the entrance against any other affection; and thus to make known to all that my heart is Thine, and that Thou alone possessest dominion over it. But, my Lord, what dost Thou hope from me, if Thou dost not do the work Thyself? I can do nothing but give Thee my poor heart, that Thou mayest dispose of me according to Thy pleasure. Behold, I give it all to Thee, I consecrate it to Thee, I sacrifice it to Thee. Do Thou possess it forever; I will no longer have any part in it. If Thou lovest it, mayest Thou be able to preserve it for Thyself. Leave it no longer in my hands, lest I should again take it from Thee. O God most gracious, O infinite love, since Thou hast so constrained me to love Thee, I pray Thee, make Thyself loved, make Thy self loved by me. I only wish to live that I may love Thee, I only wish to love Thee in order to please Thee. Thou who dost work miracles to be able to enter into my heart in this sacrament, work also this one, make my heart all Thine; but all, all, all, without division, without reserve, so that I may say, both in this life and in eternity, that Thou art the only Lord of my heart, and my only treasure : God is the God of my heart, and my portion forever?

Most holy Mary, my Mother and my hope, do thou help me, and I shall certainly be heard. Amen, amen. This I wish, this I hope. So be it.

HYMNS
I
HOLY COMMUNION

My soul, what dost thou? Answer me
Love God, who loves thee well
Love only does he ask of thee,
Canst thou his love repel?
See, how on earth for love of thee,
In lowly form of bread,
The sovereign good and majesty
His dwelling-place has made.
He bids thee now his friendship prove,

  And at his table eat;
To share the bread of life and love,
  His own true flesh thy meat.
What other gift so great, so high,
  Could God himself impart?
Could love divine do more to buy
  The love of thy poor heart?
Though once, in agonies of pain,
  Upon the cross he died,
A love so great, not even then
  Was wholly satisfied.
Not till the hour when he had found
  The sweet, mysterious way
To join his heart in closest bond
  To thy poor heart of clay.
How, then, amid such ardent flame,
  My soul, dost them not burn?
Canst thou refuse, for very shame,
  A loving heart's return?
Then yield thy heart, at length, to love
  That God of charity,
Who gives his very self to prove
  The love, he bears to thee.

II
TO JESUS AFTER COMMUNION

O bread of heaven! beneath this veil
  Thou dost my very God conceal;
  My Jesus, dearest treasure, hail!
  I love Thee, and adoring kneel
  The loving soul by Thee is fed
With Thy own self in form of bread!
O food of life! Thou who dost give
  The pledge of immortality!
  I live; no, tis not I that live,
God gives me life, God lives in me
He feeds my soul, he guides my ways
  And every grief with joy repays.
  O bond of love! that dost unite
  The servant to his loving Lord!
  Could I dare live, and not requite

Such loving then death were meet reward
I cannot live, unless to prove
Some love for such unmeasured love.
O mighty fire! thou that dost burn
To kindle every mind and heart!
For Thee my frozen soul doth yearn
Come, Lord of love, Thy warmth impart.
If thus to speak too bold appear,
Tis love like Thine has banished fear.
O sweetest dart of love divine!
If I have sinned, then vengeance take
Come, pierce this guilty heart of mine,
And let it die for his dear sake
Who once expired on Calvary,
His heart pierced through for love of me.
My dearest good! who dost so bind
My heart with countless chains to Thee I
O sweetest love, my soul shall find
In Thy dear bonds true liberty,
Thyself Thou hast bestowed on me,
Thine, Thine forever I will be!
Beloved Lord! in heaven above,
There, Jesus, Thou awaitest me
To gaze on Thee with changeless love.
Yes, thus I hope, thus shall it be
For how can he deny me heaven,
Who here on earth himself hath given?

VISITS TO THE BLESSED SACRAMENT AND TO THE BLESSED VIRGIN

INTRODUCTION

I

The Visit to the Most Holy Sacrament

Our holy faith teaches us, and we are bound to believe, that in the consecrated Host Jesus Christ is really present under the species of bread. But we must also understand that he is thus present on our altars as on a throne of love and mercy, to dispense graces and there to show us the love which he bears us, by being pleased to dwell night and day hidden in the midst of us.

It is well known that the Holy Church instituted the festival of Corpus Christi with a solemn octave, and that she celebrates it with the many usual processions, and so frequent expositions of this Most Holy Sacrament, that men may thereby be moved gratefully to acknowledge and honor this loving presence and dwelling of Jesus Christ in the Sacrament of the Altar, by their devotions, thanksgivings, and the tender affections of their souls. O God! how many insults and outrages has not this amiable Redeemer had, and has he not daily, to endure in this sacrament on the part of those very men for whose love he remains upon their altars on earth! Of this he indeed complained to his dear servant Sister Margaret Alacoque, as the author of the Book of Devotion to the Heart of Jesus relates. One day, as she was in prayer before the Most Holy Sacrament, Jesus showed her his heart on a throne of flames, crowned with thorns, and surmounted by a cross, and thus addressed her: "Behold that heart which has loved men so much, and which has spared itself nothing; and has even gone so far as to consume itself, thereby to show them its love; but in return the greater part of men only show me in gratitude, and this by the irreverences, tepidity, sacrileges, and contempt which they offer me in this sacrament of love; and that which I feel the most acutely is, that they are hearts consecrated to me." Jesus then expressed his wish, that the first Friday after the octave of Corpus Christi should be dedicated as a particular festival in honor of his adorable heart; and that on that day all souls who loved him should endeavor, by their homage, and by the affections of their souls, to make amends for the insults which men have offered him in this sacrament of the Altar; and at the same time he promised abundant graces to all who should thus honor him.

We can thus understand what our Lord said of, old by his prophet, that his delight is to be with the children of men; since he is unable to tear himself from them even when they abandon and despise him. This also shows us how agreeable all those souls are to the heart of Jesus who frequently visit him, and remain in his company in the churches in which he is, under the sacramental species. He desired St. Mary Magdalene of Pazzi to visit him in the Most Blessed Sacrament thirty three times a day; and this beloved spouse of his faith fully obeyed him, and in all her visits to the altar approached it as near as she possibly could, as we read in her life.

But let all those devout souls who often go to spend their time with the Most Blessed

Sacrament speak; let them tell us the gifts, the inspirations which they have received, the flames of love which are there enkindled in their souls, the paradise which they enjoy in the presence of this hidden God.

The servant of God and great Sicilian missionary Father, Louis La Nusa, was, even in his youth and as a layman, so enamored of Jesus Christ, that he seemed unable to tear himself from the presence of his beloved Lord. Such were the joys which he there experienced, that his director commanded him, in virtue of obedience, not to remain there for more than an hour. The time having elapsed, he showed in obeying (says the author of his life), that in tearing himself from the bosom of Jesus Christ he had to do himself just such violence as a child that has to detach itself from its mother's breast in the very moment in which it is satiating itself with the utmost avidity; and when he had to do this, we are told that he remained standing with his eyes fixed on the altar, making repeated inclinations, as if he knew not how to quit his Lord, whose presence was so sweet and gracious to him. To St. Aloysius it was also forbidden to remain in the presence of the Most Blessed Sacrament; and as he used to pass before it, finding himself drawn, so to speak, by the sweet attractions of his Lord, and almost forced to remain there, he would, with the greatest effort, tear himself away, saying, with an excess of tender love: Depart from me, O Lord, depart! There it was also that St. Francis Xavier found refreshment in the midst of his many labors in India; for he employed his days in toiling for souls, and his nights in the presence of the Most Blessed Sacrament.

In the visits you will read other examples of the tender affection with which souls inflamed with the love of God loved to dwell in the presence of the Most Holy Sacrament. But you will find that all the saints were enamored of this most sweet devotion; since, indeed, it is impossible to find on earth a more precious gem, or a treasure more worthy of all our love, than Jesus in the Most Holy Sacrament. Certainly amongst all devotions, after that of receiving the sacraments, that of adoring Jesus in the Blessed Sacrament holds the first place, is the most pleasing to God, and the most useful to ourselves. Do not then, O devout soul, refuse to begin this devotion; and forsaking the conversation of men, dwell each day, from this time forward, for at least half or quarter of an hour, in some church, in the presence of Jesus Christ under the sacramental species. Taste and see how sweet is the Lord. Only try this devotion, and by experience you will see the great benefit that you will derive from it. Be assured that the time you will thus spend with devotion before this most divine Sacrament will be the most profitable to you in life, and the source of your greatest consolation in death and in eternity. You must also be aware, that in a quarter of an hour's prayer spent in the presence of the Blessed Sacrament, you will perhaps gain more than in all the other spiritual exercises of the day. It is true, that in every place God graciously hears the petitions of those who pray to him, having promised to do so: Ask, and you shall receive yet the disciple tells us that Jesus dispenses his graces in greater abundance to those who visit him in the Most Holy Sacrament. Blessed Henry Suso used also to say that Jesus Christ hears the prayers of the faithful more graciously in the sacrament of the altar than elsewhere. And where, indeed, did holy souls make their most beautiful resolutions, but prostrate before the Most Holy Sacrament? Who knows but that you also may one day, in the presence of the tabernacle, make the resolution to give yourself entirely to God? In this little book I feel myself bound, at least out of gratitude to my Jesus in the Holy Sacrament, to declare, that through the means of this devotion of visiting the Most Blessed Sacrament, which I practiced, though with so much tepidity and in so imperfect a manner, I abandoned the world, in which, unfortunately, I lived until I was six-and-twenty years of age. Indeed that love it is which detains him there, thus hidden and unknown, and when he is even despised by ungrateful souls! But why should we say more? "Taste and see."

II
The Visit to the Blessed Virgin

And now as to the visits to the Most Blessed Virgin, the opinion of St. Bernard is well known, and generally believed it is, that God dispenses no graces otherwise than through the hands of Mary: "God wills that we should receive nothing that does not pass through Mary's hands." Hence Father Suarez declares that it is now the sentiment of the universal Church, that "the intercession of Mary is not only useful, but even necessary to obtain graces." And we may remark that the Church gives us strong grounds for this belief, by applying the words of the Sacred Scripture to Mary, and making her say: In me is all hope of life and of virtue. Come over to me, all ye that desire me: Let all come to me; for I am the hope of all that you can desire. Hence she then adds: Blessed is the man that heareth me, and that watcheth daily at my gates, and waiteth at the posts of my doors? Blessed is he who is diligent in coming every day to the door of my powerful intercession; for by finding me he will find life and eternal salvation: He that shall find me shall find life, and shall have salvation from the Lord? Hence it is not without reason that the Holy Church wills that we should all call her our common hope, by saluting her, saying, ---

"Hail, our hope!"

"Let us then," says St. Bernard (who went so far as to call Mary "the whole ground of his hope", "seek for graces, and seek them through Mary." Otherwise, says St. Antoninus, if we ask for graces without her intercession, we shall be making an effort to fly without wings, and we shall obtain nothing: "He who asks without her as his guide, attempts to fly without wings."

We read of the graces which she granted in these visits to Blessed Albert the Great, to the Abbot Rupert, to Father Suarez, especially when she obtained for them the gift of understanding, by which they afterwards became so renowned throughout the Church for their great learning: the graces which she granted to the Venerable John Berchmans of the Society of Jesus, who was in the daily habit of visiting Mary in a chapel of the Roman college he declared that he renounced all earthly love, to love no other after God than the Most Blessed Virgin, and had written at the foot of the image of his beloved Lady: "I will never rest until I shall have obtained a tender love for my Mother;" the graces which she granted to St. Bernardine of Sienna, who in his youth also went every day to visit her in a chapel near the city-gate, and declared that that Lady had ravished his heart. Hence he called her his beloved, and said that he could not do less than often visit her; and by her means he afterwards obtained the grace to renounce the world, and to become what he afterwards was, a great saint and the apostle of Italy.

Do you, then, be also careful always to join to your daily visit to the Most Blessed Sacrament a visit to the most holy Virgin Mary in some church, or at least before a devout image of her in your own house. If you do this with tender affection and confidence, you may hope to receive great things from this most gracious Lady, who, as St. Andrew of Crete says, always bestows great gifts on those who offer her even the least act of homage.

> Mary, Queen of sweetest hope,
> Who can ever forget thee?
> By thy mercy, by thy love,
> Have pity, Queen, on me?

III
Spiritual Communion

As in all the following visits to the Most Blessed Sacrament a spiritual Communion is recommended, it will be well to explain what it is, and the great advantages which result from its practice. A spiritual Communion, according to St. Thomas, consists in an ardent desire to receive Jesus in the Most Holy Sacrament, and in lovingly embracing him as if we had actually received him.

How pleasing these spiritual Communions are to God, and the many graces which he bestows through their means, was manifested by our Lord himself to Sister Paula Maresca, the foundress of the convent of St. Catharine of Sienna in Naples, when (as it is related in her life) he showed her two precious vessels, the one of gold, the other of silver. He then told her that in the gold vessel he preserved her sacramental Communions, and in the silver one her spiritual Communions. He also told Blessed Jane of the Cross that each time that she communicated spiritually she received a grace of the same kind as the one that she received when she really communicated. Above all, it will suffice for us to know that the holy Council of Trent greatly praises spiritual Communions, and encourages the faithful to practice them.

All those who desire to advance in the love of Jesus Christ are exhorted to make a spiritual Communion at least once in every visit that they pay to the Most Blessed Sacrament, and at every Mass that they hear; and it would even be better on these occasions to repeat the Communions three times, that is to say, at the beginning, in the middle, and at the end. This devotion is far more profitable than some suppose, and at the same time nothing can be easier to practice. The above named Blessed Jane of the Cross used to say, that a spiritual Communion can be made without any one remarking it, without being fasting, without the permission of our director, and that we can make it at any time we please an act of love does all.

MANNER OF MAKING THE VISITS
ACTS TO BE MADE BEFORE EACH VISIT TO THE MOST BLESSED SACRAMENT

My Lord Jesus Christ, who, for the love which Thou bearest to men, remainest night and day in this Sacrament full of compassion and of love, awaiting, calling, and welcoming all who come to visit Thee: I believe that Thou art present in the Sacrament of the Altar: I adore Thee from the abyss of my nothingness, and I thank Thee for all the graces which Thou hast bestowed upon me, and in particular for having given me Thyself in this Sacrament, for having given me Thy most holy Mother Mary for my advocate, and for having called me to visit Thee in this church.

I now salute Thy most loving Heart; and this for three ends: 1. In thanksgiving for this great gift; 2. To make amends to Thee for all the outrages which Thou receives in this Sacrament from all Thine enemies; 3. I intend by this visit to adore Thee in all the places on earth in which Thou art present in this Sacrament, and in which Thou art the least revered and the most abandoned.

My Jesus, I love Thee with my whole heart. I grieve for having hitherto so many times offended Thy infinite goodness. I purpose by Thy grace never more to offend Thee for the time to come; and now, miserable and unworthy though I be, I consecrate myself to Thee without reserve; I give Thee and renounce my entire will, my affections, my desires, and all that I possess. From henceforward do Thou dispose of me and of all that I have as Thou pleasest. All that I ask of Thee and de sire is Thy holy love, final perseverance, and the perfect accomplishment of Thy will.

I recommend to Thee the souls in purgatory; but especially those who had the greatest devotion to the Most Blessed Sacrament and to the Most Blessed Virgin Mary. I also recommend to Thee all poor sinners.

In fine, my dear Savior, I unite all my affections with the affections of Thy most loving Heart; and I offer them, thus united, to Thy Eternal Father, and beseech him in Thy name to vouchsafe, for Thy love, to accept and grant them.

AN ACT OF SPIRITUAL COMMUNION

My Jesus, I believe that Thou art truly present in the Most Blessed Sacrament. I love Thee above all things, and I desire to possess Thee within my soul. Since I am unable now to receive Thee sacramentally, come at least spiritually into my heart. I embrace Thee as being already there, and unite myself wholly to Thee; never permit me to be separated from Thee.

A SHORTER ACT

I believe that Thou, O Jesus, art in the Most Holy Sacrament! I love Thee and desire Thee! Come into my heart. I embrace Thee; oh, never leave me!

"May the burning and most sweet power of Thy love, O Lord Jesus Christ, I beseech Thee, absorb my mind, that I may die through love of Thy love, who was graciously pleased to die through love of my love."

VISIT TO THE BLESSED VIRGIN

Read the visit of the day, and finish by the following prayer, thereby to obtain the most powerful patronage of Mary:

Most holy Immaculate Virgin and my Mother Mary, to thee who art the Mother of my Lord, the Queen of the world, the advocate, the hope, the refuge of sinners, I have recourse today, I, who am the most miserable of all. I render thee my most humble homages, O Great Queen, and I thank thee for all the graces thou hast conferred on me until now, particularly for having delivered me from hell, which I have so often deserved. I love thee, O most amiable Lady; and for the love which I bear thee, I promise to serve thee always, and to do all in my power to make others love thee also. I place in thee all my hopes; I confide my salvation to thy care. Accept me for thy servant, and receive me under thy mantle, O Mother of mercy. And since thou art so powerful with God, deliver me from all temptations, or rather obtain me the strength to triumph over them until death. Of thee I ask a perfect love for Jesus Christ. From thee I hope to die a good death. O my Mother, by the love which thou bearest to God, I beseech thee to help me at all times, but especially at the last moment of my life. Leave me not, I beseech thee, until thou seest me safe in heaven, blessing thee, and singing thy mercies for all eternity. Amen. So I hope. So may it be.

VISITS TO THE BLESSED SACRAMENT AND TO BE BLESSED VIRGIN FOR EACH DAY OF THE MONTH

FIRST VISIT
To the Blessed Sacrament

Behold the source of every good, Jesus in the Most Holy Sacrament, who says, If any man thirst, let him come to Me. Oh, what torrents of grace have the saints drawn from the fountain of the Most Blessed Sacrament for there Jesus dispenses all the merits of his Passion, as it was foretold by the Prophet: You shall draw waters with joy out of the Savior's fountains? The Countess of Feria, that illustrious disciple of the Venerable Father John d Avila, afterwards a poor Clare, and surnamed the spouse of the Most Blessed Sacrament from her long and frequent visits to it, on being asked how she employed the many hours thus passed in the presence of the Holy of holies, answered: "I could remain there for all eternity. And is not there present the very essence of God, who will be the food of the blessed? Good God! am I asked what I do in his presence? Why am I not rather asked, what is not done there? We love, we ask, we praise, we give thanks. We ask, what does a poor man do in the presence of one who is rich? What does a sick man do in the presence of his physician? What does a man do who is parched with thirst in the presence of a clear fountain? What is thee occupation of one who is starving, and is placed before a splendid table?"

O my most amiable, most sweet, most beloved Jesus, my life, my hope, my treasure, the only love of my soul; oh, what has it cost Thee to remain thus with us in this Sacrament! Thou hadst to die, that Thou mightiest thus dwell amongst us on our altars; and then, how many insults hast Thou not had to endure in this Sacrament, in order to aid us by Thy presence ! Thy love, and the desire which Thou hast to be loved by us, have conquered all.

Come then, O Lord! come and take possession of my heart; close its doors forever, that henceforward no creature may enter there, to divide the love which is due to Thee, and which it is my ardent desire to bestow all on Thee. Do Thou alone, my dear Redeemer, rule me; do Thou alone possess my whole being; and if ever I do not obey Thee perfectly, chastise me with rigor, that thenceforward I may be more watchful to please Thee as Thou wiliest. Grant that I may no longer seek for any other pleasure than that of giving Thee pleasure; that all my pleasure may be to visit Thee often on Thy altar; to entertain myself with Thee, and to receive Thee in Holy Communion. Let all who will, seek other treasures; the only treasure that I love, the only one that I desire, is that of Thy love; for this only will I ask at the foot of the altar. Do Thou make me forget myself, that thus I may only remember Thy goodness.

Visit to the Blessed Virgin Mary

In our Mother Mary we have another fountain, which is indeed fruitful to us. She is so rich in good things and in graces, says St. Bernard, that there is no one in the world who does not participate in them: "Of her fullness we have all received." The Most Blessed Virgin Mary was filled by God with grace, and as such was saluted by the angel, "Hail, full of grace;" not for herself alone, but also for us. St. Peter Chrysologus adds, that she received that great abyss of grace, that she might then impart it to all who are devout to her: "The Blessed Virgin received this grace, that she might give in return salvation to all."

SECOND VISIT
To the Blessed Sacrament

The devout Father Nuremberg says, that bread being a food which is consumed by eating, and which keeps when preserved for use, Jesus was pleased to dwell on earth under its species, that he might thus not only be consumed by uniting himself to the souls of his lovers by means of the Holy Communion, but also that he might be preserved in the tabernacle, and be present with us, and thus remind us of the love which he bears us. St. Paul says: He emptied Himself, taking the form of a servant? But what must we say when we see him "taking the form of bread"? "No tongue would suffice," says St. Peter of Alcantara, "to proclaim the greatness of the love which Jesus bears to every soul that is in a state of grace. In order, therefore, that his absence might not be to them an occasion of forgetting him, this most sweet Spouse, when he was pleased to quit this life, left as a memorial this Most Blessed Sacrament, in which he himself remained. He did not wish that between these souls and himself any other pledge but himself should remain, whereby to keep alive their remembrance of him."

Since, then, my Jesus, Thou art enclosed in this tabernacle to receive the supplications of miserable creatures who come to seek an audience of Thee, listen this day to the petition addressed to Thee by the most ungrateful sinner living on earth. I come repentant to Thy feet; for I now know the evil which I have committed in giving Thee displeasure. My first prayer and desire, then, is, that Thou wilt be pleased to pardon me all the sins that I have committed against Thee. Ah, my God, would that I had never offended Thee! After this I must tell Thee my next desire. Now that I have found out Thy sovereign goodness, I have become enamored of Thee; I feel an ardent desire to love Thee and to please Thee; but I have not the strength to do this unless Thou helpest me.

Visit to the Blessed Virgin Mary

Let us go with confidence to the throne of grace that we may obtain mercy, and find grace in seasonable aid. St. Antoninus says, that Mary is this throne, from which God dispenses all graces.

O most amiable Queen, since thou hast so great a desire to help sinners, behold a great sinner who has recourse to thee; help me much, and help me without delay!

Prayer of St. Ephrem

O Queen of the universe and most bountiful sovereign! thou art the great advocate of sinners, the sure port of those who have suffered shipwreck, the resource of the world, the ransom of captives, the solace of the weak, the consolation of the afflicted, the refuge and salvation of every creature. O full of grace enlighten my understanding, and loosen my tongue, that I may recount thy praises, and sing to thee the angelical salutation, which thou so justly deservest. Hail, thou who art the peace, the joy, the consolation of the whole world! Hail, pars disc of delight, the assured asylum of all who are in danger, the source of grace, the mediatrix between God and man.

THIRD VISIT
To the Blessed Sacrament

And My delights were to be with the children of men. Behold our Jesus, who, not satisfied with dying on earth for our love, is pleased even after his death to dwell with us in the Most Holy Sacrament, declaring that he finds his delights among men. "O men," exclaims St. Teresa, "how can you offend a God who declares that it is with you that he finds his delights!" Jesus finds his delights with us; and shall we not find ours with Jesus? And we especially who have had the honor to dwell in his palace? How greatly do those vassals esteem themselves honored to whom the king assigns an abode in his own residence! Behold the palace of the King; it is this house in which we dwell with Jesus Christ. Let us, then, learn to thank him for it, and to avail ourselves of con versing with Jesus Christ.

Behold me, then, O my Lord and God, before this altar, on which Thou dost reside night and day for my sake. Thou art the source of every good; Thou art the healer of every ill; Thou art the treasure of every poor creature. Behold now at Thy feet a sinner, who is of all the poorest and most infirm, and who asks Thy mercy; have pity upon me! Now that I see Thee in this Sacrament, come down from heaven upon earth only to do me good; I will not be disheartened at the sight of my misery. I praise Thee, I thank Thee, I love Thee; and if Thou wiliest that I should ask Thee for an alms, I will ask for this. O listen to me: I desire never more to of fend Thee; and I desire that Thou shouldst give me light and grace to love Thee with all my strength. Lord, I love Thee with my whole soul; I love Thee with all my affections. Do Thou grant that I may thus speak with truth; and that I may speak in the same way during life and for all eternity. Most holy Virgin Mary, my holy patron saints, ye angels and all ye blessed spirits of paradise, help me to love my most amiable God.

Visit to the Blessed Virgin Mary.

Her bands are a healthful binding? The devout Pelbart says that devotion to Mary is a chain of predestination. Let us beseech our sovereign Lady to bind us always more closely by the chains of love to confidence in her protection.

FOURTH VISIT
To the Blessed Sacrament

Her conversation hath no bitterness, nor her company any tediousness? Friends on earth find such pleasure in being together, that they lose entire days in each other's company with Jesus in the Most Holy Sacrament, those who love him not, get weary. After her death, St. Teresa, who was already in heaven, said to a nun: "Those who are in heaven and those who are on earth should be one and the same in purity and in love; we enjoying, and you suffering; and that which we do in heaven with the divine Essence, you should do on earth with the Most Blessed

Sacrament." Behold, then, our paradise on earth; the Most Blessed Sacrament.

O immaculate Lamb, sacrificed for us upon the cross, remember that I am one of those souls that Thou hast redeemed by so many sufferings, and by Thy death. Grant that Thou mayest be mine, and that I may never lose Thee, since Thou hast given Thyself to me, and givest Thyself every day, sacrificing Thyself for my love on the altar; and grant that I may be all Thine. I give myself to Thee without reserve, that Thou mayest dis pose of me as Thou pleasest. I give Thee my will; chain it with the sweet bonds of Thy love, that it may forever be the slave of Thy most holy will. I wish no longer to live for the satisfaction of my desires, but only to please Thy goodness. Destroy in me all that does not please Thee; grant me the grace never to have any other thought than to please Thee, any other desire than that which Thou desirest. I love Thee, O my dear Savior, with my whole heart; I love Thee because Thou desirest that I should love Thee; I love Thee because Thou art indeed worthy of my love. I grieve that I love Thee not as much as Thou deservest. I desire, Lord, to die for Thy love; accept my desire and give me thy love. Amen.

Visit to the Blessed Virgin Mary

Mary says: I am the Mother of fair love; that is to say, she is the Mother of that love which beautifies souls. St. Mary Magdalene of Pazzi saw the Most Blessed Virgin Mary going about dispensing a sweet liquid, which was divine love. This gift is dispensed only by Mary; from Mary let us seek it.

Ejaculatory Prayer. My Mother, my hope, make me belong wholly to Jesus.

FIFTH VISIT
To the Blessed Sacrament

The sparrow had found herself a house, and the turtle a nest for herself, where she may lay her young ones! Thy altars, O Lord of hosts, my King and my God? The sparrow, says David, finds a dwelling in houses; turtle-doves in nests; but Thou, my king and my God, hast made Thyself a nest and found a dwelling on earth on our altars, that we might find Thee, and that Thou mightest dwell amongst us.

Lord, we cannot but say, that Thou art too much enamored of men; Thou no longer knowest what to do to gain their love. But do Thou, my most amiable Jesus, give us the grace that we also may be passionately enamored of Thee. It would indeed be unreasonable were we cold in our love towards a God who loves us with such affection. Draw us to Thee by the sweet attractions of Thy love; make us understand the endearing claims which Thou hast on our love.

O infinite Majesty and infinite Goodness, Thou lovest men so much, Thou hast done so much that Thou mightiest be loved by men how is it, then, that amongst men there are so few who love Thee? I will no longer be as I have hitherto been, of the unhappy number of those ungrateful creatures: lam resolved to love Thee as much as I can, and to love no other than Thee: Thou deserves it; Thou commandest me with too much earnestness to do so, I am resolved to satisfy Thee. Grant, O God of my soul, that I may fully satisfy Thee. I entreat Thee to grant me this favor by the merits of Thy Passion, and I confidently hope for it. Bestow the goods of the earth on those who desire them; I desire and seek the great treasure of Thy love alone. I love Thee, my

Jesus; I love Thee, infinite Goodness. Thou art all my riches, my whole satisfaction, my entire love.

Visit to the Blessed Virgin Mary

My Lady, St. Bernard calls thee "the ravisher of hearts." He says that thou goest about stealing hearts by the charms of thy beauty and goodness. Steal also my heart and will, I beseech thee: I give them wholly to thee; offer them to God with thine own.

Ejaculatory Prayer. Mother most amiable, pray for me!

Prayer of St. Bernard

We look up to thee, O Queen of the world, for protection. After a life of so much sin and ingratitude, we have to appear before our Judge, and who shall appease his wrath? No one is so well qualified to do this as thyself, who didst love him so tenderly, and was so tenderly loved by him. O Mother of mercy, open then thy ears to our sighs and prayers. Thou dost not look with disdain on the sinner, however enormous his crimes may have been; if with sincere repentance he cries out to thee and entreats thy intercession, thou despisest him not. Thou animatest and consolest him, and dost not abandon him, until thou hast reconciled him with his Judge.

We fly, therefore, to thy protection, entreating thee to appease the indignation of thy Son, and to restore us to His grace.

Ejaculatory Prayer. O Mary! show thyself a mother to us.

SIXTH VISIT
To the Blessed Sacrament

Where your treasure is, there will your heart be also. Jesus Christ says, that where a person esteems his treasure to be, there also he keeps his affections. Therefore the saints, who neither esteem nor love any other treasure than Jesus Christ, center their hearts and all their love in the Most Blessed Sacrament.

My most amiable Jesus, hidden under the sacramental veils, who for the love which Thou bearest me remainest night and day imprisoned in this tabernacle, draw, I beseech Thee, my whole heart to Thee, that I may think of none but Thee, that I may love and seek and hope for Thee alone. Do this by the merits of Thy Passion, through which I seek and hope for it.

Ah, my sacramental Lord and divine Lover, how amicable and tender are the inventions of Thy love to gain the love of souls! O Eternal Word, Thou, in becoming man, was not satisfied with dying for us; Thou hast also given us this sacrament as a companion, as food, and as a pledge of heaven. Thou reducest Thyself so as to appear amongst us, at one time as an infant in a stable, at another as a poor man in a workshop, then as a criminal on a gibbet, and now as bread on an altar. Tell me, could Thou invent other means to win our love?

O infinite goodness, when shall I really begin to correspond with such refinements of love? Lord, I will only live to love Thee alone. And of what use is life to me, if I do not spend it wholly in loving and pleasing Thee, my beloved Redeemer, who hast poured out Thy whole life for me? And what have I to love, if it is not Thee, who art all beauty, all condescension, all goodness, all loving, all worthy of love? May my soul live only to love Thee; may the sole remembrance of Thy love dissolve my soul with love; may the very names of crib, and cross, and sacrament inflame it with the desire to do great things for Thee, O my Jesus, who hast indeed done and suffered great things for me!

Ejaculatory Prayer. Grant, my Lord, that before I die I may do something for Thee!

As a fair olive-tree in the plaint I am, says Mary, the beautiful olive-tree from which the oil of mercy always flows. And I stand in the plain, that all may see me, and that all may have recourse to me. "Remember (let us say in the words of the prayer of St. Bernard), O most compassionate Mary, that it has never been heard of in any age, that anyone having recourse to thy protection was abandoned by thee" Most merciful Queen, such a thing was never heard of, that anyone having recourse to thy aid was abandoned: I will not be the first unfortunate creature who, having recourse to thee, was abandoned.

Ejaculatory Prayer. O Mary, grant me the grace always to have recourse to thee!

Behold I am with you all days, even to the consummation of the world? Thus our loving shepherd, who has given his life for us who are His sheep, would not separate himself from us by death. Behold me, he says, beloved sheep; I am always with you; for you I have remained on earth in this Sacrament; here you find me whenever you please, to help and console you by my presence: I will not leave you until the end of the world, as long as you are on earth. The Bridegroom, says St. Peter of Alcantara, wished to leave his bride company, that she might not remain alone during so long an absence; and therefore he left this Sacrament, in which he himself, the best companion he could leave her, remains.

My sweetest Lord, my most amiable Savior, I am now visiting Thee on this altar; but Thou return me the visit with far other love when Thou enter my soul in the Holy Communion. Thou art then not only present to me, but Thou becomes my food; Thou unites and give Thy whole self to me, so that I can then say with truth, My Jesus, Thou art now all mine. Since, then,

Thou give Thyself all to me, it is reasonable that I should give myself all to Thee. I am a worm, and Thou art God. O God of love! O love of my soul! when shall I find myself all Thine, in deeds, and not only in words? Thou canst do this; by the merits of Thy blood increase my confidence, that I may at once obtain this grace of Thee, that I may find myself all Thine, and in nothing mine own. Thou graciously nearest, O Lord, the prayers of all; hear now the prayers of a soul that indeed desires really to love Thee. I desire to love Thee with all my strength, I desire to obey Thee in all that Thou wiliest, without self-interest, without consolations, without reward.

Visit to the Blessed Virgin Mary

O our own most amiable Lady, the whole Church pro claims and salutes thee as "hope"! Thou, then, who art the hope of all, be also my hope. St. Bernard called thee "the whole ground of his hope," and said: "Let him who despairs hope in thee." Thus also will I address thee: My own Mary, thou save even those who are in despair; in thee I place all my hope.

Ejaculatory prayer. Mary, Mother of God, pray to Jesus for me!

To every soul that visits Jesus in the Most Holy Sacrament, he addresses the words which he said to the Sacred Spouse: Arise, make haste, my love, mv dove, my beautiful one, and come. Thou. O soul, that visit me, "arise" from thy miseries; I am here to enrich thee with graces. "Make haste," approach, come near me; fear not my majesty, which has humbled itself in this

Sacrament in order to take away thy fear, and to give thee confidence. "My beloved" thou art no longer my enemy, but my friend; since thou loves me and I love thee. "My beautiful one," my grace has made thee fair. "And come," draw near and cast thyself into my arms, and ask me with the greatest confidence for whatever thou wiliest.

St. Teresa says that this great king of glory has dis guised himself in the Sacrament under the species of bread, and that he has concealed his majesty to encourage us to approach his divine heart with greater confidence. Let us, then, draw near to Jesus with great condense and affection; let us unite ourselves to him, and let us ask him for graces.

O Eternal Word made man, and present for my sake in this Sacrament, what joy should be mine now that I stand in Thy presence, who art my God, who art infinite majesty and infinite goodness, and hast so tender an affection for my soul ! Ye souls who love God, wherever you may be, either in heaven or on earth, love him for me also. Mary, my Mother, help me to love him. And Thou, most beloved Lord, make Thyself the object of all my love. Make Thyself the Lord of my entire will; possess my entire self. I consecrate my whole mind to Thee, that it may always be occupied with the thought of Thy goodness; I also consecrate my body to Thee, that it may help me to please Thee; I consecrate my soul to Thee, that it may be all Thine. Would, O be loved of my soul, that all men could know the tender ness of the love which Thou bears them, that all might live only to honor Thee and to please Thee, as Thou desires and deserves. Grant that at least I may always live enamored of Thy infinite beauty. From this day forward my desire is to do all that I can to be pleasing to Thee. I now resolve to abandon everything, be it what it may, as soon as I perceive that it displeases Thee, however much it may cost me, even should it be necessary for this purpose to lose all, or even to lay down my life. Fortunate indeed shall I be, if I lose all to gain Thee, my God, my treasure, my love, my all!

Ejaculatory prayer. Jesus, my love, take all that I have; take full possession of me!

Visit to the Blessed Virgin Mary

Whoever is a little one, let him come to me? Mary invites all children who need a mother to have recourse to her, as to the most loving of all mothers. The devout Nieremberg says, that the love of all mothers is a shadow in comparison with the love which Mary bears to each one of us. My Mother, mother of my soul, thou who loves me, and desires my salvation more than any other after God, O Mother, "show thyself a Mother."

Ejaculatory prayer. My Mother, grant that I may always remember thee!

NINTH VISIT
To the Blessed Sacrament

St. John says that he saw our Lord girt up with a golden girdle, which supported his breasts: I saw the Son of Man girt about the pans with a golden girdle? Thus also is Jesus in the Sacrament of the Altar, with his breasts all filled with milk; that is to say, with the graces which, in his mercy, he desires to bestow upon us. And as a mother, whose breasts are overcharged with milk, goes about seeking for children who may draw it off, and relieve her of its weight, so also does he call out to us, You shall be carried at the breasts?

The Venerable Father Alvarez saw Jesus in the Blessed Sacrament with his hands filled with graces, and seeking to whom he might dispense them. Of St. Catharine of Sienna it is related, that when she approached the Most Holy Sacrament, she did so precisely with the same loving avidity with which a child flies to its mother s breast.

O most beloved and only-begotten Son of the Eternal Father, I know that Thou art the object most worthy of being loved. I desire to love Thee as much as Thou deserves to be loved, or at least as much as a soul can ever desire to love Thee. I fully understand that I, who am a traitor, and so great a rebel to Thy love, deserve not to love Thee, neither do I deserve to approach Thee so near as I now am in this church. But I feel that Thou, for all this, seeks my love; I hear Thee say, My son, give me thy heart. 1 Thou shall love the Lord thy God with thy whole heart? I understand that it is for this end that Thou hast spared my life, and not sent me to hell, that I might be converted and turn all my affections to Thee. Since, then, Thou art pleased that even I should love Thee, oh, yes, my God, I will do so. Behold me: to Thee I yield myself up; I give myself to Thee; I love Thee. O God ! all goodness, all love, I choose Thee for the only king and lord of my poor heart. Thou desires it, and my will is to give it to Thee : it is cold, it is loathsome ; but if Thou accepts it, Thou wilt change it. Change me, my Lord, change me; I no longer have courage to live as I have hitherto done, ungrateful, and with so little love towards Thy infinite goodness, which loves me so much, and deserves an infinite love.

TENTH VISIT
To the Blessed Sacrament

O foolish ones of the world, says St. Augustine, miser able creatures, where are you going to satisfy your hearts? Come to Jesus; for by him alone can that pleasure which you seek be bestowed. "Unhappy creatures, whither are you going ? The good you seek for comes from him." 1 My soul, be not of the number of these foolish ones; seek God alone: "seek for that one good in which are all good things." And if thou desires soon to find him, behold, he is close to thee; tell him what thou desires, since for this end it is that he is in the ciborium, to console thee, and to grant thy prayer. St. Teresa says that all are not allowed to speak to their king : the most that can be hoped for is to communicate with him through a third person. To converse with Thee, O King of glory, no third person is needed; Thou art always ready in the Sacrament of the Altar to give audience to all. All who desire Thee always find Thee there, and converse with Thee face to face. And even if anyone at length succeeds in speaking with a king, how many difficulties

has he had to overcome before he can do so! Kings grant audiences only a few times in the year; but Thou, in this Sacrament, grants audience to all night and day, and whenever we please.

O Sacrament of love, Thou who, whether Thou gives Thyself in the Communion, or dwells on the altar, knows, by the tender attractions of Thy love, how to draw so many hearts to Thyself, who, enamored of Thee, and filled with amazement at the sight of such love, burn with joy, and think always of Thee; draw also my miserable heart to Thyself; for it desires to love

Thee, and to live enslaved by Thy love. For my part, I now and henceforward place all my interests, all my hopes, and all my affections, my soul, my body, I place all in the hands of Thy goodness. Accept me, O Lord, and dispose of me as Thou pleases. I will never again complain, O my love, of Thy holy dispensations; I know that, as they all take their source in Thy loving heart, they all will be full of love, and for my good. It is enough for me to know that Thou wiliest them; I will them also in time and in eternity. Do all that Thou wiliest in me and with me ; I unite my entire self to Thy will, which is all holy, all good, all beautiful, all perfect, all loving. O will of my God, how dear art thou to me! My will is ever to live and die united to and bound up with Thee. Thy pleasure is my pleasure. I will that Thy desires shall also be my desires. My God, my God, help me; make me henceforward live for Thee alone; make me will only what Thou wiliest, and make me live only to love Thy amiable will. Grant that I may die for Thy love, since Thou hast died and become food for me. I curse those days in which I did my own will, so much to Thy displeasure. I love thee, O will of God, as much as I love God, since thou art one with him. I love Thee, then, with my whole heart, and give myself all to Thee. Ejaculatory prayer. O will of God, thou art my love!

ELEVENTH VISIT
To the Blessed Sacrament

"Let us be careful," says St. Teresa, "never to be at a distance from Jesus our beloved Shepherd, nor to lose sight of him; for the sheep which are near their shepherd are always more caressed and better fed, and always receive some choice morsels of that which he himself eats. If by chance the shepherd sleeps, still the lamb remains near him, and either waits until his slumber ends, or itself awakens him; and it is then caressed with new favors.

My Redeemer, present in this Most Holy Sacrament, behold me near Thee: the only favor which I ask of Thee is, fervor and perseverance in Thy love. I thank thee, O holy faith; for thou teaches and assures me that in the divine Sacrament of the Altar, in that heavenly bread, bread does not exist; but that my Lord Jesus Christ is all there, and that he is there for love of me. My Lord and my all, I believe that Thou art present in the Most Holy Sacrament; and though unknown to eyes of flesh, by the light of holy faith I discern Thee in the consecrated Host, as the monarch of heaven and earth, and as the Savior of the world. Ah, my most sweet Jesus! as Thou art my hope, my salvation, my strength, my consolation, so also I will that Thou should be all my love, and the only subject of all my thoughts, of my desires, and of my affections. I rejoice more in the supreme happiness which Thou enjoys, and wilt enjoy forever, than in any good thing which I could ever have in time or in eternity. My supreme satisfaction is, that Thou, my beloved Redeemer, art supremely happy, and that Thy happiness is infinite. Reign, reign, my Lord, over my whole soul; I give it all to Thee; do Thou ever possess it. May my will, my senses, and my faculties be all servants of Thy love, and may they never in this world serve for anything else than to give Thee satisfaction and glory.

TWELFTH VISIT
To the Blessed Sacrament

God is charity ; and he that abides in charity, abides in God, and God in him. He who loves Jesus dwells with Jesus, and Jesus with him. If anyone love Me... My Father will love him; and We will come to him, and will make Our abode with him? When St. Philip Neri received the Holy Communion as Viaticum, on seeing the Most Blessed Sacrament enter his room, he exclaimed: "Behold my love! behold my love!" Let each one of us, then, say, here in the presence of Jesus in the Blessed Sacrament: Behold my love! Behold the object of all my love for my whole life and for all eternity!

Since, then, my Lord and my God, Thou hast said in the Gospel that he who loves Thee will be beloved by Thee, and that Thou wilt come and dwell in him, and never more leave him, I love Thee above every other good: do Thou, then, also love me; for I, indeed, esteem being loved by Thee above all the kingdoms of the world. Come and fix Thy dwelling in the poor house of my soul in such a way that Thou may no more depart from me; or rather, so that I may never more drive Thee from me. Thou dost not go, if Thou art not expelled; but as I have already done this, so I might do again.

Visit to the Blessed Virgin Mary

They that work by me shall not sin. He, says Mary, who endeavors to honor me shall persevere to the end. They that explain me shall have life everlasting and those who endeavor to make me known and loved by others will be of the number of the elect. Promise, then, that whenever you can, be it in public or in private, you will speak of the glories of Mary, and of devotion to her.

Ejaculatory prayer. Vouchsafe that I may praise Thee, most sacred Virgin!

THIRTEENTH VISIT
To the Blessed Sacrament

My eyes and my heart shall be there always? Behold, Jesus has verified this beautiful promise in the Sacrament of the Altar, wherein he dwells with us night and day.

My Lord, would it not have been enough had Thou remained in this Sacrament only during the day, when Thou could have had adorers of Thy presence to keep Thee company; but why remain also the whole night, when the churches are all closed, and when men retire to

their homes, leaving Thee quite alone ? Ah, yes! I already understand Thee: love has made Thee our prisoner; the excessive love which Thou bears us has so bound Thee down on earth, that neither night nor day can Thou leave us. Ah, most amiable Savior, this refinement of love alone should oblige all men ever to stay with Thee in the sacred ciboriums, and to remain with Thee until forcibly compelled to leave Thee; and when they do so, they should all leave at the foot of the altar their hearts and affections inflamed with love towards an Incarnate God, who remains alone and enclosed in a tabernacle, all eyes to see and provide for them in their necessities, and all heart to love them, and who awaits the coming day to be again visited by his beloved souls.

O Love, O God of love, reign, triumph over my entire self; destroy and sacrifice all in me which is mine and not Thine. Permit not, O my Love, that my soul, which, having received Thee in the Holy Communion, is filled with the Majesty of God, should again attach itself to creatures. I love Thee, my God, I love Thee; and I will love Thee alone and forever.

Ejaculatory prayer. Draw me by the chains of Thy love!

Visit to the Blessed Virgin Mary

St. Bernard exhorts us, saying: "Let us seek for grace, and let us seek it by Mary." "She," says St. Peter Damian, "is the treasure of divine graces." She can en rich us, and she desires to do so. She therefore invites and calls us, saying: Whosoever is a little one, let him come to me." Most amiable Lady, most exalted Lady, most gracious Lady, look on a poor sinner who recommends himself to Thee, and who places all his confidence in Thee.

Ejaculatory prayer. We fly to thy patronage, O holy Mother of God!

Prayer of St. Ildefonsus.

Most humble handmaid of thy divine Son! I prostrate myself before thee, conjuring thee to obtain pardon of my sins, that I may be cleansed from all the imperfections of my life. I entreat thee to procure me the grace of being always united to God and to thee, and to be ever a faithful servant of thy Son and of thee: of thy Son, as my Lord and my Redeemer; and of thee, as the cause of my redemption: for if he has paid the price of my redemption, it was with the body which he received from thee.

Ejaculatory prayer. O Mary! Obtain for me confidence in thy intercession, and the grace that I may continually have recourse to thee.

FOURTEENTH VISIT
To the Blessed Sacrament

Most amiable Jesus, I hear Thee say from this tabernacle in which Thou art present, This is my rest forever and ever; here will I dwell, for I have chosen it? Since, then, Thou hast chosen Thy dwelling on our altars in the midst of us, remaining there in the Most Holy Sacrament, and since Thy love for us makes Thee there find Thy repose, it is but just that our hearts also should ever dwell with Thee in affection, and should find all pleasure and repose in Thee. Blessed are you, O loving souls, who can find no sweeter repose in the world than in remaining near to your Jesus in the Most Holy Sacrament! And blessed should I be, my Lord, did I from this time forward find no greater delight than in remaining always in Thy presence, or in always thinking of Thee, who in the Most Holy Sacrament art always thinking of me and of my welfare.

Ah, my Lord! And why have I lost so many years, in which I have not loved Thee? O miserable years, I curse you; and I bless Thee, O infinite patience of my God, for having for so many years borne with me, though so ungrateful to Thy love. And still, notwithstanding this ingratitude, Thou waits for me: and why, my God, why? It is, that one day, overcome by Thy mercies and by Thy love, I may yield wholly to Thee. Lord, I will no longer resist, I will no longer be ungrateful. It is but just that I should consecrate to Thee the time, be it long or short, which I have still to live. I hope for Thy help, O my Jesus, to become entirely Thine. Thou didst favor me so much when I fled from Thee and despised Thy love; how much more may I now hope that Thou wilt favor me, now that I seek and desire to love Thee! Give me, then, the grace to love Thee, O God, worthy of infinite love. I love Thee with my whole heart; I love Thee above all things; I love Thee more than myself, more than my life. I am sorry for having offended Thee, O infinite goodness: pardon me; and with Thy pardon grant me the grace to love Thee much in this life until death, and in the next life for all eternity. O Almighty God, show the world the greatness of Thy power, in the prodigy of a soul ungrateful as mine has been becoming one of Thy greatest lovers. Do this by Thy merits, my Jesus.

Visit to the Blessed Virgin Mary

St. Germanus, addressing the Most Blessed Virgin Mary, says: "No one is saved but through thee; no one is delivered from evils but through thee; there is no one on whom any gift is bestowed but through thee." Therefore, my Lady and my hope, if thou dost not help me I am lost, and shall be unable to bless thee in heaven. But, Lady, I hear all the saints say that thou never abandons those who have recourse to thee. He only is lost who has not recourse to thee. I, then, miserable creature that I am, have recourse to thee, and in thee place all my hopes.

Ejaculatory prayer, in the words of St. Bernard. Mary is my whole confidence; she is the whole ground of my hope!

FIFTEENTH VISIT
To the Blessed Sacrament

I am come to cast fire on the earth; and what will I but that it be kindled? Father Francis Olimpio, the Theatine, used to say that there was nothing on earth which en kindled so ardent flames of divine love in the hearts of men as the Most Holy Sacrament of the Altar. Hence our Lord showed himself to St. Catharine of Sienna in this Blessed Sacrament as a furnace of love, from which issued forth torrents of divine flames, spreading themselves over the whole earth : so much so, indeed, that the saint, in perfect astonishment, wondered how it was possible that men could live without burning with love for such love on the part of God towards them.

My Jesus, make me burn with the desire of Thee; grant that all my thoughts, and sighs, and desires, and seeking, may be for Thee alone. Oh, happy should I be, did this Thy heavenly fire fully possess me, and as I advance in years, gradually consume all earthly affections in me!

O divine Word! O my own Jesus! I see Thee all sacrificed, all annihilated, and so to say destroyed on the altar, for my love. It is, then, but right that, as Thou sacrifices Thyself as a victim of love for me, I at least should consecrate myself wholly to Thee. Yes, my God and my sovereign Lord, I now sacrifice to Thee my whole soul, my entire self, my whole will and my whole life. I unite this poor sacrifice of mine, O Eternal Father, to the infinite sacrifice of himself which Jesus, Thy Son and my Savior, once offered to Thee on the cross, and which he now offers to Thee so many times every day on our altars. Accept it, then, through the merits of Jesus; and grant me the grace to renew it every day of my life, and to die sacrificing my whole self to Thy honor. I de sire the grace granted to so many martyrs, to die for Thy love. But if I am unworthy of so great a grace, grant at least, my Lord, that I may sacrifice my life to Thee, together with my entire will, by accepting the death which Thou sends me. Lord, I desire this grace; I desire to die with the intention of honoring and pleasing Thee thereby: and from this moment I sacrifice my life to Thee; and I offer Thee my death, when or wheresoever it may take place.

Visit to the Blessed Virgin Mary

Allow me also, my most sweet Queen, to call thee, with thine own St. Bernard, "the whole ground of my hope," 1 and to say with St. John Damascene, "I have placed my whole hope in thee." Thou hast to obtain for me the forgiveness of my sins; thou, perseverance until death; thou, deliverance from purgatory. All who are saved obtain salvation through thee: thou, then, O Mary, hast to save me." He will be saved whom thou will. "Will, then, my salvation, and I shall be saved. But thou saves all who invoke thee ; behold, then, I invoke thee, and say:

Ejaculatory prayer. O salvation of those who invoke Thee, save me!

SIXTEENTH VISIT
To the Blessed Sacrament

Had men but always recourse to the Most Blessed Sacrament to seek from it the remedy for their ills, they certainly would not be so miserable as they are. The prophet Jeremias, lamenting, exclaimed: Is there no balm in Galaad? Or is there no physician there? Galaad, a mountain of Arabia, rich in aromatical spices, according to venerable Bede, is a figure of Jesus Christ, who in this Sacrament keeps in readiness all the remedies for our woes. Why, then, our Redeemer seems to ask, do you complain of your misfortunes, O sons of Adam, when you have the physician and the remedy for them all in this Sacrament? Come to Me, and I will refresh you. I will, then, address Thee in the words of the sisters of Lazarus: Behold, he whom Thou loves is sick. Lord, I am that miserable creature whom Thou loves; my soul is all wounded by the sins which I have committed; my divine physician, I come to Thee, that Thou may heal me; if Thou wilt, Thou canst cure me: Heal my soul; for I have sinned against Thee. I Draw me wholly to Thyself, my most sweet Jesus, by the all-winning attractions of Thy love. Far rather would I be bound to Thee than become the Lord of the whole earth. I desire nothing else in the world but to love Thee. I have but little to give Thee; but could I gain possession of all the kingdoms of the world, I would do so, that I might renounce them all for Thy love. For Thee, then, I renounce what I can; I give up all relatives, all comforts, all pleasures, and even spiritual consolations: for Thee I renounce my liberty and my will. On Thee I desire to bestow all my love. I love Thee, infinite goodness; I love Thee more than myself, and I hope to love Thee for all eternity.

Ejaculatory prayer. My Jesus, I give myself to Thee: do Thou accept me!

Visit to the Blessed Virgin Mary

My Lady, though didst say to St, Bridget: However much a man sins, if he returns to me with a real purpose of amendment, I am instantly ready to welcome him: neither do I pay attention to the greatness of his sins, but to the intention alone with which he comes. I do not disdain to anoint and heal his wounds; for I am called, and truly am, the Mother of mercy. "Since, then, thou hast both the power and the will to heal me, behold, I have recourse to thee, O heavenly physician; heal the many wounds of my soul: with a single word addressed by thee to thy Son I shall be restored.

Ejaculatory prayer. O Mary, have pity on me!

SEVENTEENTH VISIT
To the Blessed Sacrament

Loving souls can find no greater delight than to be in the company of those whom they love. If we, then, love Jesus Christ much, behold we are now in his presence. Jesus in the Blessed Sacrament sees us and hears us: shall we, then, say nothing to him? Let us console ourselves in his company; let us rejoice in his glory, and in the love which so many enamored souls bear him in the Most Holy Sacrament. Let us desire that all should love Jesus in the Holy Sacrament, and consecrate their hearts to him; at least let us consecrate all our affections to him. He should be all our love and our whole desire. Father Salesius, of the Society of Jesus, felt consolation in only speaking of the Most Blessed Sacrament; he could never visit it enough. When called to the parlor, on returning to his room, when going about the house, he always profited by these occasions to repeat his visits to his beloved Lord; so much so, that it was remarked that scarcely an hour of the day passed without his visiting him. At length he obtained the favor to die by the hands of heretics while defending the truth of the real presence in the Blessed Sacrament.

Oh, had I but the happiness to die for so noble a cause as the defense of this Sacrament, in which, O most amiable Jesus, Thou hast taught us the tenderness of the love which Thou bears us! But since, my Lord, Thou works so many miracles in this Sacrament, work this one also: draw my entire self to Thee. Thou indeed desires that I should be all Thine, and Thou dost also indeed deserve that I should be so. Give me the strength to love Thee with all the affection of my soul. Give the goods of this world to whomsoever Thou wiliest. I renounce them all: I sigh after and desire Thy love alone; this alone do I now and will always seek. I love Thee, my Jesus; grant me the grace always to love Thee, and grant me this alone.

Ejaculatory prayer. My Jesus, when shall I really love Thee?

Visit to the Blessed Virgin Mary

My most sweet Queen, how pleasing to me is that beautiful name by which thy devout clients address thee: "Most amiable Mother!" Yes, my Lady, thou art truly and indeed amiable. Thy beauty has captivated thy Lord himself: And the king shall greatly desire thy beauty. St. Bernard says that thy very name is so amiable to thy lovers, that when they pronounce or hear it they are inflamed with a fresh desire to love thee: "sweet, O pious, O exceedingly amiable Mary! Thou cannot be named without inflaming, neither can thy name be heard without enkindling, the affections of those who love thee." It is, then, reasonable, my most amiable Mother, that I should love thee. But I am not satisfied with only loving thee: I desire in the first place on earth, and then in heaven, to be, after God, thy greatest lover. If my desire is presumptuous, it is thou thyself who art to blame, on account of thy amiability, and the special love which thou hast shown me. If thou wert less amiable, my desire to love thee would be less. Accept, then, O Lady, this my desire; and in token that thou hast accepted it, do thou obtain me from God this love for which I ask thee, since he is so well pleased with the love which is borne thee.

Ejaculatory prayer. My most amiable Mother, I love thee much.

Prayer of St. Damian

O Mother of God ! cast upon us one look of compassion. I know that thou art full of goodness, and that thou loves us in a measure that surpasses all other love. How often dost thou appease the anger of our Judge, when the hand of his justice is raised to strike us? All the treasures of mercy are in thy hands, and thou seeks every opportunity to save miserable sinners and to make them partakers of thy glory. Ah! Never cease to interest thyself in our regard, that we may one day arrive at the happiness of seeing Thee in heaven ; as the greatest good that we can enjoy, next to that of seeing God, is to see thee, to love thee, and to be under thy protection. Since thy Son desires to honor thee by refusing nothing that thou asks, hear our prayer, and intercede in our behalf.

Ejaculatory prayer. O Mary! I love thee as the most amiable of the works of God, and place my confidence in thee.

EIGHTEENTH VISIT
To the Blessed Sacrament

One day Jesus will be seated on a throne of majesty in the valley of Josaphat ; but now, in the Most Blessed Sacrament, he is seated on a throne of love. Did a king, to show his love for a poor shepherd, go and live in his village, how great would be the ingratitude of this peas ant did he not often go to visit him, knowing the king wish to see him, and that for this purpose he had come to reside there! Ah, my Jesus, for love of me Thou dwells in the Sacrament of the Altar. Could I, then, do so, my desire would be to remain night and day in Thy presence. If the angels, O my Lord, filled with astonishment at the love which Thou bears us, remain always around Thee, it is but reasonable that I, seeing Thee for my sake on this altar, should endeavor to please Thee, at least by remaining in Thy presence, to praise the love and goodness which Thou hast for me: I will sing praise to Thee in the sight of the angels; I will worship towards Thy holy temple, and I will give glory to Thy name : for Thy mercy and for Thy truth? God, present in this Most Holy Sacrament, O bread of angels, O heavenly food, I love Thee; but Thou art not, neither am I, satisfied with my love. I love Thee ; but I love Thee too little. Do Thou, my Jesus, make known to me the beauty, the immense goodness which I love: make my heart banish from itself all earthly affections, and give place to Thy divine love. To fill me with Thy love, and to unite Thyself all to me, Thou descends every day from heaven on our altars: it is, then, but just that I should think of nothing else but of loving, adoring, and pleasing Thee. I love Thee with my whole soul, I love Thee with all my affections. If Thou art graciously pleased to make me a return for this love, increase my love; render its flames more ardent; that thus I may always love Thee more, and desire more and more to please Thee.

Ejaculatory prayer. Jesus, my love, give me love!

Visit to the Blessed Virgin Mary

As poor sick persons, who on account of their miseries are abandoned by all, find shelter in the public hospitals; so also do the most miserable sinners, who, although discarded by all, find protection in the mercy of Mary, by whom they are never rejected; for God has placed her in the world as a receptacle and as a public hospital for sinners, as Si. Basil of Seleucia gives us to understand. Hence St. Ephrem also calls her "the asylum of sinners," Therefore, my Queen, if I have recourse to thee, thou canst not reject me on account of my sins; nay, even the more wretched I am, the greater is the claim which I have upon thy protection, since God has created thee as the refuge of the most miserable. Therefore to thee I have recourse, O Mary; I place myself under thy mantle. Thou art the refuge of sinners; thou art, then, my refuge, the hope of my salvation. If thou reject me, to whom shall I have recourse?

Ejaculatory prayer. Mary, my refuge, save me!

NINETEENTH VISIT
To the Blessed Sacrament

It is sweet to everyone to be in the company of a dear friend; and shall we not find it sweet, in this valley of tears, to remain in the company of the best friend we have, and who can do us every kind of good; who loves us with the most tender affection, and therefore dwells always with us? Behold, in the Most Blessed Sacrament we can converse at pleasure with Jesus, we can open our hearts to him, we can lay our wants before him, and we can ask him for his graces; in a word, in this Sacrament we can treat with the King of Heaven, in all confidence and without restraint. Joseph was only too happy when, as the sacred Scripture tells us, God descended by his grace into his prison to comfort him: She went down with him into the pit, and in bands she left him not? But we are yet more highly favored; for we have always with us in this land of miseries our God made Man, who, by his real presence, is with us all the days of our life, and comforts and helps us with the greatest affection and com passion. What a consolation it is to a poor prisoner to have an affectionate friend, who keeps him company, consoles him, gives him hope, succors him, and thinks of relieving him in his misery! Behold our good friend Jesus Christ, who in this Sacrament encourages us, saying: Behold, I am with you all days! Behold me, he says, all thine: I am come from heaven into thy prison expressly to console thee, to help thee, to deliver thee. Welcome me, and do so always; cling to me and thus thou wilt never feel thy miseries; and afterwards thou will come with me to my kingdom, where I shall make thee perfectly happy. O God, O incomprehensible ocean of love, since Thy condescension towards us is so great, that in order to dwell near us Thou descends upon our altars, I propose often to visit Thee; I am determined, as often as I possibly can, to enjoy Thy most sweet presence, which is the beatitude of the saints in heaven. Oh, could I but always remain in Thy presence, to adore Thee and to make Thee acts of love! Arouse, I beseech Thee, my soul, when through tepidity or worldly affairs it neglects to visit Thee. Enkindle in me a great desire always to remain near Thee in this Sacrament. Ah, my loving Jesus, would that I had always loved Thee! Would that I had always pleased Thee! I console myself that I still have time to do so, not only in the next

life, but also in this. I am determined to do so; I am determined to love Thee indeed, my sovereign good, my love, my treasure, my all. I will love Thee with all my strength.

Ejaculatory prayer. My God, help me to love Thee!

Visit to the Blessed Virgin Mary

The devout Bernardine de Bustis says: "O sinner, whoever you may be, despair not ; but with confidence have recourse to this Lady: you will find her hands filled with mercies and graces." "And know also," he adds, "that this most compassionate Queen has a greater desire to do you good than you can have to be succored by her," I will ever, O my Lady, thank God for having taught me to know thee. Unfortunate indeed should I be, did I not know thee, or did I forget thee. I would it fare with my salvation. But, my Mother, I bless thee, I love thee; and so great is my confidence in thee, that I place my whole soul in thy hands.

Ejaculatory prayer. O Mary, blessed is he who knows thee, and puts his trust in thee!

Prayer of the Abbot of Celles

Draw me after thee, O Virgin Mary! That I may run in the odor of thy perfumes. Draw me because I am impeded by the weight of my sins, and by the malice of my enemies. As no one can go to thy divine Son who is not conducted by his heavenly Father, so I presume also to say, that no one can approach this same Jesus but through thy intercession. Thou art the teacher of true wisdom : through thee sinners obtain grace because thou art their advocate; thou promises to obtain help for those who honor thee, because thou art the treasure of God and the depository of all his graces.

Ejaculatory prayer. O thou, who art the salvation of those who invoke thee, save me.

TWENTIETH VISIT
To the Blessed Sacrament

The prophet Zacharias says that day there shall be a fountain open to the house of David, and to the inhabitants of Jerusalem, for the washing of the sinner. 1 Jesus in the Holy Sacrament is the fountain foretold by the prophet as open to all, and to which we can go whenever we please, to wash our souls from all the stains of sin which are daily contracted. When any one falls into some fault, what more beautiful remedy is there than to have immediate recourse to the Most Blessed Sacrament? Yes, my Jesus, I resolve always to do this; for I know that the waters of this fountain of Thine not only cleanse me, but also give me light, and strengthen me not to fall, and enable me cheerfully to bear contradictions, and also inflame me with Thy love. I know that for this end it is that Thou awaits my visits, and recompenses those of Thy lovers with so many graces. My Jesus, delay not; but wash me now from all the defects that I have committed this day, and for which I am grieved because they have displeased Thee ; strengthen me against relapse by giving me a great desire to love Thee much. Oh, could I but always dwell near Thee, as did Thy faithful servant Mary Diaz, who lived in the time of St. Teresa, and had permission from the Bishop of Avila to inhabit the tribune of a church, where she remained almost always in the presence of the Most Blessed Sacrament, which she called her neighbor, and which she only left to go to confession and Communion. When the Venerable Brother Francis of the Infant Jesus, of the Order of the Discalced Carmelites, passed before a church in which the Blessed Sacrament was kept, he could not refrain from entering to visit it, saying: "That it was not becoming for a friend to pass before the door of a friend without entering, at least to salute him and exchange a word." But a word did not satisfy him; he always remained as long as obedience allowed him in the presence of his beloved Lord. My only and infinite good, I see that Thou hast instituted this Sacrament, and that Thou remains on this altar, to be loved by me ; and that for this end Thou hast given me a heart capable of loving Thee much. Why is it, then, that I am so ungrateful as not to love Thee? Or that I love Thee so little? Now it is not just that such goodness as Thou art should be so little loved. The love, at least, which Thou bears me, deserves other and greater love on my part. Thou art an infinite God, and I am a miserable worm. It would be little, did I die for Thee, or wear myself out for Thee, who didst die for me, and dost sacrifice Thy entire self for me every day on the altar. Thou deserves to be much loved; I will love Thee much: help me, my Jesus, help me to love Thee, and to do that which pleases Thee so much, and

which Thou so earnestly seeks of me. Ejaculatory prayer. My Beloved to me, and I to my Beloved!

Visit to the Blessed Virgin Mary

My most sweet, most compassionate, most amiable Queen, oh, how great is the confidence with which St. Bernard inspires me when I have recourse to thee! He says that thou dost not go examining the merits of those who have recourse to thy compassion ; but that offers thyself to help all who pray to thee: "Mary does not discuss merits, but shows herself ready to hear and welcome all." Therefore, if I pray to thee, thou dost graciously hear me. Well, then, listen to what I have to ask thee: I am a poor sinner, deserving of a thousand hells. I wish to change my life; I wish to love my God, whom I have so greatly offended. I dedicate myself to

thee as thy slave; to thee I give myself, miserable as I am; save, then, a poor creature who is no longer his own, but thine. My Lady, dost thou understand me? Yes; I trust that thou hast understood me, and graciously heard my prayer.

Ejaculatory prayer. O Mary, I am thine; save me!

Prayer of the Abbot of Celles

Most sweet Virgin, thou hast found grace and favor with God, in having been preserved from original sin, filled with the Holy Ghost, and chosen to be the Mother of the Son of God. Thou boldest in thy hands all the treasures of grace, not only for thy own benefit, but also for ours; and thou fails not to distribute them according to our necessities, Thou assists the good, by obtaining for them grace to persevere, and thou helps the wicked by preparing them to receive the divine mercy; thou aids the dying by defending them against the snares of the devil, and, after death, thou receives their souls, and conducts them to the mansions of the blessed.

Ejaculatory prayer. O Mary! happy is he who serves thee and trusts in thee.

TWENTY-FIRST VISIT
To the Blessed Sacrament

Wheresoever the body shall be, thither will the eagles also be gathered together. The saints generally understand by this body that of Jesus Christ; and by the eagles, souls who, being detached from creatures, rise above the things of the earth, and fly towards heaven, after which they always sigh in thought and affection, and where they constantly dwell. These eagles also find their paradise on earth wherever they find Jesus in the Most Holy Sacrament; so much so, indeed, that they seem never to tire hovering around him. If eagles, says St. Jerome, on scenting a dead body go from afar to seek it, how much more should we run and fly to Jesus in the Most Blessed Sacrament, as to the most delicious food of our hearts ! Hence saints in this valley of tears have always as parched harts run to this fountain of paradise. Father Balthasar Alvarez, of the Society of Jesus, in whatever occupation he was engaged, used often to cast his eyes towards the place in which he knew that the Blessed Sacrament was; he often visited it, and even spent entire nights before it. He used to weep when he saw the palaces of the great ones of this world filled with people, who courted a man from whom they hoped for some miserable earthly good, and the churches so abandoned, in which the supreme sovereign of the world dwells, and remains with us as on a throne of love, rich in immense and eternal treasures. He used also to say, that religious persons were indeed fortunate, because in the very houses in which they reside, they can, whenever they please, either night or day, visit this great Lord in the Most Blessed Sacrament; and this lay people cannot do. Since, then, my most loving Lord, notwithstanding that Thou sees me as a leper, and so ungrateful to Thy love, Thou invites me to approach Thee, I will not be discouraged at the sight of my miseries: I come and approach Thee;

but do Thou wholly change me. Drive from me every love which is not for Thee, every desire which displeases Thee, every thought which does not tend toward Thee. My Jesus, my love, my treasure, my all, I am determined to please Thee alone. I will give pleasure only to Thee. Thou alone deserves all my love; Thee only will I love with my whole heart. Detach me from everything, my Lord, and bind me to Thyself alone; but bind me so firmly, that I may never more be able to separate myself from Thee, either in this life or in the next.

Ejaculatory prayer. My most sweet Jesus, never allow me to be separated from Thee!

Visit to the Blessed Virgin Mary

Denis, the Carthusian, calls the Most Blessed Virgin "the advocate of all the wicked who have recourse to her." Since, then, O great Mother of God, thy office is to defend the causes of the most guilty criminals who have recourse to thee, behold me now at thy feet; to thee I have recourse, and I address thee in the words of St. Thomas of Villanova. "O gracious advocate, fulfil thy charge." Now quickly enter upon thy office, under-take my cause : it is true that I have indeed been guilty before my Lord, having offended him, after the many benefits and graces he has conferred upon me; but the evil is done; thou canst save me. Thou hast only to tell thy God that thou defends me, and then I shall be forgiven, and shall be saved.

Ejaculatory prayer. My dear Mother, thou hast to save me!

Prayer of William Bishop of Paris

I address my petitions to thee, O Mother of God! Whom the whole Church styles the Mother of mercy. Canst thou, whose prayers are always acceptable to God, refuse thy intercession in behalf of sinners? Justly does St. Bernard say, that we may cease to call thee the Mother of Mercy, if any one ever invokes thee in the hour of need, without experiencing thy assistance. Thou wilt not, therefore, exclude me from a share in thy compassion. Thou wilt intercede for me with more earnestness than I can for myself ; and thou wilt procure more abundant graces than I could presume to ask. O Mother of mercy! Can that clemency, which never abandoned any one, refuse me its assistance in the danger to which I am exposed of being eternally lost?

Ejaculatory prayer. O Mary! I am thine: save me.

TWENTY-SECOND VISIT
To the Blessed Sacrament.

The Spouse in the sacred Canticles went about seeking for her Beloved; and not finding him, she asked all whom she met: Have you seen Him whom my soul love? Jesus was not then on earth; but now, if a soul that loves him seeks him, she can always find him in the Most Blessed Sacrament. The Venerable Father John Avila used to say, that amongst all sanctuaries he could neither find nor desire a more delightful one than a church in which the Most Blessed Sacrament is reserved. O infinite love of my God, worthy of infinite love! And how could Thou, my Jesus, ever abase Thyself so far as, in order to dwell amongst men, and to unite Thyself to their hearts, to humble Thyself to such a degree as to conceal Thyself under the species of bread? O incarnate Word, Thou art supreme in Thy humility, because Thou art supreme in Thy love ! How can I do otherwise than love Thee with my entire self, knowing as I do how much Thou hast done to captivate my love? I love Thee much; and therefore I give Thy good pleasure the preference above every interest and every satisfaction of my own. My pleasure is to give Thee pleasure, my Jesus, my God, my love, my all. Make me hunger to be continually in Thy presence in the Blessed Sacrament, to receive Thee into myself, and to keep Thee company. I should be indeed ungrateful did I not accept so sweet and gracious an invitation. Ah, Lord, annihilate in me all affection for created things! Thou wiliest that Thou alone, my Creator, should be the object of all my sighs, of all my love. I love Thee, most amiable goodness of my God. I ask nothing of Thee but Thyself. I desire not my own pleasure; Thy pleasure is all my desire, and sufficient for me. Accept, my Jesus, this good desire of a sinner who wishes to love Thee. Help me by Thy grace. Grant that I, a miser able slave of hell, may from this day forward be the happy slave of Thy love.

Ejaculatory prayer. I love Thee, Jesus, my treasure, above every other treasure! Visit to the Blessed Virgin Mary. My most sweet Lady and Mother, I am a vile rebel to thy great Son; but I come repentant to thy mercy, that thou may obtain for me pardon. Say not that thou cannot do so; for St. Bernard calls thee "the minister of propitiation." To thee also it belongs to succor those who are in dangers, St. Ephrem calling thee "the helper of those in peril." My Lady, who is in greater danger than I am? I have lost God: it is certain that it may have been condemned to hell. I know not whether God has yet pardoned me. I may again lose him. But thou canst obtain me all; and from thee I hope for every good, for forgiveness, perseverance, and heaven. I hope to be one of those who, in the kingdom of the blessed, will most praise thy mercies, O Mary, for having saved me by thy intercession.

Ejaculatory prayer. I will sing the mercies of Mary for all eternity; I will sing them forever and ever! Amen, amen.

Prayer of William, Bishop of Paris

Mother of God! Thy goodness never despises the sinner who recommends himself to thy patronage, however enormous his crimes may have been: and hence the Church justly calls thee her advocate and the refuge of sinners. Let not, then, my crimes prevent thee from fulfilling this office of mercy, whereby thou becomes the mediatrix of peace, the hope and secure asylum of all who are in affliction. Let it not be said that the Mother of God, who, for the sake of the world, brought forth the source of mercy, can refuse to look down with pity on any wretch that flies to her for assistance. Thou art employed as the mediatrix between God and man : let me experience a share of thy great compassion."

Ejaculatory prayer. O Mary, my loving Mother, may I, under God, owe my salvation to thee!

TWENTY-THIRD VISIT
To the Blessed Sacrament

Many Christians submit to great fatigue, and expose themselves to many dangers, to visit the places in the Holy Land where our most loving Savior was born, suffered, and died. We need not undertake so long a journey, or expose ourselves to so many dangers; the same Lord is near us, and dwells in the church, only a few steps distant from our houses. If pilgrims, says St. Paulinus, consider it a great thing to bring back a little dust from the crib, or from the holy sepulchre in which Jesus was buried, with what ardor should not we visit the Most Blessed Sacrament, where the same Jesus is in person, and where we can go without encountering so much fatigue and so many dangers! A religious person, to whom God had given great love for the Most Blessed Sacrament, amongst other things wrote as follows in a letter: "I see that every good thing that I have comes to me from the Most Blessed Sacrament. I have given and consecrated my whole self to Jesus in this Sacrament. I see innumerable graces, which are not granted because people do not go to this divine Sacrament. I see the great desire that our Lord has to dispense his graces in the Sacrament. O holy mystery! O sacred Host! Where is it that God manifests his power the most, if it is not in this Host? For this Host contains all that God has ever done for us. Let us not envy the blessed who are in heaven, since on earth we have the same Lord, with greater wonders of his love. Induce all with whom you speak to devote themselves to the Most Blessed Sacrament. I speak thus because this Sacrament enraptures my soul. Nor can I cease to speak of the Most Blessed Sacrament, which deserves so greatly to beloved. I know not what to do for Jesus in this Sacrament." Thus the letter ends. O ye Seraphim, who remain sweetly burning with love around your and my Lord; though it is not indeed for love of you but of me that this King of Heaven is pleased to be present in this Sacrament O loving Angels, let me also burn with love; and do you enkindle your love in me, that with you I also may burn! O my

Jesus, teach me to know the greatness of the love which Thou bears to men, that at the sight of so great love my desire to love Thee and please Thee may go on always increasing! I love Thee, most amiable Lord, and will always love Thee; and this alone to please Thee.

Ejaculatory prayer. My Jesus, I believe in Thee, I hope in Thee, I love Thee, and I give myself to Thee!

Visit to the Blessed Virgin Mary

Most amiable Virgin, St. Bonaventure calls thee, "the Mother of orphans" and St. Ephrem, moreover, calls thee "the receiver of orphans." Alas, these wretched orphans are no others than poor sinners who have lost God! Behold, then, I have recourse to thee, most holy Mary. I have lost my Father; but thou art my Mother, who must enable me to recover him. In this my so great misfortune I call thee to my aid; do thou succor me. Shall I remain disconsolate? No; for Innocent III., speaking of thee, asks, "Whoever called upon her, and was not graciously heard by her?" And whoever prayed to thee, and was not heard and helped by thee? Who was ever lost who had recourse to thee? He alone is lost who has not recourse to thee. Then, my Queen, if thou desires my salvation, enable me always to invoke and confide in thee.

Ejaculatory prayer. My own most holy Mary, give me confidence in thee! I shall say with St. Augustine, Remember, O Mary, full of goodness! That no sinner has ever been heard of that has had recourse to thy protection and been abandoned by thee. Let us, then, says St. Bernard, seek for grace through the means of Mary, because she can obtain what she asks, and her demands never meet with a refusal. 1 O Mother of God! thou prays for all; vouchsafe to pray for me, who am the greatest of sinners, and therefore have the greatest need of thy intercession.

Ejaculatory prayer. I fly to thy protection, O sacred Mother of God!

TWENTY-FOURTH VISIT
To the Blessed Sacrament

Verily Thou art a hidden God? In no other work of divine love are these words so fully verified as in this adorable mystery of the Most Holy Sacrament, where our God is entirely hidden. When the Eternal Word took flesh, he hid his divinity, and appeared as a man on earth; but remaining with us in this Sacrament, he hides even his humanity, and, as remarks St. Bernard, appears only under the form of bread, to show thereby the tenderness of the love which he bears us: "The divinity is hid, the humanity is hid; the bowels of charity alone appear." O my Beloved Redeemer, at the sight of the excessive tenderness Thou hast for men, I am beside myself, my Lord, and know not what to say. In this Sacrament Thou goes so far for their love as to hide Thy majesty and lower Thy glory; Thou goes so far as even to consume and annihilate Thy divine life. And whilst Thou art on the altar Thou seems to have nothing else to do than to love men, and to show them the love which Thou bears them. And what gratitude do they show Thee in return, O great Son of God? Jesus, O too great a lover of men, allow me to say so, for I see that Thou prefers their advantage to Thine own glory. And didst Thou not know to how much contempt this loving design of Thine would ex pose Thee? I see, and before me Thou didst see it full well Thyself, that the greater part of men adore Thee not, neither will they acknowledge Thee for what Thou art in this Sacrament. I know that these very men have gone so far as to trample on the consecrated Hosts, that they have thrown them on the ground, into water, and into fire. And I see the greater part even of those who believe in Thee, O God, who, so far from repairing so many outrages by the homage of their devotion, either come to the church to offend Thee still more by their irreverence, or else abandon Thee on Thy altar, and sometimes even leave it unprovided with a lamp or the necessary ornaments! Oh, could I, my most sweet Savior, but wash with my tears, or even with my blood, those unhappy places in which, in this Sacrament, Thy love and Thy enamored heart have been so greatly outraged ! But if so much is

not granted me, I desire at least, my Lord, and deter mine, to visit Thee often, in order to adore Thee as I now adore Thee, and this in compensation for the insults which Thou receives in this most divine mystery. Accept, O Eternal Father, this scanty honor, which I, the most miserable of men, now offer Thee in reparation of the outrages offered to Thy Son in the Most Holy Sacrament; accept it in union with that infinite honor which Jesus Christ gave Thee on the cross, and which he daily gives Thee in the Most Blessed Sacrament. O my Sacramental Jesus, would that I could fill all men with love for the Most Blessed Sacrament!

Ejaculatory prayer. O amiable Jesus, make Thyself known, make Thyself loved!

Visit to the Blessed Virgin Mary

My most powerful Lady, in the midst of my misgivings as to my eternal salvation, how great is the confidence which I feel when I have recourse to thee; and when I think that thou, my Mother, art, on the one hand, so rich in graces, that St. John Damascene calls thee "a sea of graces;" St. Bonaventure, "the assemblage of graces," that is, the source in which all graces are congregated; St. Ephrem, "a fountain of grace and of all consolation;" and St. Bernard, "the fullness of every good," and when, on the other hand, I reflect that thy desire to do us good is so great, that thou esteems thyself offended, as St. Bonaventure says, by him who does not ask thee for thy graces: "they sin against thee, O Lady," he says, "who do not ask of thee." O most rich, O most wise, and most merciful Queen, I see that thou knows far better than I do the wants of my soul, and that thou loves me far more than I can love thee! Know, then, the grace for which I now ask thee; obtain me the grace which thou knows to be the most expedient for my soul. Ask this favor from God, and I am satisfied.

Ejaculatory prayer. My God, grant me the graces which Mary asks Thee for me!

Let us go, says St. Paul, to the throne of grace, that we may obtain mercy in the time of need. I Thou, divine Mary, art this throne of grace, from which God dispenses all his blessings. Most amiable Queen, thy delight is to assist those who are in the wretched state of sin : behold, then, at thy feet a grievous sinner, imploring the aid of thy prayers. Help me to the utmost of thy power, and without delay: the wonders of thy mercy will be enhanced by saving one that has deserved a thousand hells. Thy Son cannot withstand thy intercession. I entreat thee, therefore, by the love which thou entertains for Jesus, to procure pardon for me for the past, and grace to lead a holy life for the future. O Mary, thou art my strength, and the ground of my hope.

Ejaculatory prayer. O Mary, cast a look of compassion on me.

TWENTY-FIFTH VISIT
To the Blessed Sacrament

St. Paul praises the obedience of Jesus Christ, saying, that he obeyed his Eternal Father even to death: becoming obedient even unto death? But in this sacrament he has gone still farther; for here he has been pleased to become obedient, not only to his Eternal Father, but also to man; and not only to death, but as long as the world shall last; so that we can say: "He has become obedient even unto the consummation of the world." He, the King of Heaven, comes down from heaven in obedience to man, and then seems to dwell and converse there, in order to obey men: And I do not resist. There he remains without moving himself; he allows himself to be

placed where men will, be it for exposition in the re monstrance, or to be enclosed in the tabernacle. He allows himself to be carried wheresoever he is borne, be it into houses or through the streets; he allows himself to be given in Communion to whomsoever he is administered, be they just or sinners. St. Luke says that whilst he dwelt on earth he obeyed the Most Blessed Virgin Mary and St. Joseph; but in this Sacrament he obeys as many creatures as there are priests on earth: and I do not resist.

Permit me now to address Thee, O most loving Heart of my Jesus, from which indeed all the Sacraments flowed forth, but principally this Sacrament of love. I would gladly give Thee as much glory and honor as Thou gives in the Holy Sacrament in our churches to the Eternal Father. I know that on this altar Thou still loves me with that same love with which Thou didst love me when Thou didst close Thy divine life in the midst of so much anguish on the cross. O divine Heart, enlighten all those who know Thee not with the knowledge of Thyself! Through Thy merits deliver from purgatory, or at least relieve, the pains of the afflicted souls, who are already Thy spouses for all eternity. I adore Thee, I thank Thee, I love Thee, in union with all souls who at this moment love Thee, be they on earth or in heaven. O most pure Heart, purify my heart from attachment to creatures, and fill it with Thy holy love! Most sweet Heart, possess my whole heart, so that henceforward it may be all Thine, and always been able to say: Who, then, shall separate us from the love of God, which is in Jesus Christ our Lord? Write, O most sacred Heart, upon my heart all the bitter sorrows, which for so many years Thou didst endure on earth with so much love for me, that, on seeing them, I may hence forward desire, or at least endure with patience, all the sorrows of this life. Most humble Heart of Jesus, give me a share of Thy humility. Most meek Heart, impart Thy sweetness to me, Take from my heart all that displeases Thee; convert it wholly to Thee, so that I may no longer will or desire other than what Thou wiliest. In a word, grant that I may live only to obey Thee, only to love Thee, only to give Thee pleasure. I know that I, indeed, owe Thee much; and that Thou hast indeed placed me under great obligations: it will be but little if I consume and wear myself out for Thee.

Ejaculatory prayer. O Heart of Jesus, Thou art the sole Lord of my heart!

Visit to the Blessed Virgin Mary

St. Bernard says, that Mary is that heavenly ark, in which if we take timely refuge, we shall certainly be delivered from the shipwreck of eternal damnation: "She is the ark in which we escape shipwreck." The ark in which Noe escaped from the general wreck of the world was indeed a type of Mary. But Hesychius says, that Mary is a more spacious, stronger, and more compassionate ark. Only a few men and a few beasts were received and saved by the former; but Mary, our ark, receives all who take refuge under her mantle, and with certainty saves them all. Unfortunate should we be had we not Mary! But still, my Queen, how many are lost! And why? Because they have not recourse to thee. And who would ever be lost had he recourse to thee?

Ejaculatory prayer. Grant, most holy Mary, that we may all and always have recourse to thee!

My sovereign Queen ! thou art the treasure of God, 1 and in thy hands are deposited those stores of mercy which he wishes to bestow upon us. Thou hast said, by the mouth of the prophet, that thou holds in thy hands the treasures of heaven, to enrich those who love thee. My loving Mother, I am an unfortunate sinner, and in the greatest need of help. Remember that I love thee with all my heart; yes, next to God, there is no object that I love so much as thee, because I know that this is due to thy unrivalled perfections. Have pity on me, and forsake me not; help me during life, and help me at the hour of death, that I may one day arrive at the enjoyment of thy happy society in the kingdom of heaven.

Ejaculatory prayer. O Mary ! all my hopes are directed towards thee.

TWENTY-SIXTH VISIT.
To the Blessed Sacrament

Rejoice, and praise, O thou habitation of Sion; for great is He that is in the midst of thee, the Holy One of Israel. O God, and what joy ought not we men to conceive, what "Thesaurus et Thesauraria gratiarum." Idiot. Cont. de V. M. hopes and what affections, in knowing that in the midst of our land, in our churches, near our houses, the Holy of holies, the true God, dwells and lives in the Most Holy Sacrament of the Altar ! He who by his presence alone renders the saints in heaven blessed! He who is love itself. "It is not so much that he has love, as that he is love itself," says St. Bernard. This Sacrament is not only a sacrament of love, but is love itself; it is God himself, who, for the immense love which he bears his creatures, calls himself, and is, love itself: God is love? But I hear Thee complain, O my Sacramental Jesus: I was a stranger, and you took Me not in; that Thou earnest on earth to be our guest for our good, and that we have not welcomed Thee. Thou art right, Lord, Thou art right; and I am one of these ungrateful creatures who have left Thee alone, without even visiting Thee. Chastise me as Thou pleases; but not by depriving me of Thy presence, which is the chastisement I deserve: no, I will repair my fault, and the indignities which I have heaped upon Thee. From this day forward I will not only visit Thee often, but will remain with Thee for as long a time as I can. O most compassionate Savior, be pleased to make me faithful to Thee; and grant that I may also, by my example, excite others to keep Thee company in the Most Blessed Sacrament. I hear the Eternal Father, who says: This is my beloved Son: in whom I am well pleased? A God, then, finds all his complacency in Thee; and shall not I, a miserable worm, find mine in dwelling with Thee in this valley of tears! O consuming fire, destroy in me all affections for earthly things; for they alone can render me unfaithful, and take me away from Thee. Thou canst do so, if Thou will: Lord, if Thou wilt, Thou canst make me clean. Thou hast already done so much for me, do this also: banish from my heart all love which does not tend towards Thee. Behold, I give myself all to Thee: I now dedicate the whole remainder of my life to the love of the Most Blessed Sacrament. Thou, O Sacramental Jesus, hast to be my comfort, my love in life, and at the hour of my death, when Thou wilt come to be my Viaticum and my guide to Thy blessed kingdom. Amen, amen. So do I hope; so may it be!

Ejaculatory prayer. When, O my Jesus, shall I behold Thy beautiful face!

Visit to the Blessed Virgin Mary

In thee, our own most holy Mother, we find the remedy for all our woes; in thee we find strength in our weakness; for St. Germanus calls thee the "strength itself of our weakness." In thee we find a door by which to make our exit from the slavery of sin; for St. Bonaventure calls thee "the gate of liberty." In thee we find our certain peace; for the same saint calls thee "the safe repose of men. "In thee we find relief in our miserable life. Thou art "the solace of our pilgrimage," as St. Laurence Justinian calls thee. In thee, in a word, we find divine grace and God himself, for St. Bonaventure calls thee "the throne of God s grace;" and St. Proclus, "the bridge by which God descends to men;" that happy bridge by which God, who had been driven to a distance by our sins, returns to dwell by his grace in our souls.

Ejaculatory prayer. O Mary, thou art my strength, my deliverance, my peace, and salvation!

Mary! I will say to thee in the words of thy servant St. Bernard: Thou art the queen of mercy. And who are the subjects of thy mercy but such as are in misery and affliction? Yes, thou art truly the queen of mercy, and I, the most wretched of sinners, am thy subject. I, therefore, of all, am the best entitled to thy compassion. Turn then, O my advocate, those eyes of mercy towards me, and after my days of exile, show me Jesus, the blessed fruit of thy womb.

Ejaculatory prayer. O Mary, my refuge, pray for me to Jesus.

TWENTY-SEVENTH VISIT
To the Blessed Sacrament

The holy Church sings in the Office of the Most Blessed Sacrament: "There is no other country, however great, whose gods are nigh it as our God is nigh to us." When the Gentiles heard how far our God carried his works of love, they exclaimed: Oh, how good a God is this God of the Christians! And, indeed, although the Gentiles imagined their gods according to their own caprices, yet, if you read history, you will never find in all their fables, and. among the many gods they invented, that they went so far as even to imagine a god as enamored of men as is our true God ; who, to show his love for his adorers, and to enrich them with graces, has worked such a prodigy of love as to become their constant companion, and to remain night and day concealed on their altars, seeming as if he knew not how to separate himself from them, even for a moment: He hath made a remembrance of His wonderful works? Thou, then, my most sweet Jesus, hast been pleased to work the greatest of Thy miracles in order to satisfy the

excessive desire which Thou hast to remain always near and present to us. Why, then, do men fly from Thy presence? And how can they live for so long a time at a distance from Thee, or visit Thee so seldom? How is it that when in Thy presence they get so weary that a quarter of an hour appears an age? Oh, patience of my Jesus, how great art Thou! Yes, my Lord, I understand Thee; Thy patience is great, because the love Thou bears to men is great: and this it is which, so to say, forces Thee to dwell always in the midst of creatures so ungrateful. Ah, my God, who, because Thou art infinite in perfections art also infinite in love, permit not that I should for the future be, as I have hitherto been, of the number of these ungrateful ones. Grant me a love equal to Thy merits and to my own obligations. At one time I also was weary in Thy presence, either because I loved Thee not, or because I loved Thee too little; but if by Thy grace I am enabled to love Thee much, I shall no longer find it tedious to remain even for whole days and nights at Thy feet in the Most Holy Sacrament. O Eternal Father, I offer Thee Thine own Son himself; accept him for me, and through his merits give me so ardent and tender a love towards the Most Blessed Sacrament, that, constantly turning towards some church in which had wells, I may think of, and desire with longing anxiety, the time when I may be able to go and entertain myself in his presence.

Ejaculatory prayer. My God, for the love of Jesus, give me a great love towards the Most Blessed Sacrament!

Visit to the Blessed Virgin Mary

Mary is that tower of David, of which the Holy Ghost says in the sacred Canticles is built with bulwarks; a thousand bucklers hang upon it, all the armor of valiant men. A tower built with a thousand fortresses, and containing a thousand shields and weapons, for the benefit of those who have recourse to it. Thou art, then, according to an expression of St. Ignatius, martyr, O most holy Mary, a most powerful defense for all those who are engaged in battle. Oh, how constantly are my enemies attacking me, in order to deprive me of the grace of God and of thy protection, my most dear Lady! But thou art my strength. Thou, indeed, dost not disdain to battle for those who trust in thee; for St. Ephrem calls thee "the bulwark of all who confide in thee." Do thou, then, defend and fight for me, who have such great hope and confidence in thee.

Ejaculatory prayer. Mary, Mary, thy name is my defense!

My queen! Thou hast said to thy servant St. Bridget, that as often as a man sins, if he returns to thee with sincere repentance, thou wilt receive him and restore him to the friendship of God that thou dost not consider the greatness of his crimes, but the sincerity of his repentance ; and that thou art ever ready to apply dwells, I may think of, and desire with longing anxiety, the time when I may be able to go and entertain myself in his presence.

Ejaculatory prayer. My God, for the love of Jesus, give me a great love towards the Most Blessed Sacrament!

Therefore, O Savior of the world, O Incarnate Word, if I desire to have Thee, I can really think that Thou art mine, and all mine. But can I at the same time say that I am all Thine, as Thou desires? Ah, my Lord, prevent it ; and never let the world witness such disorder and such ingratitude, as that I should not be Thine when Thou desires me! Ah, no, let it never be! If it has been so hitherto, let it never be so again. I now, with the utmost determination, consecrate myself entirely to Thee; for time and eternity I consecrate my life, my will, my thoughts, my actions, my sufferings, to Thee. Behold me Thine; as a victim consecrated to Thee, I bid farewell to all creatures, and offer my whole self to Thee. Consume me with the flames of Thy divine love. No, I am determined that creatures shall no longer share my heart. The proofs which Thou hast

given me of the love which Thou bears me, even at a time when I did not love Thee, make me hope that Thou certainly accepts me now that I love Thee, and out of love give myself to Thee.

Eternal Father, I now offer Thee all the virtues, the actions, the affections, of the Heart of Thy dear Jesus. Accept them, and by his merits, which are all mine, for he has given them to me, grant me the graces which Jesus asks Thee for me. With these merits I thank Thee for the many mercies which Thou hast shown me; with these I satisfy for what I owe Thee for my sins; through these I hope for every grace from Thee, pardon, perseverance, Paradise, and above all, the crowning gift of Thy pure love. I well see that to all these gifts I myself place impediments; but do Thou also remedy this. I ask it of Thee in the name of Jesus Christ, who has promised: Whatsoever you shall ask the Father in My name, that will I do? Then Thou canst not refuse me. Lord, my only desire is to love Thee, to give myself to Thee without reserve, and no longer to be ungrateful to Thee, as I have hitherto been. Behold me, and graciously hear me; grant that this may be the day of my entire conversion to Thee, so that I may never more cease to love Thee. I love Thee, my God! I love Thee, Infinite Goodness! I love Thee, my love, my paradise, my good, my life, my all!

Ejaculatory prayer. My Jesus, who art all mine, Thou desires me, and I desire Thee!

Visit to the Blessed Virgin Mary

What relief do I feel in my miseries, and what consolation in my tribulations, what strength do I not find in the midst of temptations, when I remember and call thee to my aid, O my most sweet and most holy Mother Mary ! Yes, indeed, you were right, O ye saints, in calling my Lady "the haven of those who are in tribulation," with St. Ephrem; "the repairer of our calamities," and "the solace of the miserable," with St. Bonaventure; and "the rest from our mourning, "with St. Germanus. My own Mary, do thou console me. I see myself loaded with sins, and surrounded by enemies; without virtue, and cold in my love towards God. Com fort me, comfort me; and let my consolation be to make me begin a new life a life which will be really pleasing to thy Son and to thee.

Ejaculatory prayer. Change me, O Mary my Mother: change me; thou canst do it. Servants:

most amiable Mother. Yes, thou art truly amiable: thy beauty and thy goodness have won the heart of the King of kings, even of God himself. He has said to thee, How beautiful thou art, my beloved; and again, Thou art all beautiful, and there is no spot in thee? If, then, thou art so dear to God, how can I, a miserable sinner, and indebted to thee for so many benefits, refuse to love thee? I love thee, therefore, my most amiable Queen, and I desire to be of the number of thy most devoted lovers. Accept my desire, and obtain for me from God the love which I ask, since nothing is more pleasing to him than to love thee.

Ejaculatory prayer. O my amiable Mother, grant that I may love thee with the greatest ardor.

TWENTY-NINTH VISIT
To the Blessed Sacrament

Behold, I stand at the gate, and knock? O most loving shepherd, who, not satisfied with sacrificing Thyself once to death on the altar of the cross for the love of Thy sheep, hast moreover been pleased to hide Thyself in this divine Sacrament on the altars of our churches, to be always near, and to knock at the doors of our hearts, and thus obtain Thy admission! Ah, did I but know how to enjoy Thy nearness to me as did the Sacred Spouse in the Canticles, who says: I sat down under His shadow, whom I desired. Ah, did I but love Thee, did I but really love Thee, my most amiable Sacrament, I also should wish never to leave the foot of a tabernacle either night or day; and fixing myself near Thy Majesty, concealed under the apparent shadow of

the sacred species, I also should find those divine sweetness and that happiness which souls enamored of Thee there find. Ah, do Thou be graciously pleased to draw me by the odor of Thy beauties, and of the immense love which Thou manifests in this Sacrament: Draw me: we will run after Thee to the odor of Thy ointments. Yes, my Savior, I will leave creatures and all earthly pleasures, to run after Thee in this Sacrament: As olive-plants, round about Thy table? Oh, what abundant fruits of virtues do those happy souls, like olive-plants, bring forth to God, who assist with love before the sacred tabernacle! But I am ashamed to appear before Thee, O my Jesus, so naked and so devoid of all virtues. Thou hast commanded that all who approach the altar to honor Thee should present a gift: Thou shalt not appear empty before Me. What, then, am I to do? Am I no more to appear before Thee? Ah, no; this would not please Thee. Poor as I am, I will approach Thee; and do Thou provide me with the gifts which Thou desires. I see that Thou dwells in the Sacrament, not only to reward Thy lovers, but also to provide for the poor out of Thy riches.

Be it so, then; let us now begin. I adore Thee, O King of my heart, and true lover of men. O shepherd, loving Thy sheep beyond all bounds, to this throne of Thy love I now approach; and having nothing else to present to Thee, I offer Thee my miserable heart, that it may be entirely consecrated to Thy love and to Thy good pleasure. With this heart I can love Thee, and I will love Thee as much as I can. Draw it, then, to Thy-self, and bind it wholly to Thy will, so that, filled with consolation, it may be able from henceforth to say, as Thy dear disciple said, that it is bound by the chains of Thy love, Paul, the prisoner of Jesus Christ. Unite me, my Lord, entirely to Thyself, and make me forget myself, that I may have the happiness one day to lose all things, and even myself, to find Thee alone, and to love Thee forever. I love Thee, my Sacramental

Lord; to Thee do I bind myself, to Thee do I unite myself; make me find Thee, make me love Thee, and never more separate Thyself from me.

Ejaculatory prayer. My Jesus, Thou alone art sufficient for me!

Visit to the Blessed Virgin Mary

St. Bernard calls Mary u the royal road of the Savior "the safe road by which to find the Savior and salvation. Since, then, it is true, O Queen, that thou art, as the same saint says, "the chariot in which our souls go to God," the one who guides us to him, ah, Lady, thou must not suppose that I shall advance towards God, if thou dost not carry me in thine arms! Carry me, carry me; and if I resist, carry me by main force ; do all the violence that thou canst by the sweet

attractions of thy charity to my soul and to my rebellious will, that they may leave creatures, to seek for God alone and his divine will. Show the court of heaven the greatness of thy power. After so many wonders of thy mercy, show this one more: make a poor creature who is far from God wholly his.

Ejaculatory prayer. O Mary, thou canst make me a saint; I hope for this grace from thee!

O charitable Queen, thou art styled by thy servants the advocate of sinners. 1 Since, then, thou art employed in defending sinners, who place themselves under thy protection, I fly to

thee, and address thee in the language of one of thy most devoted servants, St. Thomas of Villanova: O loving advocate, exercise thy office in my behalf; undertake my defense. It is true that I have been a rebel to thy beloved Son; but the evil is committed: save me, then, from the dreadful consequence of my rebellion. If thou tell thy divine Son that thou hast taken me under thy protection, I shall be pardoned and saved.

Ejaculatory prayer. O my Mother, my dear Mother, save me.

THIRTIETH VISIT
To the Blessed Sacrament.

Why Judest Thou Thy face's Job feared when he saw that God hid his face : but to know that Jesus Christ veils his majesty in the Most Blessed Sacrament should not inspire us with fear, but rather with greater love and confidence; since it is precisely to increase our confidence, and with greater evidence to manifest his love, that he remains on our altars concealed under the appearance of bread. Novarinus says "that whilst God hides his face in this Sacrament, he discloses his love."

And who would ever dare approach him with confidence, and lay bare before him his affections and desires, did this King of heaven appear on our altars in the splendor of his glory?

Ah, my Jesus! What loving invention was this of the Most Blessed Sacrament, to hide Thyself under the appearance of bread, in order to make Thyself loved and that Thou might be found on earth by all who desire Thee! The prophet was right in saying that men should speak and raise their voices throughout the world, in order to make known to all men to what an excess the inventions of the love of our good God go for us: Make His works known among the people? O most loving Heart of my Jesus, worthy to possess the hearts of all creatures, Heart all and ever full of flames of most pure love! O consuming fire, consume me all, and give me a new life of love and grace! Unite me to Thyself in such a way that I may never more be separated from

Thee. O Heart open to be the refuge of souls, receive me! O Heart, which on the cross was so agonized for the sins of the world, give me true sorrow for my sins! I know that in this Sacrament Thou preserves the same sentiments of love for me which Thou had for me when dying on Calvary; and therefore Thou hast an ardent desire to unite me wholly to Thyself. And is it possible that I should any longer resist yielding up my entire self to Thy love and to Thy desire? Ah, by Thy merits, my beloved Jesus, be pleased Thyself to wound me, to bind me, to force me, to unite me in all things to Thy Heart. I am now determined by Thy grace to give

Thee all the pleasure that I possibly can, by trampling under foot all human respect, inclinations, repugnance, all my tastes and conveniences, which may prevent me from entirely pleasing Thee. Do Thou, my Lord, so help me, that I may execute this determination in such a way, that henceforward all my works, opinions, and affections, may be all in conformity with Thy good pleasure. O love of God, do Thou drive all other loves from my heart ! O Mary, my hope, thou art all-powerful with God, obtain me the grace to be a faithful servant of the pure love of Jesus until death. Amen, amen. So I hope: so may it be in time and in eternity!

Ejaculatory prayer. Who shall separate me from the love of Christ!

Visit to the Blessed Virgin Mary

St. Bernard affirms, that the love of Mary towards us cannot be greater or more powerful than it is; hence by her affection she is always abundant in her compassion for us, and by her power she is plentiful in the relief she affords us: "The most powerful and compassionate charity of the Mother of God abounds in tender com passion, and in kind relief : she is equally rich in both."

So that, my most pure Queen, thou art rich in power, and rich in compassion ; thou art able to save, and desires to save all. I therefore beseech thee, now and always, in the words of the devout Blosius, saying: "Lady! Protect me in my combats, and confirm me when I am wavering." O most holy Mary, in this great battle in which I am now engaged with hell, do thou always help me; but when thou sees me wavering and likely to fall, O my Lady! Do thou then extend thy hand with greater promptitude, and sustain me with greater vigor. O God! How many temptations have I still to overcome before my death! Mary, my hope, my refuge, my strength, do thou protect me, and never allow me to lose the grace of God. And on my part I resolve always and instantly to have recourse to thee in all temptations, saying:

Ejaculatory prayer. Help me, Mary! Mary, help me! O Mary, we are taught by thy servant St. Bonaventure to regard thee as the Mother of orphans? Those unfortunate sinners, who have lost God, their Father, are orphans indeed. I fly then to thee, O merciful Mother: I have by my sins lost my Father; all my hope rests in thee, who still remains as my Mother. I feel fresh confidence arise within me when I hear Innocent III. ask, Who has ever called on Mary without being heard? Who was ever lost that had sincere recourse to her? I fly, therefore, to thy holy protection; have compassion on me; help me, and do not forsake me.*

Ejaculatory prayer. O Mother of my God, augment daily my confidence in thee.

THIRTY-FIRST VISIT
To the Blessed Sacrament

Oh, how beautiful a sight was it to behold our sweet Redeemer on that day when, fatigued by his journey, lie sat down, all engaging and loving, beside the well to await the Samaritan woman, that he might convert and save her! Jesus, therefore, sat thus on the well. It is precisely thus that this same Lord seems sweetly to dwell with us all the day long, having come down from heaven upon our altars as upon so many fountains of graces, where he awaits and invites souls to keep him company, at least for a while, that he may thus draw them to his perfect love. From every altar on which Jesus remains in the Most Holy Sacrament he seems to speak and address all, saying: O men! Why do you fly my presence? Why do you not come and draw near to me, who love you so much, and who remain thus annihilated for your sake? Why do you fear? I am not now come on earth to judge; but I have hid myself in this Sacrament of love only to do good, and to save all who have recourse to me: I came not to judge the world, but to save the world. Let us, then, understand, that as Jesus Christ in heaven is always living to make intercession for us so in the Sacrament of the Altar he is continually, both night and day, exercising the compassionate office of our Advocate; offering himself as a victim for us to the Eternal Father, thus to obtain for us his mercies and innumerable graces. Therefore the devout Thomas a Kern says, that we ought to approach and converse with Jesus in the Blessed Sacrament without the fear of chastisement, and unrestrained, as to a beloved friend, "as one who loves speaks to his beloved, as a friend to a friend." Since, then, Thou thus gives me permission, let me, O my hidden King and Lord, now open my heart to Thee with confidence, and say: O my Jesus! O enamored of souls, I well know the injustice that men do Thee. Thou loves them, and art not beloved by them; Thou does good, and receives! contempt; Thou desires to make them hear Thy voice, and they give Thee no ear; Thou offers them Thy graces, and they refuse them.

Ah, my Jesus! and is it true that I also at one time joined these ungrateful creatures in thus displeasing Thee? O God, it is but too true? But I am determined to amend, and to endeavor during the time that I still have to live, to make up for the displeasure which I have caused Thee, by doing all that I possibly can to please Thee and to give Thee pleasure. Tell me, Lord, what Thou asks of me, I will execute all without any reserve: make it known to me by the means of holy obedience, and I hope to do it. My God, I now resolutely promise Thee that I will never, from this day forward, omit anything which I know to be, rather than another, pleasing to Thee, even were I thereby to lose all -parents, friends, esteem, health, and even life. Let all perish, provided Thou art pleased. Happy is that loss, when all is lost and sacrificed to satisfy Thy heart,

O God of my soul! I love Thee, O sovereign good, worthy of love above every other good; and in loving Thee I unite my poor heart to all the hearts with which the seraphim love Thee; I unite it to the heart of Mary, to the Heart of Jesus. I love Thee with my entire self; Thee alone will I love, and Thee alone will I always love.

Ejaculatory prayer. My God, my God! I am Thine, and Thou art mine!

Visit to the Blessed Virgin Mary.

Blessed Amadeus says that our most blessed Queen, Mary, is always in the divine presence, acting as our advocate, and interposing with God by her prayers, which are most powerful: "The most blessed Virgin stands before the face of her Creator, interceding with her most powerful prayers for us. For" he adds, "she well sees our miseries and our dangers, and the most clement and sweet Lady compassionates and succors us with a mother's love. "Thou, my advocate and my most loving Mother, thou even now sees the miseries of my soul; thou sees my dangers, and prays for me. Pray, pray, and cease not to pray, until thou sees me saved and thanking thee in heaven. The devout Blosius tells me that thou, O most sweet Mary, art, after Jesus, the certain salvation of those who are thy faithful servants. Ah! This grace I now ask thee: grant me the happy lot of being thy faithful servant until death; that after death I may go to bless thee in heaven, where I shall be certain never more, as long as God is God, to leave thy sacred feet.

Ejaculatory prayer. O Mary, my Mother, grant that I may be ever thine!

O Mary, thou art the tower of David, and therefore art able to defend those who take refuge under thee. Protect all who are engaged in the contest. I experience continual assaults from my enemies, who are striving to deprive me of the grace of God, and to withdraw me from thy protection. But thou art the fortress and the bulwark of our hope; thou dost not disdain to fight in behalf of those who trust in thee. O Mary, defend me, then, against all my enemies, and tight my battles for me, because I rely with confidence on thee.

Ejaculatory prayer. O Mary, thou art my protectress. My Good, my God, all mine Thou art; Myself I give Thee, all my heart; For Thee, and Thee alone, I sigh. What have I in heaven? And besides Thee, what do I desire upon earth? Thou art the God of my heart, and the God that is my portion forever.

HYMNS
I.

Jesus in the Blessed Sacrament enclosed in the Tabernacle.
O flowers, O happy flowers, which day and night
So near to my own Jesus silent stay,
And never leave him, till before his sight
At length your life in fragrance fades away!
Could I, too, always make my dwelling-place
In that dear spot to which your charms you lend.
Oh, what a blessed lot were mine! What grace,
Close to my truest Life, my life to end!
O lights! O happy lights, which burn away,
The presence of our Jesus to proclaim;
Ah! Could I see my heart become one day
Like you, all fire of love and burning flame,
Then, as you waste away, so would I die,
Like you, consumed with fire of love divine;
Oh! How I envy you! How blest were I
Could I but change your happy lot with mine!
O sacred pyx! thou art more favored still,
For thou my love concealed dost here enclose;

What nobler, happier part could creature fill?
In thee thy very God deigns to repose!
Ah! Were thy office but for one brief day
On this my poor and frozen breast bestowed,
Then would my heart be melted all away,
Of love and fire become the blest abode!
But ah, sweet flowers, bright lights, and so blest!
Far, far more fortunate than you am I,
When my Beloved comes within my breast,
All loving like a tender lamb to lie;
And I, poor worm, in this frail host receive
My good, my all, the God of Majesty!
Why then not burn? My life why then not give,
Since here my treasure gives himself to me?
Away, like fluttering moth around the light,
My raptured soul, about thy Jesus fly,
Inflamed with faith and love; and at the sight
Of thy beloved ever burn and sigh!
And when the hour arrives, and he is thine
Whose very sight make Paradise above,
Oh, press him to thy heart with fire divine,
And say thou wilt but love, love, only love!

II.
The Visit to Jesus on the Altar
When the loving Shepherd,
Ere he left the earth,
Shed, to pay our ransom,
Blood of priceless worth,
These his lambs so cherish d,
Purchased for his own,
He would not abandon
In the world alone.
Ere he makes us partners
Of his realm on high,
Happy and immortal
With him in the sky,
Love immense, stupendous,
Makes him here below
Partner of our exile
In this world of woe.

Lest one heart that loves him
E'er should sigh with pain,
Pining for his presence,
Seeking him in vain,
He on earth would tarry
Near to everyone,
That each heart might find him
On his altar-throne.
Yes, upon that altar,
Captive in his cell,
Burning with affection,
Jesus deigns to dwell.
Thence he seeks to kindle
With his heavenly fires
Every heart that truly
To his love aspires.
How that fire enkindles,
Piercing like a dart,
He alone is witness
Who has felt its smart ;
Though the heart approaches
Cold as falling snow,
Soon it melts and kindles
From the furnace glow.
Say, ye souls enamored,
What blest flames you feel:
Say, what fiery arrows
Pierce you as you kneel,
When you come to worship
Where your Jesus lies,
All your love awaiting,
Hid from mortal eyes.
Jesus, food of angels!
Monarch of the heart,
Oh, that I could never
From Thy face depart!
Yes, Thou ever dwells
Here for love of me,
Hidden Thou remains,
God of Majesty!

Soon I hope to see Thee,
And enjoy Thy love,
Face to face, sweet Jesus,
In Thy heaven above.
But on earth an exile
My delight shall be,
Ever to be near Thee,
Veiled for love of me

Mediations for the Octave of Corpus Christi

MEDITATION I

The Love of Jesus in the Most Holy Sacrament

Our most loving Redeemer, knowing that he must leave this earth and return to his Father as soon as he should have accomplished the work of our redemption by his death, and seeing that the hour of his death was now come, Jesus knowing that His hour was conic, that He should pass out of this world unto the Father would not leave us alone in this valley of tears, and therefore what did he do? He instituted the Most Holy Sacrament of the Eucharist, in which he left us his whole self. "No tongue," said St. Peter of Alcantara, "is able to declare the greatness of the love that Jesus bears to every soul: and therefore this Spouse, when he would leave this earth, in order that his absence might not cause us to forget him, left us as a memorial this Blessed Sacrament, in which he himself remained; for he would not that there should be any other pledge to keep alive our remembrance of him than he himself." Jesus, therefore, would not be separated from us by his death; but he instituted this Sacrament of love in order to be with us even to the end o the world: Behold I am with you even to the consummation of the world? Behold him, then, as faith teaches us, be hold him on so many altars shut up as in so many prisons of love, in order that he may be found by every one that seeks him. But, O Lord, says St. Bernard, this does not become Thy majesty. Jesus Christ answers, It is enough that it becomes my love.

They feel great tenderness and devotion who go to Jerusalem and visit the cave where the Incarnate Word was born, the hall where he was scourged, the hill of Calvary on which he died, and the sepulchre where he was buried; but how much greater ought our tenderness to be when we visit an altar on which Jesus remains in the Most Holy Sacrament! The Ven. Father John

Avila used to say, that of all sanctuaries there is not one to be found more excellent and devout than a church where Jesus is sacramentally present.

Affections and Prayers

O my beloved Jesus, O God, who hast loved men with so exceeding love! What more canst Thou do to make Thyself loved by these ungrateful men? Oh, if men loved Thee, all the churches would be continually filled with people prostrate on the ground adoring and thanking Thee, and burning with love for Thee at seeing Thee with the eyes of faith hidden in a tabernacle. But no; men, forgetful of Thee and of Thy love, are ready enough to court a man from whom they hope for some miserable advantage, while they leave Thee, O my Lord, abandoned and alone. Oh that I could by my devotion make reparation for such ingratitude! I am sorry that I also have hitherto been, like them, careless and ungrateful. But for the future I will not be so any longer, and I will devote myself to Thy service as much as I possibly can. Do Thou inflame me

with Thy holy love, so that from this day forth I may live only to love and to please Thee. Thou deserves the love of all hearts. If at one time I have despised Thee, I now desire nothing but to love Thee. O my Jesus, Thou art my love and my only good, "my God and my all."

Most holy Virgin Mary, obtain for me, I pray thee, a great love for the Most Holy

Sacrament.

MEDITATION II
Jesus remains on the Altar, that Every One may be able to find Him

St. Teresa said, that in this world it is impossible for all subjects to speak to the king. As for the poor, the most they can hope for is, to speak with him by means of some third person. But to speak with Thee, O King of Heaven, there is no need of third persons; for every one that wishes can find Thee in the Most Holy Sacrament, and can speak to Thee at his pleasure and without restraint. For this reason, said the same saint, Jesus Christ has concealed his majesty in the Sacrament, under the appearance of bread, in order to give us more confidence, and to take away from us all fear of approaching him.

Oh, how Jesus seems continually to exclaim from the altar: Come to Me, all you that labor and are burdened, and I will refresh you. Come, he says, come, ye poor: come, ye infirm; come, ye afflicted; come, ye just and ye sinners, and you shall find in me a remedy for all your losses and afflictions: such is the desire of Jesus Christ; to console everyone who has recourse to him, he remains day and night on our altars, that he maybe found by all, and that he may bestow favors upon all. Hence the saints experienced in this world such pleasure in remaining in the presence of Jesus in the Blessed Sacrament, that days and nights appeared to them as moments. The Countess of Feria having become a nun of the Order of St. Clare, was never wearied of remaining in the choir in sight of the tabernacle: being asked one day what she was doing so long before the Most Holy Sacrament, she answered with surprise: "What do I do before the Blessed Sacrament? what do I do ? I return thanks, I love and I pray!" St. Philip Neri being in the presence of the Blessed Sacrament, exclaimed: "Behold my love, behold all my love?" Ah, if Jesus were thus our whole love, days and nights in his presence would appear also to us as moments.

Affections and Prayers

O my Jesus, from this day forward I also hope to say always to Thee, when I come to visit Thee on Thy altars: "Behold my love, behold all my love!" Yes, my beloved Redeemer, I will love none other but Thee; I desire that Thou should be the only love of my soul. I seem to die of sorrow when I think that hitherto I have loved creatures and my own pleasures more than Thee, and have turned my back upon Thee, the sovereign good. But Thou wouldst not have me lost, and therefore hast Thou borne with me with so much patience; and instead of chastising me, Thou hast pierced my heart with so many darts of love, that I could no longer resist Thy kindness, but have given myself up to Thee; I see that Thou wouldst have me to be entirely Thine. But since Thou wouldst have it to be so, do Thou make me so Thyself ; for it is Thou who must do it. Do Thou detach my heart from all earthly affections and from myself, and grant that I may seek none other but Thee, that I may think of none but Thee, that I may speak of none but Thee, and that I may only desire and sigh to burn with love for Thee, and to live and die for Thee alone. O love of my Jesus, come and occupy my whole heart, and expel from it all other love" but that of God! I love Thee, O Jesus in the Sacrament, I love Thee, my treasure, my love, my all.

O Mary, my hope, pray for me, and make me belong entirely to Jesus.

MEDITATION III

The Great Gift which Jesus has made us by Giving Himself to us in the Blessed Sacrament. The love of Jesus Christ was not satisfied with sacrificing for us his divine life in the midst of a sea of ignominies and torments, in order to prove to us the affection that he bore us; but besides all this, in order to oblige us to love him more, on the night before his death he would leave us his whole self as our food in the Holy Eucharist. God is omnipotent; but after he has given himself to a soul in this Sacrament of love, he has nothing more to give her. The Council of Trent says, that Jesus, in giving himself to us in the Holy Communion, pours forth, as it were, all the riches of his infinite love in this gift: "He has, as it were, poured forth the treasures of his love towards man." How would that vassal esteem himself honored, writes St. Francis de Sales, were his prince, whilst he was at table, to send him a portion of his own dish; and what would it be if this portion were a piece torn out from his own arm? Jesus in the Holy Communion gives us for our food, not only a portion of his own meal and of his most sacred flesh, but all his body: Take and eat, this is My Body? And together with his body he gives us also his soul and his divinity; so that, as St. Chrysostom says, our Lord, in giving himself to us in the Blessed Sacrament, gives us all that he has, and nothing more remains for him to give us: "He gave all to Thee, and left nothing for himself." O wonderful prodigy of divine love, that God, who is the Lord of all, makes himself entirely ours!

Affections and Prayers

My dear Jesus, what more canst Thou do to make us love Thee? Oh, make us understand what an excess of love Thou hast shown us in reducing Thyself to food, in order to unite Thyself thus to us poor sinners! Thou, therefore, my dear Redeemer, hast had so much affection for me, that Thou hast not refused to give Thyself again and again entirely for me in Holy Communion. And yet I have had the courage to drive Thee so many times away from my soul! But Thou canst not despise an humble and a contrite heart. Thou didst become man for my sake, Thou didst die for me, Thou didst even go so far as to become my food; and what more can there remain for Thee to do to gain my love? Oh, that I could die with grief every time that I remember to have thus despised Thy grace! I repent, my love, with my whole heart for having offended Thee. I love Thee, O infinite goodness! I love Thee, O infinite love! I desire nothing but to love Thee, and I fear nothing but to live without Thy love. My beloved Jesus, do not refuse to come for the future into my soul. Come, because I would rather die a thousand times than drive Thee away again, and I will do all I can to please Thee. Come and inflame my whole soul with Thy love. Grant that I may forget everything, to think only of Thee, and to aspire to Thee alone, my sovereign and my only good.

Mary, my Mother, pray for me; and by thy prayers make me grateful for all the love of Jesus towards me.

MEDITATION IV

The Great Love which Jesus Christ has shown us in the Blessed Sacrament. Jesus, knowing that His hour was come, that He should pass out of this world to the Father: having loved His own who were in the world, He loved them to the end? Jesus, knowing that the hour of his death was come, desired to leave us, before he died, the greatest pledge of his affection that he could give us; and this was the gift of the Most Holy Sacrament: He loved them to the end; which St. Chrysostom explains, "He loved them with extreme love." He loved men with the greatest love with which he could love them, by giving them his whole self. But at what time did Jesus institute this great Sacrament, in which he has left us himself? On the night preceding his death: The same night in which He was betrayed (writes the Apostle), He took bread; and giving thanks, broke and said, Take ye and eat; this is My Body. "At the very time that men were preparing to put him to death, he gave them this last proof of his love. The marks of affection which we receive from our friends at the time of their death remain more deeply impressed on our hearts; for this reason did Jesus bestow on us this gift of the Blessed Sacrament just before his death. With reason, then, did St. Thomas call this gift "sacrament and pledge of love" and St. Bernard, "the love of loves;" because in this Sacrament Jesus Christ united and accomplished all the other acts of love which he had shown us. Hence St. Mary Magdalene of Pazzi called the day on which Jesus instituted this Sacrament "the day of love."

Affections and Prayers

O infinite love of Jesus, worthy of being loved with a like in finite love! Thou, my Lord, dost love men so much; how is it, then, that men love Thee so little in return? What more could Thou do to make Thyself loved by them? O my Jesus, Thou art so amiable and so loving; make thyself, I pray Thee, known; make Thyself loved. When shall I love Thee as Thou has love me? Oh, discover to me more and more the great ness of Thy mercy, in order that I may burn ever more and more with Thy love, and always seek to please Thee. O be loved one of my soul, would that I had always loved Thee! Alas, there was a time when I not only did not love Thee, but despised Thy grace and Thy love! I am consoled by the sorrow which I feel for it, and I hope for pardon through Thy promise to forgive him that repents of his sins. To Thee, O my Savior, do I turn all my affections; help me, through the merits of Thy Passion, to love Thee with my whole strength. Oh, that I could die for Thee, as Thou didst die for me!

Mary, my Mother, do thou obtain for me the grace hence forth to love God alone.

MEDITATION V

The Union of the Soul with Jesus in the Holy Communion

St. Dionysius the Areopagite says that the principal effect of love is to tend to union. For this very purpose did Jesus institute the Holy Communion, that he might unite himself entirely to our souls. He had given himself to us as our master, our example, and our victim; it only remained for him to give himself to us as our food, that he might become one with us; as food becomes one with the person that eats it. This he did by instituting this Sacrament of love: "The last degree of love"; (says St. Bernardine of Sienna) "is when he gave himself to us to be our food; because he gave himself to be united with us in every way, as food and he who takes it are mutually united."

So that Jesus Christ was not satisfied with uniting himself to our human nature; but he would, by this Sacrament, find a way of uniting himself also to each one of us, so as to make himself wholly one with him who receives him. Hence St. Francis de Sales writes: "In no other action can our Savior be considered more tender or more loving than in this, in which he, as it were, annihilates himself, and reduces himself to food, that he may penetrate our souls, and unite himself to the hearts of his faithful." Because Jesus loved us ardently, he desired to unite himself to us in the Holy Eucharist, in order that we might become the same thing with him; thus writes St. Chrysostom: "He mingled himself with us, that we might be one; for this belongs to those who love greatly."

And Jesus himself said this: He that eateth My flesh abideth in Me, and I in him? He, therefore, that communicates, abides in Jesus, and Jesus abides in him; and this union is not of mere affection, but it is a true and real union. As two wax tapers, when melted, says St. Cyril of Alexandria, unite themselves into one, so he that communicates becomes one with Jesus Christ. Let us, therefore, imagine, when we communicate, that Jesus Christ says to us that which he said one day to his beloved servant, Margaret of Ypres: "Behold, O my daughter, the beautiful union between me and thee; come, then, love me, and let us remain constantly united in love, and never more be separated."

Affections and Prayers

O my Jesus, this is what I seek of Thee, and what I will always seek for from Thee in the Holy Communion: "Let us be always united, and never more be separated." I know that Thou wilt not separate Thyself from me, if I do not first separate myself from Thee. But this is my fear, lest I should in future separate myself from Thee by sin, as I have done in times past. O my blessed Redeemer, permit it not: "Suffer me not to be separated from Thee." As long as I am alive, I am in danger of this; oh, through the merits of Thy death, I beseech Thee let me die, rather than repeat this great injury against Thee. I repeat it, and pray Thee to grant me Thy grace always to repeat: "Suffer me not to be separated from Thee; suffer me not to be separated from Thee." O God of my soul, I love Thee; I love Thee, and will always love Thee, and will love Thee alone. I protest before heaven and earth that I desire Thee alone, and nothing but Thee. O my Jesus, hear me; I desire Thee alone, and nothing but Thee.

O Mary, Mother of mercy, pray for me now; and obtain for me the grace never more to separate myself from Jesus, and to love only Jesus.

MEDITATION VI

The Desire which Jesus Christ has to Unite Himself to us in the Holy Communion

Jesus knowing that His hour was come. This hour, which Jesus called. His hour, "was the hour of that night in which his Passion was to begin. But why did he call so sad an hour his hour? Because this was the hour for which he had sighed during his whole life, having determined to leave us in this night the Holy Communion, by which he desired to unite himself entirely to the souls whom he loved, and for whom he was soon to give his blood and his life. Behold how he spoke on that night to his disciples: With desire have I desired to eat this Pasch with you? By which words he would express to us the desire and anxiety that he had to unite himself to us in this Sacrament of love. With desire have I desired these words, said St. Laurence Justinian, were words which came from the Heart of Jesus, which was burning with infinite love: This is the voice of the most ardent charity."

Affections and Prayers

My adorable Jesus, Thou canst not give us greater proofs of Thy love, to show us how much Thou lovest us. Thou hast given Thy life for us; Thou hast bequeathed Thyself to us in the Holy Sacrament, in order that we may come and nourish ourselves with Thy flesh ; and Thou art most anxious that we should receive Thee. How, then, can we behold all these proofs of Thy love, and not burn with love for Thee? Begone, ye earthly affections, begone from my heart; it is you that hinder me from burning with love for Jesus as he burns with love for me. And what other pledges of Thy love can I expect, O my Redeemer, than those which Thou hast already given me? Thou hast sacrificed Thy whole life for the love of me; Thou hast embraced for my sake a most bitter and infamous death; Thou hast for my sake reduced Thyself almost to annihilation, by becoming food in the Holy Eucharist in order to give Thyself entirely to us. O Lord, let me no longer live ungrateful for such great goodness. I thank Thee for having given me time to bewail the offences I have committed against Thee, and to love Thee during the days that remain to me in this life. I repent, O sovereign good, for having hitherto despised Thy love. I love Thee, O infinite goodness! I love Thee, O infinite treasure! I love Thee, O infinite love who art worthy of infinite love! Oh, help me, my Jesus, to discard from my heart all affections that are not directed to Thee; so that from this day forward I may not desire, nor seek, nor love any other but Thee. My beloved Lord, grant that I may always find Thee, grant that I may always love Thee. Do Thou take possession of my whole will, in order that I may never desire anything but what is pleasing to Thee. My God, my God, whom shall I love, if I love not Thee, who art the supreme good? I do indeed desire Thee, and nothing more. O Mary, my Mother, take my heart into thy keeping, and fill it with pure love for Jesus Christ.

MEDITATION VII

Holy Communion Obtains for us Perseverance in Divine Grace

When Jesus comes to the soul in Holy Communion, he brings to it every grace, and specially the grace of holy perseverance. This is the principal effect of the Most Holy Sacrament of the Altar, to nourish the soul that receives it with this food of life, and to give it great strength to advance unto perfection, and to resist those enemies who desire our death. Hence Jesus calls himself in this Sacrament heavenly bread: I am the living Bread which came down from heaven; if any man eat of this Bread, he shall live forever? Even as earthly bread sustains the life of the body, so this heavenly bread sustains the life of the soul, by making it persevere in the grace of God.

Affections and Prayers

Miserable sinner that I am, O Lord, wherefore do I lament my weakness when I consider my many falls from grace? How was it possible that I should have resisted the assaults of the devil while I stayed away from Thee, who art my strength? If I had oftener approached the Holy Communion, I should not have been so often overcome by my enemies. But in future it shall not be so: In Thee, O Lord, have I hoped; I shall not be confounded forever. No, I will no longer rely on my own resolution. Thou alone art my hope, O my Jesus; Thou wilt give me strength, that I may no more fall into sin. I am weak; but Thou, by Holy Communion, wilt make me strong against every temptation I can do all things in Him who strengthened me? Forgive me, O my Jesus, all the offences I have committed against Thee, of which I repent with my whole heart. I resolve rather to die than ever to offend Thee again; and I trust, in Thy Passion, that Thou wilt give me Thy help to persevere in Thy grace to the end of my life In Thee, O Lord, have I hoped; I shall not be confounded forever.

And with St. Bonaventure I will say the same to thee, O Mary, my Mother: "In thee, O Lady, have I hoped; I shall not be confounded forever."

MEDITATION VIII
Preparation for Communion and Thanksgiving after it

Cardinal Bona asks wherefore it happens that so many souls, after so many Communions, make so little advance in the way of God and he answers: "The fault is not in the food, but in the disposition of him who eats it;" that is to say, in the want of due preparation on the part of the communicant. Fire soon burns dry wood, but not that which is green, because the latter is not fit to burn. The saints derived great profit from their Communions, because they were very careful in their preparation for it.

There are two principal things which we should endeavor to obtain in order to prepare ourselves for Holy Communion.

The first is, detachment from creatures, by driving from our heart everything that is not of God and for God. Although the soul may be in a state of grace, yet if the heart is occupied by earthly affections the more there is of earth in the soul, so much less room will there be for divine love. St. Gertrude once asked our Lord what preparation he required of her for Holy Communion, and Jesus answered her: "I require none other from thee than that thou shouldst come to receive me void of thyself."

The second thing that is necessary in order to reap great fruit from Communion is, the desire to receive Jesus Christ with the view, of loving him more. Gerson says that at this banquet none are satiated but those who feel great hunger. Hence St. Francis de Sales writes, that the principal intention of a soul in receiving Communion should be to advance in the love of God. "He" (says the saint) "should be received for love, who out of pure love alone gives himself to us." And therefore Jesus said to St. Mechtilde: "When thou art going to communicate, desire all the love that any soul ever had for me, and I will receive it according to thy desire, as if it were thine own."

It is also necessary to make a thanksgiving after Communion. There is no prayer more dear to God than that which is made after Communion. We must occupy this time in acts of love and prayers. The devout acts of love which we then make have greater merit in the sight of God than those which we make at other times, because they are then animated by the presence of Jesus Christ, who is united to our souls. And as to prayers, St. Teresa says that Jesus, after Communion, remains in the soul as on a throne of grace, and says to it: What wilt thou that I should do for thee? Soul, I am come from heaven on purpose to bestow graces upon thee; ask me what thou wilt, and as much as thou wilt, and thou shalt be heard. Oh, what treasures of grace do they lose who pray but a short time to God after Holy Communion!

Affections and Prayer

O God of love, dost Thou, then, so much desire to dispense Thy favors to us, and yet are we so little anxious to obtain them? Oh, what sorrow we shall feel at the hour of death, when we think of this negligence, so pernicious to our souls! O my Lord, forget, I beseech Thee, all that is past; for the future, with Thy help, I will prepare myself better, by endeavoring to detach my affections from everything that prevents me from receiving all those graces which Thou desirest to bestow upon me. And after Communion I will lift up my heart to Thee as much as I can, in order to obtain Thy help that I may advance in Thy love, oh, grant me grace to accomplish this. O my Jesus, how negligent have I hitherto been in loving Thee! The time which Thou in Thy mercy mayest yet allot to me in this life, is the time to prepare myself for death, and to make amends by my love for the offences I have committed against Thee. I will spend it entirely in lamenting my sins and in loving Thee. I love Thee, my Jesus, my love; I love Thee, my only Good; have pity on me, and do not forsake me.

And thou, O Mary, my hope, do not cease to help me by thy holy intercession.

NOVENA TO THE SACRED HEART OF JESUS
NOTICE ON THE DEVOTION TO THE ADORABLE HEART OF JESUS

The devotion of all devotions is love for Jesus Christ, and frequent meditation on the love which this amiable Redeemer has borne and still bears to us.

A devout author laments, and most justly, the sight of so many persons who pay much attention to the practice of various devotions, but neglect this; and of many preachers and confessors, who say a great many things, but speak little of love for Jesus Christ: whereas love for Jesus Christ ought to be the principal, indeed the only, devotion of a Christian; and therefore the only object and care of preachers and confessors towards their hearers and penitents ought to be to recommend to them constantly, and to inflame their hearts with, the love of Jesus Christ. This neglect is the reason why souls make so little progress in virtue, and remain groveling in the same defects, and even frequently relapse into grievous sins, because they take but little care, and are not sufficiently admonished to acquire the love of Jesus Christ, which is that golden cord which unites and binds the soul to God.

For this sole purpose did the Eternal Word come into this world, to make himself loved: I am conic to cast fire on the earth, and what will I but that it be kindled? And for this purpose also did the Eternal Father send him into the world, in order that he might make known to us his love, and thus obtain ours in return; and he protests that he will love us in the same proportion as we love Jesus Christ: For the Father Himself loveth you, because you have loved Me.

For this same purpose it is related in the life of the Venerable Sister Margaret Alacoque, a nun of the Order of the Visitation, that our Savior revealed to this his servant his wish that in our times the devotion and feast of his Sacred Heart should be established and propagated in the Church, in order that devout souls should by their adoration and prayer make reparation for the injuries his heart constantly receives from ungrateful men when he is exposed in the Sacrament upon the Altar. It is also related in the life of the same venerable sister, written by the learned

Monseigneur Languet, Bishop of Sens, that while this devout virgin was one day praying before the Most Holy Sacrament, Jesus Christ showed her his heart surrounded by thorns, with a cross on the top and in a throne of flames; and then he said thus to her: "Behold the heart that has so much loved men, and has spared nothing for love of them, even to consuming itself to give them pledges of its love, but which receives from the majority of men no other recompense but ingratitude, and insults towards the Sacrament of love; and what grieves me most is, that these hearts are consecrated to me." And then he desired her to use her utmost endeavors in order that a particular feast should be celebrated in honor of his divine heart on the first Friday after the Octave of Corpus Christi. And this for three reasons: 1. In order that the faithful should return thanks to him for the great gift which he has left them in the adorable Eucharist; 2. In order that loving souls should make amends by their prayers and pious affections for the irreverences and insults which he has received and still receives from sinners in this Most Holy Sacrament; 3. In order that they might make up also for the honor which he does not receive in so many churches where he is so little adored and reverenced. And he promised that he would make the riches of his Sacred Heart abound towards those who should render him this honor, both on the day of this feast, and on every other day when they should visit him in the Most Holy Sacrament.

This devotion to the Sacred Heart of Jesus Christ is nothing more than an exercise of love towards this amiable Savior. But as to the principal object of this devotion, the spiritual object is the love with which the heart of Jesus Christ is inflamed towards men, because love is generally attributed to the heart, as we read in many places of Scripture: My son, give Me thy heart. My heart and my flesh have rejoiced in the living God? The God of my heart, and the God that is my portion forever? The charity of God is poured forth in our hearts by the Holy Ghost who is given to us. But the material or sensible object is the most Sacred Heart of Jesus, not taken separately by itself, but united to his sacred humanity, and consequently to the divine Person of the Word.

But the hope we entertain that this concession will someday be granted in favor of the heart of our Lord, is not built upon the above-mentioned opinion of the ancients, but on the com
mon opinion of philosophers, both ancient and modern, that the human heart, even though it may not be the seat of the affections and the principle of life, is, notwithstanding, as the most learned Muratori writes in the same place, "One of the primary fountains and organs of the life of man." For the generality of modern physicians agree in saying that the fountain and the principle of the circulation of the blood is the heart, to which are attached the veins and arteries; and therefore there is no doubt that the other parts of the body receive their principle of motion from the heart. If, therefore, the heart is one of the "primary fountains"; of human life, it cannot be doubted that the heart has a principal share in the affections of man. And, indeed, one may observe from experience, that the internal affections of sorrow and love produce, a much greater impression on the heart than on all the other parts of the body. And especially with regard to love, without naming many other saints, it is recorded of St. Philip Neri, that in his fervors of love towards God, heat came forth from his heart so that it might be felt on his chest, and his heart palpitated so violently that it beat against the head of any one that approached him; and by a supernatural prodigy our Lord enlarged the ribs of the saint round his heart, which, agitated by

the ardor he felt, required a greater space to be able to move. St. Teresa herself writes in her life, that God sent several times an angel to pierce her heart, so that she remained afterwards inflamed with divine love, and felt herself sensibly burning and fainting away, a thing to be well pondered on, as we perceive from this that the affections of love are in a special manner impressed by God in the hearts of the saints; and the Church has not objected to grant to the Discalced Carmelites the proper Mass in honor of the wounded heart of St. Teresa.

But, however this may be, let us now endeavor to satisfy the devotion of souls enamored of Jesus Christ, who are desirous to honor him in the most Holy Sacrament, by a Novena of holy meditations and affections to his Sacred Heart.

Affections and Prayers

O my amiable Redeemer, what object more worthy of love could Thy Eternal Father command me to love than Thee? Thou art the beauty of paradise, Thou art the love of Thy Father, Thy heart is the throne of all virtues. O amiable heart of my Jesus, Thou dost well deserve the love of all hearts; poor and wretched is that heart which loves Thee not! Thus miser able, O my God, has my heart been during all the time in which it hath not loved Thee. But I will not continue to be thus wretched; I love Thee, I will always continue to love Thee, O my Jesus. O my Lord, I have hitherto forgotten Thee, and now what can I expect? That my ingratitude will oblige Thee to forget me entirely, and forsake me forever? No, my Savior, do not permit this. Thou art the object of the love of God; and shalt Thou not, then, be loved by a miserable sinner, such as I am, who have been so favored and loved by Thee? O lovely flames that burnt in the loving heart of my Jesus, enkindle in my poor heart that holy fire which Jesus came down from heaven to kindle on earth. Consume and destroy all the impure affections that dwell in my heart, and prevent it from being entirely his. O my God, grant that it may only exist to love Thee, and Thee alone, my dearest Savior. If at one time I despised Thee, Thou art now the only object of my love. I love Thee, I love Thee, I love Thee, and I will never love anyone else but Thee. My beloved Lord, do not disdain to accept the love of a heart which has once afflicted Thee by my sins. Let it be Thy glory to exhibit to the angels a heart now burning with the love of Thee, which hitherto shunned and despised Thee.

Most holy Virgin Mary, my hope, do thou assist me, and beseech Jesus to make me, by his grace, all that he wishes me to be.

MEDITATION II
The Loving Heart of Jesus

Oh, if we could but understand the love that burns in the heart of Jesus for us! He has loved us so much, that if all men, all the angels, and all the saints were to unite, with all their energies, they could not arrive at the thousandth part of the love that Jesus bears to us. He loves us infinitely more than we love ourselves.

He has loved us even to excess: They spoke of His decease (excess) which He was to accomplish in Jerusalem. And what greater excess of love could there be than for God to die for his creatures? He has loved us to the greatest degree: Having loved His own. He loved them unto the end; since, after having loved us from eternity, for there never was a moment from eternity when God did not think of us and did not love each one of us: I have loved thee with an everlasting love for the love of us he made himself man, and chose a life of sufferings and the death of the cross for our sake. Therefore he has loved us more than his honor, more than his repose, and more than his life; for he sacrificed everything to show us the love that he bears us. And is not this an excess of love sufficient to stupefy with astonishment the angels of paradise for all eternity?

This love has induced him also to remain with us in the Holy Sacrament as on a throne of love; for he remains there under the appearance of a small piece of bread, shut up in aciborium, where he seems to remain in a perfect annihilation of his majesty, without movement, and without the use of his senses; so that it seems that he performs no other office there than that of loving men. Love makes us desire the constant presence of the object of our love. It is this love and this desire that makes Jesus Christ reside with us in the Most Holy Sacrament. It seemed too short a time to this loving Savior to have been only thirty-three years with men on earth; therefore, in order to show his desire of being constantly with us, he thought right to perform the greatest of all miracles, in the institution of the Holy Eucharist. But the work of redemption was already completed, men had already become reconciled to God; for what purpose, then, did Jesus remain on earth in this Sacrament? Ah, he remains there because he cannot bear to separate himself from us, as he has said that he takes a delight in us.

Affections and Prayers

O adorable heart of my Jesus, heart inflamed with the love of men, heart created on purpose to love them, how is it possible that Thou canst be despised, and Thy love so ill corresponded to by men ? Oh, miserable that I am, I also have been one of those ungrateful ones that have not loved Thee. Forgive me, my Jesus, this great sin of not having loved Thee, who art so amiable, and who hast loved me so much that Thou canst do nothing more to oblige me to love Thee. I feel that I deserve to be condemned not to be able to love Thee, for having renounced Thy love, as I have hitherto done. But no, my dearest Savior, give me any chastisement, but do not inflict this one upon me. Grant me the grace to love Thee, and then give me any affliction Thou pleasest. But how can I fear such a chastisement, whilst I feel that Thou continuest to give me the sweet, the pleasing precept of loving Thee, my, Lord and my God? Love the Lord thy God with thy whole heart. Yes, O my God, Thou wouldst be loved by me, and I will love Thee; indeed I will love none but Thee, who hast loved me so much. O Love of my Jesus. Thou art my Love. O burning heart of my Jesus, do thou inflame my heart also. Do not permit me in future, even for a single moment, to live without Thy love; rather kill me, destroy me; do not let the world behold the spectacle of such horrid ingratitude as that I, who have been so beloved by Thee, and received so many favors and lights from Thee, should begin again to despise Thy love. No, my Jesus, do not permit this. I trust in the blood that Thou hast shed for me, that I shall always love Thee, and that Thou wilt always love me, and that this love between Thee and me will not be broken off for eternity.

O Mary, Mother of fair love, thou who desirest so much to see Jesus loved, bind me, unite me to thy Son; but bind me to him, so that we may never again be separated.

MEDITATION III
The Heart of Jesus Christ Panting to be Loved

Jesus has no need of us; he is equally happy, equally rich, equally powerful with or without our love; and yet, as St. Thomas says, he loves us so, that he desires our love as much as if man was his God, and his felicity depended on that of man. This filled holy Job with astonishment: What is man that Thou shouldst magnify him or why dost Thou set Thy heart upon him?

What can God desire or ask with such eagerness for the love of a worm? It would have been a great favor if God had only permitted us to love him. If a vassal were to say to his king, "Sire, I love you," he would be considered impertinent. But what would one say if the king were to tell his vassal, "I desire you to love me?" The princes of the earth do not humble themselves to this; but Jesus, who is the King of Heaven, is he who with so much earnestness demands our love: Love the Lord thy God with thy whole heart. So pressingly does he ask for our heart: My son, give Me thy heart? And if he is driven from a soul, he does not depart, but he stands outside of the door of the heart, and he calls and knocks to be let in: I stand at the gate arid knock. And he beseeches her to open to him, calling her sister and spouse: Open to Me, My sister, My love. In short, he takes a delight in being loved by us, and is quite consoled when a soul says to him, and repeats often, "My God, my God, I love Thee."

All this is the effect of the great love he bears us. He who loves necessarily desires to be loved. The heart requires the heart; love seeks love: "Why does God love, but that he might be loved himself," said St. Bernard; and God himself first said, What doth the Lord thy God re quire of thee, but that thou fear the Lord thy God, and love Him? 4 Therefore he tells us that he is that Shepherd who, having found the lost sheep, calls all the others to rejoice with him: Rejoice with Me, because I have found My sheep that was lost. He tells us that he is that Father who, when his lost son returns and throws himself at his feet, not only forgives him, but embraces him tenderly.

He tells us that he that loves him not is condemned to death: He that loveth not abideth in death? And, on the contrary, that he takes him that loves him and keeps possession of him: He that abideth in charity, abideth in God, and God in him? Oh, will not such invitations, such en treaties, such threats, and such promises move us to love God, who so much desires to be loved by us?

Affections and Prayers

My dearest Redeemer, I will say to Thee, with St. Augustine, Thou dost command me to love Thee, and dost threaten me with hell if I do not love Thee; but what more dreadful hell, what greater misfortune, can happen to me than to be deprived of Thy love! If, therefore, Thou desirest to frighten me, Thou shouldst threaten me only that I should live without loving Thee; for this threat alone will frighten me more than a thousand hells. If, in the midst of the flames of hell, the damned could burn with Thy love, O my God, hell itself would become a paradise; and if, on the contrary, the blessed in heaven could not love Thee, paradise would become hell. Thus St. Augustine expresses himself.

I see, indeed, my dearest Lord, that I, on account of my sins, did deserve to be forsaken by Thy grace, and at the same time condemned to be incapable of loving Thee; but still I understand that

Thou dost continue to command me to love Thee, and I also feel within me a great desire to love Thee. This my desire is a gift of Thy grace, and it comes from Thee. Oh, give
me also the strength necessary to put it in execution, and make me, from this day forth, say to Thee earnestly, and from the bottom of my heart, and to repeat to Thee always, My God, I love Thee, I love Thee, I love Thee. Thou desirest my love; I also desire Thine. Blot out, therefore, from thy remembrance, O my Jesus, the offences that in past times I have committed against Thee; let us love each other henceforth forever. I will not leave Thee, and Thou wilt not leave me. Thou wilt always love me, and I will always love Thee. My dearest Savior, in Thy merits do I place my hope; oh, do Thou make Thyself to be loved forever, and loved greatly, by a sinner who has offended Thee greatly.

O Mary, Immaculate Virgin, do thou help me, do thou beseech Jesus for me.

MEDITATION IV
The Sorrowful Heart of Jesus

It is impossible to consider how afflicted the heart of Jesus was for love of us and not to pity him. He himself tells us that his heart was overwhelmed with such sorrow, that this alone would have sufficed to take his life away, and to make him die of pure grief, if the virtue of his divinity had not, by a miracle, prevented his death: My soul is sorrowful even unto death.

The principal sorrow which afflicted the heart of Jesus so much was not the sight of the torments and infamy which men were preparing for him, but the sight of their ingratitude towards his immense love. He distinctly foresaw all the sins which we should commit after all his sufferings and such a bitter and ignominious death. He foresaw, especially, the horrible insults which men would offer to his adorable heart, which he has left us in the Most Holy Sacrament as a proof of his affection. O my God, what affronts has not Jesus Christ received from men in this Sacrament of love? One has trampled him under foot, another has thrown him into the gutters, others have availed themselves of him to pay homage to the devil!

And yet the sight of all these insults did not prevent him from leaving us this great pledge of his love. He has a sovereign hatred of sin; but still it seems as if his love towards us had overcome the hatred he bore to sin, since he was content to permit these sacrileges, rather than to deprive the souls that love him of this divine food. Shall not all this suffice to make us love a heart that has loved us so much?

Affections and Prayers

My adorable and dearest Jesus, behold at Thy feet one who has caused so much sorrow to Thy amiable heart. O my God, how could I grieve this heart, which has loved me so much, and has spared nothing to make itself loved by me? But console Thyself, I will say, O my Savior, for my heart having been wounded, through Thy grace, with Thy most holy love, feels now so much regret for the offences I have committed against Thee, that it would fain die of sorrow. Oh, who will give me, my Jesus, that sorrow for my sins which Thou didst feel for them in Thy life! Eternal Father, I offer Thee the sorrow and abhorrence Thy Son felt for my sins; and, for his sake, I beseech Thee to give me so great a sorrow for the offences I have committed against Thee, that I may lead an afflicted and sorrowful life at the thought of having once despised Thy friend ship. And Thou, O my Jesus, do Thou give me, from this day forth, such a horror of sin, that I may abhor even the lightest faults, considering that they displease Thee, who dost not de serve to be offended much or little, but dost deserve an infinite love. My beloved Lord, I now detest everything that displeases Thee, and in future I will love only Thee, and that which Thou lovest. Oh, help me, give me the strength, give me the grace to invoke Thee constantly, O my Jesus, and always to repeat to Thee this petition: My Jesus, give me Thy love, give me Thy love, give me Thy love.

And thou, most holy Mary, obtain for me the grace to pray to thee continually, and to say to thee, O my Mother, make me love Jesus Christ.

MEDITATION V
The Compassionate Heart of Jesus

Where shall we ever find a heart more compassionate or tender than the heart of Jesus, or one that had a greater feeling for our miseries?

This pity induced him to descend from heaven to this earth; it made him say that he was that good shepherd who came to give his life to save his sheep. In order to obtain the pardon of our sins, he would not spare himself, but would sacrifice himself on the Cross, that by his sufferings he might satisfy for the chastisement that we have deserved. This pity and compassion makes him say even now: Why will ye die, O house of Israel return ye, and live. O men, he says, my poor children, why will you damn yourselves by flying from me? Do you not see that by separating yourselves from me you are hastening to eternal death? I desire not to see you lost; do not despair; as often as you wish to return, return, and you shall recover your life: Return, and live.

This compassion even makes him say that he is that loving Father who, though he sees himself despised by his son, yet, if that son returns a penitent, he cannot reject him, but embraces him tenderly and forgets all the injuries He has received: I will not remember all his iniquities? It is not thus that men behave; for though they may forgive, yet they nevertheless retain the remembrance of the offence received, and feel inclined to revenge themselves; and even if they do not revenge themselves, because they fear God, at least they always feel a great repugnance against conversing and entertaining themselves with those persons who have vilified them.

O my Jesus, Thou dost pardon the penitent sinners, and dost not refuse in this world to give them everything in Holy Communion during their life, and everything in the other world, even in heaven, with eternal glory, without retaining the slightest repugnance towards being united to the soul that has offended Thee, for all eternity. Where, then, is there to be found a heart so amiable and compassionate as Thine, O my dearest Savior?

Affections and Prayers

O compassionate heart of my Jesus, have pity on me: "Most sweet Jesus, have mercy on me." I say so now, and beseech Thee to give me the grace always to say to Thee, "Most sweet Jesus, have mercy on me." Even before I offended Thee, O my Redeemer, I certainly did not deserve any of the favors Thou hast bestowed upon me. Thou hast created me, Thou hast given me so much light and knowledge; and all without any merit of mine. But after I had offended Thee, I not only did not deserve Thy favor, but I deserved to be forsaken by Thee and cast into hell. Thy compassion has made Thee wait for me and preserve my life even when I had offended Thee. Thy compassion has enlightened me, and offered me pardon; it has given me sorrow for my sins, and the desire of loving Thee; and now I hope from Thy mercy to remain always in Thy grace. O my Jesus, cease not to show Thy compassion towards me. The mercy which I implore of Thee is that Thou wouldst grant me light and strength to be no longer ungrateful towards Thee. No, O my love, I do not expect that Thou shouldst again forgive me, if I again turn my back towards Thee; this would be presumption, and would prevent Thee from showing mercy to me anymore. For what pity could I expect any more from Thee if I were so ungrateful as to despise Thy friendship again, and to separate myself from Thee. No, my Jesus, I love Thee, and I will always love Thee; and this is the mercy which I hope for and seek from Thee: "Permit me not to be separated from Thee, permit me not to be separated from Thee."

And I beseech thee also, O Mary my Mother, permit me not to be ever again separated from my God.

MEDITATION VI
The Generous Heart of Jesus

It is the characteristic of good-hearted people to desire to make everybody happy, and especially those most distressed and afflicted. But who can ever find one who has a better heart than Jesus Christ? He is infinite goodness, and has therefore a sovereign desire to communicate to us his riches: With Me are riches, that I may enrich them that love Me. 1 He for this purpose made himself poor, as the Apostle says, that he might make us rich: He became poor for your sakes, that through His poverty you might be rich. For this purpose also he chose to remain with us in the most Holy Sacrament, where he remains constantly with his hands full of graces, as was seen by Father Balthazar Alvarez, to dispense them to those who come to visit him. For this reason also he gives himself wholly to us in Holy Communion, giving us to understand from this that he cannot refuse us any good gifts, since he even gives himself entirely to us: How hath He not also, with Him, given us all things?

For in the heart of Jesus we receive every good, every grace that we desire: In all things you are made rich in Christ, so that nothing is wanting to you in any grace? And we must understand that we are debtors to the heart of Jesus for all the graces we have received graces of redemption, of vocation, of light, of pardon, the grace to resist temptations, and to bear patiently with contradictions; for without his assistance we could not do anything good: Without me you can do nothing?

Affections and Prayers

Ah, my Jesus, Thou hast not refused to give me Thy blood and Thy life, and shall I refuse to give Thee my miserable heart? No, my dearest Redeemer, I offer it entirely to Thee. I give Thee all my will; do Thou accept it, and dispose of it at Thy pleasure. I can do nothing, and have nothing; but I have this heart which Thou hast given me, and of which no one can deprive me. I may be deprived of my goods, my blood, my life, but not of my heart. With this heart I can love Thee; with this heart I will love Thee. I beseech Thee, O my God, teach me a perfect forgetfulness of myself; teach me what I must do to arrive at Thy pure love, of which Thou in Thy goodness hast inspired me with the desire. I feel in myself a determination to please Thee; but in order to put my resolve into execution, I expect and implore help from Thee. It de pends on Thee, O loving heart of Jesus, to make entirely Thine my poor heart, which hitherto has been so ungrateful, and through my own fault deprived of Thy love. Oh, grant that my heart may be all on fire with the love of Thee, even as Thine is on fire with the love of me. Grant that my will may be entirely united to Thine, so that I may will nothing but what Thou wiliest, and that from this day forth Thy holy will may be the rule of all my actions, of all my thoughts, and of all my desires. I trust, O my Savior, that Thou wilt not refuse me Thy grace to fulfil this resolution which I now make prostrate at Thy feet, to receive with submission whatever Thou mayest ordain for me and my affairs, as well in life as in death. Blessed art thou, O Immaculate Mary, who hadst thy heart always and entirely united to the heart of Jesus; obtain for me, O my Mother, that in future I may wish and desire that which Jesus wills and thou wiliest.

MEDITATION VII
The Grateful Heart of Jesus

The heart of Jesus is so grateful, that it cannot behold, the most trifling works done for the love of him our smallest word spoken for his glory, a single good thought directed towards pleasing him without giving to each its own reward. He is besides so grateful, that he always returns a hundredfold for one: You shall receive a hundredfold.

Men, when they are grateful, and recompense any benefit done to them, recompense it only once; they, as it were, divest themselves of all the obligation, and then they think no more of it. Jesus Christ does not do thus with us; he not only recompenses a hundredfold in this life every good action that we perform to please him, but in the next life he recompenses it an infinite number of times throughout eternity. And who will be so negligent as not to do as much as he can to please this most grateful heart?

Affections and Prayers

O my beloved Jesus, behold at Thy feet an ungrateful sinner. I have been grateful indeed towards creatures; but to Thee alone I have been ungrateful to Thee, who hast died for me, and hast done the utmost that Thou couldst do to oblige me to love Thee. But the thought that I have to do with a heart full of goodness and infinite in mercy, of one who proclaims that he forgives all the offences of the sinner who repents and loves him, consoles me and gives me courage. My dearest Jesus, I have in times past offended Thee and despised Thee; but now I love Thee more than everything more than myself. Tell me what Thou wouldst have me to do; for I am ready to do everything with Thy help. I believe that Thou hast created me. Thou hast given Thy blood and Thy life for the love of me. I believe also that for my sake Thou dost remain in the Blessed Sacrament; I thank Thee for it, O my love. Oh, permit me not to be ungrateful in future for so many benefits and proofs of Thy love. Oh, bind me, unite me to Thy heart; and permit me not, during the years that remain to me, to offend Thee or grieve Thee any more. I have displeased Thee sufficiently. O my Jesus, it is time that I should love Thee now. Oh, that those years that I have lost would return! But they will return no more, and the life that remains for me may be short; but whether it be short or long, my God, I desire to spend it all in loving Thee, my sovereign good, who dost deserve an eternal and infinite love.

O Mary, my Mother, let me never again be ungrateful to thy Son. Pray to Jesus for me.

MEDITATION VIII
The Despised Heart of Jesus

There is not a greater sorrow for a heart that loves, than to see its love despised; and so much the more when the proofs given of this love have been great, and, on the other hand, the ingratitude great.

If every human being were to renounce all his goods, and to go and live in the desert, to feed on herbs, to sleep on the bare earth, to macerate himself with penances, and at last give himself up to be murdered for Christ's sake, what recompense could he render for the sufferings, the blood, the life that this great Son of God has given for his sake? If we were to sacrifice ourselves every moment unto death, we should certainly not recompense in the smallest degree the love that Jesus Christ has shown us, by giving himself to us in the most Holy Sacrament. Only conceive that God should conceal himself under the species of bread to become the food of one of his creatures!

But, O my God, what recompense and gratitude do men render to Jesus Christ? What but ill-treatment, contempt of his laws and his maxims, injuries such as they would not commit towards their enemy, or their slave, or the greatest villain upon earth. And can we think of all these injuries which Jesus Christ has received, and still receives every day, and not feel sorrow for them and not endeavor, by our love, to recompense the infinite love of his divine heart, which remains in the most Holy Sacrament, inflamed with the same love towards us, and anxious to communicate every good gift to us, and to give himself entirely to us, ever ready to receive us into his heart whenever we go to him? Him that cometh to Me, I will not cast out.

Affections and Prayers

O Heart of Jesus, abyss of mercy and love, how is it that, at the sight of the goodness Thou hast shown me, and of my ingratitude, I do not die of sorrow? Thou, O my Savior, after having given me my being, hast given me all Thy blood and Thy life, giving Thyself up, for my sake, to ignominy and death; and, not content with this, Thou hast invented the mode of sacrificing Thyself every day for me in the Holy Eucharist, not refusing to expose Thyself to the injuries which Thou shouldst receive, and which Thou didst foresee, in this Sacrament of love. O my God, how can I see myself so ungrateful to Thee without dying with confusion! O Lord, put an end, I pray Thee, to my ingratitude, by wounding my heart with Thy love, and making me entirely Thine. Remember the blood and the tears that Thou hast shed for me, and forgive me. Oh, let not all Thy sufferings be lost upon me. But though Thou hast seen how ungrateful and unworthy of Thy love I have been, yet Thou didst not cease to love me even when I did not love Thee, nor even desire that Thou shouldst love me; how much rather, then, may I not hope for Thy love, now that I desire and sigh after nothing but to love Thee, and to be loved by Thee. Oh, do Thou fully satisfy this my desire; or rather this Thy desire, for it is Thou that hast given it to me. Grant that this day may be the day of my thorough conversion; so that I may begin to love

Thee, and may never cease to love Thee, my sovereign good. Make me die in everything to myself, in order that I may live only to Thee, and that I may always burn with Thy love.

O Mary, thy heart was the blessed altar that was always on fire with divine love my dearest Mother, make me like to thee; obtain this from thy Son, who delights in honoring thee, by denying thee nothing that thou askest of him.

MEDITATION IX
The Faithful Heart of Jesus

Oh, how faithful is the beautiful heart of Jesus towards those whom he calls to his love: He is faithful who hath called you, who also will perform?

The faithfulness of God gives us confidence to hope all things, although we deserve nothing. If we have driven God from our heart, let us open the door to him, and he will immediately enter, according to the promise he has made: If any one open to me the door, I will come in to him, and will sup with him? If we wish for graces, let us ask for them of God, in the name of Jesus Christ, and he has promised us that we shall obtain them: If you shall ask the Father anything in My name, He will give it you? If we are tempted, let us trust in his merits, and he will not permit our enemies to strive with us beyond our strength: God is faithful, who will not suffer you to be tempted above that which you are able?

Affections and Prayers

Oh, that I had been as faithful towards Thee, my dearest Redeemer, as Thou hast been faithful to me. Whenever I have opened my heart to Thee, Thou hast entered in, to forgive me and to receive me into Thy favor; whenever I have called Thee, Thou hast hastened to my assistance. Thou hast been faithful with me, but I have been exceedingly unfaithful towards Thee. I have promised Thee my love, and then have many times refused it to Thee; as if Thou, my God, who hast created and redeemed me, wert less worthy of being loved than Thy creatures and those miserable pleasures for which I have forsaken Thee. Forgive me, O my Jesus. I know my ingratitude, and abhor it. I know that Thou art infinite goodness, who deserves an infinite love, especially from me, whom Thou hast so much loved, even after all the offences I have committed against Thee. Unhappy me if I should damn myself; the graces Thou hast vouchsafed to me, and the proofs of the singular affection which Thou hast shown me, would be, O God, the hell of hells to me. Ah, no, my love, have pity on me; suffer me not to forsake Thee again, and then by damning myself, as I should deserve, continue to repay in hell with injuries and hatred the love that Thou hast borne me. O loving and faithful heart of Jesus, inflame, I beseech Thee, my miserable heart, so that it may burn with love for Thee, as Thine dost for me. My Jesus, it seems to me that now I love Thee; but I love Thee but little. Make me love Thee exceedingly, and remain faithful to Thee until death. I ask of Thee this grace, together with that of always praying to Thee for it. Grant that I may die rather than ever betray Thee again.

O Mary, my Mother, help me to be faithful to thy Son.

AFFECTIONS OF LOVE TOWARDS THE HEART OF JESUS

O amiable Heart of my Savior! thou art the seat of all virtues, the source of all graces, the burning furnace in which are inflamed all holy souls. Thou art the object of all God's love; thou art the refuge of the afflicted, and the abode of the souls that love thee. O heart worthy of reigning over all hearts, and of possessing the affection of all hearts! O heart that was wounded for me on the Cross by the lance of my sins, and that remained afterwards continually wounded for me on the altar in the Blessed Sacrament, but not by any other lance than that of the love that thou entertainest for me! O loving heart, that loves men with so much tenderness, and that is so little loved by men! Do thou apply a remedy to so great an ingratitude, inflame thou our hearts with a true love for thee. Ah! why can I not go all over the world to make known the graces, the sweetness, the treasures that thou dispenses! to those who truly love thee? Accept the desire that I have of seeing all hearts burning with love for thee, O divine heart! be thou my consolation in trials, my repose in labors, my solace in anxieties, my haven in tempests. I consecrate to thee my body and my soul, my heart and my life, together with all that I am. I unite to thine all my thoughts, all my affections, all my desires. O eternal Father! I offer Thee the pure affections of the heart of Jesus. If Thou dost reject mine, Thou canst not reject those of Thy Son, who is sanctity itself; may they supply what is wanting in me, and may they render me pleasing in Thy eyes!

St. Catharine of Genoa was one day permitted to see the heart of Jesus in his breast, and she saw it all on fire.

One day our Lord deigned to approach St. Mechtilde, and she heard the heart of Jesus palpitating violently, as if someone had struck him blows on the breast. The Lord told her that his heart had thus palpitated from his infancy, on account of the love with which it was in flamed for mankind. Father Nuremberg also assures us that if Jesus had left to his love for us the liberty of producing its own effects, he would have died of love in his infancy.

Jesus said to St. Gertrude: "Were it expedient, I would for thee alone suffer all that I have suffered for the whole world." And to St. Mechtilde: "My love for souls is yet the same as that love which I bore them at the time of my Passion; I would die as many times as there are souls to save."

St. Carpus appeared as if he desired to condemn to the abyss all sinners. Jesus said to him: "For my part, O Carpus, I am still ready to allow myself to be crucified for man."

St. John of the Cross said: "Jesus loves each one of us as much as he loves all men."

HYMNS ON THE SACRED HEART OF JESUS

I

The Loving Spouse
Fly, my soul, ah, fly away

To Jesus heart so kind;
There love s captive thou shalt stay,
And truest freedom find.
See, thy foes are all around;
Thou art pursued, poor thing!
Safety in the ark is found,
Then thither, dove, take wing.
Why delay? The world is woe,
And care, and cold deceit;
God alone can joy bestow,
And happiness complete.
Give me, Lord, a place to dwell
Within Thy heart so meek;
This shall be my prison cell,
Where true repose I seek.
All on earth I now disdain,
And for Thy love resign;
This the fruit of every pain,
To bind my heart to Thine.
If within Thy heart divine
To die my lot should be,
Oh, what happy death were mine!
Such death were life to me.

II

The Loving Spouse in the Heart of Jesus

I dwell a captive in this heart,
On fire with love divine;
Tis here I live alone in peace,
And constant joy is mine.
It is the Heart of God s own Son,
In his humanity,
Who, all enamored of my soul,
Here burns with love of me.
Here, like the dove within the ark,
Securely I repose;
Since now the Lord is my defense,
I fear no earthly foes.
Now I have found this happy home,
God s love alone I prize;
All else is torment to my heart,

The world I now despise.
What though I suffer, still in love
I ever true will be;
My love of God shall deeper grow
When crosses fall on me.
Then he who longs with me to seek
Repose within this nest,
All love that is not love for God,
Must banish from his breast.
Ye haughty lovers of the world,
Full of self-love, depart!
Away, away! no place is found
For you within this heart.
Each vile and earthly chain impedes
The soul's true heavenward flight;
All, all the heart belongs to God,
Love claims his sovereign right.
From every bond of earth, dear Lord,
Thy grace has set me free;
My soul, delivered from the snare,
Enjoys true liberty.
I cannot love Thee as I ought,
This pains me, this alone;
For all my love must have an end;
Thy goodness, Lord, has none.
One thought brings comfort to my heart
I love a good so great,
That though I love him all I can,
More love he merits yet.
Naught more can I desire than this,
To see his face in heaven;
And this I hope, since he on earth
His heart in pledge has given.

THE PRACTICE OF THE LOVE OF JESUS CHRIST

INTRODUCTION

I

How deserving Jesus Christ is of our Love, on Account of the Love He has shown us in His Passion

The whole sanctity and perfection of a soul consists in loving Jesus Christ, our God, our sovereign good, and our Redeemer. Whoever loves me, says Jesus Christ himself, shall be loved by my Eternal Father: My Father loves you because you have loved Me. Some, says St. Francis de Sales, make perfection consist in an austere life; others in prayer; others in frequenting the Sacraments; others in alms-deeds. But they deceive themselves perfection consists in loving God with our whole heart. The Apostle wrote: Above all things, have charity, which is the bond of perfection? It is charity which keeps united and preserves all the virtues that render a man perfect. Hence St. Augustine said: "Love God, and do whatever you please;" because a soul that loves God is taught by that same love never to do anything that will displease him, and to leave nothing undone that may please him.

But perhaps God does not deserve all our love? He has loved us with an everlasting love? O man, says the Lord, behold I was the first to love thee. Thou was not yet in the world, nay, the world itself was not, and I already loved thee. As long as I am God, I loved thee; as long as I have loved myself, I have also loved thee. With good reason, therefore, did St. Agnes, that young holy virgin, reply to those who wished to unite her to an earthly spouse: "I am engaged to another lover." "Go," said she, "O lovers of this world, cease to sue my love; my God was the first to love me. He has loved me from all eternity: it is but just, then, for me to give him all my affections, and to love none other but him."

As Almighty God knew that man is won by kindness, he determined to lavish his gifts upon him, and so take captive the affections of his heart. For this reason he said, I will draw them with the cords of Adam, with the bands of love? I will catch men by those very snares by which they are naturally caught, that is, by the snares of love. And such exactly are all the favors of God to man. After having given him a soul created in his own image, with memory, understanding, and will, and a body with its senses, he created heaven and earth for him, yes, all that exists, all for the love of man, the firmament, the stars, the planets, the seas, the rivers, the fountains, the hills, the plains, metals, fruits, and a countless variety of animals and all these creatures that they might minister to the uses of man, and that man might love him in gratitude for so many admirable gifts.

And so, likewise, the Son, through his love towards us, has given himself wholly to us: Who loved me, and delivered Himself for me? In order to redeem us from everlasting death, and to recover for us the divine grace and heaven which we had forfeited, he became man, and put

on flesh like our own: And the Word was made flesh. Behold, then, a God reduced to nothingness: But emptied Himself, taking the form of a servant, and in habit found as a man. Behold the sovereign of the world humbling himself so low as to assume the form of a servant, and to subject himself to all the miseries which the rest of men endure.

But what is more astonishing still is, that he could very well have saved us without dying and without suffering at all; but no: he chose a life of sorrow and con tempt, and a death of bitterness and ignominy even to the expiring on a cross, the gibbet of infamy, the award of vilest criminals: He humbled Himself, becoming obedient unto death, even to the death of the cross. But why, if he could have ransomed us without suffering, why should he choose to die, and to die on a cross? To show us how he loved us. He loved us, and delivered Himself for us? He loved us, and because he loved us, he delivered himself up to sorrows, and ignominies, and to a death more cruel than ever any man endured in this world.

Hence that great lover of Jesus Christ, St. Paul, took occasion to say: The charity of Christ presseth us? Wishing to show us by these words that it is not so much the sufferings themselves of Jesus Christ as his love in enduring them, that obliges us, and, as it were, constrains us to love him. Let us hear what St. Francis de Sales says on this text: "When we remember that Jesus Christ, true God, has loved us to such an excess as to suffer death, and the death of the cross, for us, our hearts are, as it were, put in a wine-press, and suffer violence, until love be extorted from them, but a violence which, the stronger it is, becomes the more delightful." He then goes on to say, "Ah! why do we not therefore cast ourselves on Jesus crucified, to die on the cross with him, who has chosen to die for love of us? I will hold him (should we say), and I will never let him go; I will die with him, and will be consumed in the flames of his love. One flame shall consume this divine Creator and his miserable creature. My Jesus gives himself unreservedly to me, and I give myself unreservedly to him."

The love of Jesus Christ towards men created in him a longing desire for the moment of his death, when his love should be fully manifested to them; hence he was wont to say in his lifetime: I have a baptism wherewith I am to be baptized, and how am I straitened till it be accomplished! I have to be baptized in my own blood; and how do I feel myself straitened with the desire that the hour of my Passion may soon arrive; for then man will know the love which I bear him! Hence St. John, speaking of that night in which Jesus began his Passion, writes: Jesus knowing that His hour was come, that He should pass out of this world to the Father, having loved His own who were in the world, He loved them unto the end. The Redeemer called that hour His own hour, because the time of his death was the time desired by him; as it was then that he wished to give mankind the last proof of his love, by dying for them upon a cross overwhelmed by sorrows.

But what could have ever induced a God to die as a malefactor upon a cross between two sinners, with such insult to his divine majesty? "Who did this?" asks St. Bernard; he answers, "It was love, careless of its dignity." Ah, love indeed, when it tries to make itself known, does not seek what is becoming to the dignity of the lover, but what will serve best to declare itself to the object loved. St. Francis of Paula therefore had good reason to cry out at the sight of a crucifix, "O charity, O charity, O charity!" And in like manner, when we look upon Jesus on the cross, we should all exclaim, O love, O love, O love!

Ah, if faith had not assured us of it, who could ever have believed that a God, almighty, most happy, and the Lord of all, should have condescended to love man to such an extent that he seems to go out of himself for the love of him? We have seen Wisdom itself, that is the Eternal Word, become foolish through the excessive love he bore to man! So spoke St. Laurence Justinian: "We see Wisdom itself infatuated through excess of love." St. Mary Magdalene of Pazzi said the same: One day, being in ecstasy, she took a wooden crucifix in her hands, and then cried out: "Yes, my Jesus, Thou art mad with love: I repeat it, and I will say it forever: My Jesus, thou art mad with love." But no, says St. Denis the Areopagite; "no, it is not madness, but the ordinary effect of divine love, which makes him who loves go out of himself, in order to give himself up entirely to the object of his love: divine love causes ecstasy."

The Venerable John of Avila, who was so possessed with the love of Jesus Christ that he never failed in any of his sermons to speak of the love which Jesus Christ bears towards us, in a treatise on the love which this most loving Redeemer has for men, has expressed him self in sentiments so full of the fire of devotion, and of such beauty, that I desire to insert them here. He says as follows:

"Thou, O Redeemer, hast loved man in such a manner, that whoso reflects upon this love cannot do less than love Thee; for Thy love offers violence to hearts: as the Apostle says: The charity of Christ presseth us? The source of the love of Jesus Christ for men is his love for God. Hence he said on Monday Thursday, That the world may know that I love the Father, arise, let us go hence. But whither? To die for men upon the cross."

"O robber of hearts, the strength of Thy love has broken the exceeding hardness of our hearts! Thou hast inflamed the whole world with Thy love. O most loving Lord, inebriate our hearts with this wine, consume them with this fire, pierce them with this dart of Thy love! Thy Cross is indeed an arrow which pierces hearts. May all the world know that my heart is smitten! O sweetest love, what hast Thou done? Thou hast come to heal me, and Thou hast wounded me. Thou hast come to teach me, and Thou hast made me well-nigh mad. O madness full of wisdom, may I never live without you! All, O Lord, that I behold upon the cross invites me to love Thee the wood, the figure, the wounds of Thy body; and above all, Thy love, engages me to love Thee, and never to forget Thee more."

But in order to arrive at the perfect love of Jesus Christ, we must adopt the means. Behold, then, the means which St. Thomas Aquinas gives us:

1. To have a constant remembrance of the benefits of God, both general and particular.

2. To consider the infinite goodness of God, who is ever waiting to do us good, and who ever loves us, and seeks from us our love.

3. To avoid even the smallest tiling that could offend him.

4. To renounce all the sensible goods of this world, riches, honors, and sensual pleasures.

Father Tauler says that meditation on the sacred Passion of Jesus Christ is a great means also for acquiring his perfect love.

Who can deny that, of all devotions, devotion to the Passion of Jesus Christ is the most useful, the most tender, the most agreeable to God, one that gives the greatest consolation to sinners, and at the same time most powerfully enkindles loving souls? Whence is it that we receive so many blessings, if it be not from the Passion of Jesus Christ? Whence have we hope of

pardon, courage against temptations, confidence that we shall go to heaven? Whence are so many lights to know the truth, so many loving calls, so many spurrings to change our life, so many desires to give ourselves up to God, except from the Passion of Jesus Christ? The Apostle therefore had but too great reason to declare him to be excommunicated who did not love Jesus Christ. If any man love not our Lord Jesus Christ, let him be anathema?

St. Bonaventure says there is no devotion more fitted for sanctifying a soul than meditation on the Passion of Jesus Christ; whence he advises us to meditate every day upon the Passion, if we would advance in the love of God. "If you would make progress, meditate daily on the Passion of the Lord; for nothing works such an entire sanctification in the soul, as the meditation of the Passion of Christ." And before him St. Augustine, as Bustis relates, said, that one tear shed in memory of the Passion is worth more than to fast weekly on bread and water fora year. Wherefore the saints were always occupied in considering the sorrows of Jesus Christ: it was by this means that St. Francis of Assisi became a seraph.

Affections and Prayers

O Eternal Word! Thou hast spent three-and-thirty years in labors and fatigues; Thou hast given Thy life and Thy blood for man s salvation; in short, Thou hast spared nothing to make men love Thee; and how is it possible that there should be those who know this, and yet do not love Thee? O God, amongst these ungrateful ones I also may be numbered! I see the wrong I have done Thee; O my Jesus, have pity upon me! I offer Thee this ungrateful heart ungrateful it is true, but penitent. Yes, I repent above every other evil, O my dear Redeemer, for having despised Thee! I repent, and I am sorry with my whole heart. O my soul, love a God who is bound like a criminal for thee; a God scourged like a slave for thee; a God made a mock-king for thee; a God, in short, dead upon a cross, as the vilest outcast for thee! Yes, my Savior, my God, I love Thee, I love Thee! Bring continually to my remembrance, I beseech Thee, all that Thou hast suffered for me, so that I may never more forget to love Thee. O cords that bound my Jesus, bind me to Jesus; thorns that crowned my Jesus, pierce me with the love of Jesus; nails that transfixed my Jesus, nail me to the Cross of Jesus, that I may live and die united to Jesus. O blood of Jesus, inebriate me with his holy love! O death of Jesus, make me die to every earthly affection! Pierced feet of my Lord, I embrace you; deliver me from hell, which I have deserved; my Jesus, in hell I could no more love Thee, and yet I desire to love Thee always. Save me, my dearest Savior; bind me to Thyself, that I may never again lose Thee. O Mary, refuge of sinners, and Mother of my Savior! help a sinner who wishes to love God, and who recommends himself to thee; succor me for the love thou bearest to Jesus Christ.

II

How much Jesus Christ deserves to be Loved by us, on Account of the Love He has shown us in Instituting the most Holy Sacrament of the Altar

Jesus, knowing that His hour was come, that He should pass out of this world to the Father: having loved His own. He loved them unto the end. Our most loving Savior, knowing that his hour was now come for leaving this earth, desired, before he went to die for us, to leave us the greatest possible mark of his love; and this was the gift of the most Holy Sacrament.

St. Bernardine of Sienna remarks, that men remember more continually and love more tenderly the signs of love which are shown to them in the hour of death. Hence it is the custom that friends, when about to die, leave to those persons whom they have loved some gift, such as a garment or a ring, as a memorial of their affection. But what hast Thou, O my Jesus, left us, when quitting this world, in memory of Thy love? Not, indeed, a garment or a ring, but Thine own body, Thy blood, Thy soul, Thy divinity, Thy whole self, without reserve. "He gave thee all," says St. John Chrysostom; "He left nothing for himself."

The Council of Trent says, that in this gift of the Eucharist Jesus Christ desired, as it were, to pour forth all the riches of the love he had for men. And the Apostle observes, that Jesus desired to bestow this gift upon men on the very night itself when they were planning his death: The same night in which He was betrayed, He took bread; and giving thanks, broke and said: Take ye, and eat: this is My body? St. Bernardine of Sienna says, that Jesus Christ, burning with love for us, and not content with being prepared to give his life for us, was constrained by the excess of his love to work a greater work before he died; and this was to give his own body for our food.

This Sacrament, therefore, was rightly named by St. Thomas, "Sacrament of love, the pledge of love." Sacrament of love; for love was the only motive which induced Jesus Christ to give us in it his whole self, Pledge of love; so that if we had ever doubted his love, we should have in this sacrament a pledge of it: as if our Redeemer, in leaving us this gift, had said: O souls, if you ever doubt my love, behold, I leave you myself in this Sacrament: with such a pledge, you can never any more doubt that I love you, and love you to excess. But more, St. Bernard calls this sacrament "the love of loves;" because this gift comprehends all the other gifts bestowed upon us by our Lord, creation, redemption, predestination to glory; so that the Eucharist is not only a pledge of the love of Jesus Christ, but of paradise, which he desires also to give us. "In which," says the Church, "a pledge of future glory is given us." Hence St. Philip Neri could find no other name for Jesus Christ in the Sacrament save that of love; and so, when the holy Viaticum was brought to him, he was heard to exclaim, "Behold my love; give me my love."

The prophet Isaias desired that the whole world should know the tender inventions that our God has made use of, wherewith to make men love him. And who could ever have thought if he himself had not done it that the Incarnate Word would hide himself under the appearances of bread, in order to become himself our food? "Does it not seem foil" says St. Augustine, "to say, Eat my flesh; drink my blood?" When Jesus Christ revealed to his disciples the sacrament he desired to leave them, they could not bring themselves to believe him; and they left him, saying: How can this Man give us His flesh to eat? This saying is hard, and who can hear it? But that which men could neither conceive nor believe, the great love of Jesus Christ hath thought of and accomplished.

In order, then, to excite us to receive him in the Holy Communion, he not only exhorts us to do so by so many invitations, Come, eat My bread; and drink the wine which I have mingled for you? Eat, O friends, and drink speaking of this heavenly bread and wine, but he even gives us a formal precept: Take ye, and eat; this is My body. And more than this; that we may go and receive him, he entices us with the promise of paradise. He that eat. My flesh hath everlasting life. He that eat this bread shall live forever? And still more, he threatens us with hell, and exclusion from paradise, if we refuse to communicate. Except you eat the flesh of the Son of Man, you shall not have life in you. These invitations, these promises, these threats, all proceed from the great desire he has to come to us in this sacrament.

But why is it that Jesus Christ so desires that we should receive him in the Holy Communion? Here is the reason. St. Denis says that love always sighs after and tends to union, and so also says St. Thomas, "Lovers desire of two to become one." Friends who really love each other would like to be so united as to become one person. Now this is what the infinite love of God for man has done; that he would not only give us himself in the eternal kingdom, but even in this life would permit men to possess him in the most intimate union, by giving them himself, whole and entire, under the appearances of bread in the sacrament. He stands there as though behind a wall; and from thence he beholds, as it were, through a closed lattice: Behold He standeth behind our wall, looking through the windows, looking through the lattices: It is true, we do not see him; but he sees us, and is there really present: he is present, in order that we may possess him but he hides himself from us to make us desire him and as long as we have not reached our true country, Jesus desires to give himself wholly to us, and to remain united with us.

"It was Thy wish, in short," says St. Laurence Justinian, "O God, enamored of our souls, to make, by means of this sacrament, Thine own heart, by an inseparable union, one and the same heart with ours! St. Bernardine of Sienna adds, that "the gift of Jesus Christ to us as our food was the last step of his love; since he gives himself to us in order to unite himself wholly to us; in the same way as food becomes united with him who partakes of it." Oh, how delighted is Jesus Christ to be united with our souls! He one day said to his beloved servant, Margaret of Ypres, after Communion, "See, my daughter, the beautiful union that exists between me and thee come, then, love me; and let us remain ever united in love, and let us never separate again."

We must, then, be persuaded that a soul can neither do, nor think of doing, anything which gives greater pleasure to Jesus Christ than to communicate frequently, with dispositions suitable to the great guest whom she has to receive into her heart. I have said suitable, not indeed worthy dispositions; for if worthy were necessary, who could ever communicate? Another God would alone be worthy to receive God. By suitable, I mean such dispositions as become a miserable creature, clothed with the unhappy flesh of Adam. Ordinarily speaking, it is sufficient if a person communicates in a state of grace, and with a great desire of growing in the love of Jesus Christ. St. Francis de Sales said, "It is by love alone that we must receive Jesus Christ in the Communion, since it is through love alone that he gives himself to us." For the rest, with regard to the number of times a person should communicate, in this he should be guided by the advice of his spiritual Father. Nevertheless, we should be aware that no state of life or employment, neither the married state nor business, prevents frequent Communion, when the director thinks it advisable, as Pope Innocent XI has declared in his decree of 1679, when he says, "Frequent Communion must be left to the judgment of the confessors who, for lay persons in business, or in the marriage state, must recommend it according as they see it will be profitable for their salvation."

This Sacrament, moreover, above all others, inflames our souls with divine love. God is love. And he is a fire which consumes all earthly affections in our hearts. He is a consuming fire. And for this very purpose, namely, to enkindle this fire, the Son of God came upon earth. I am come to send fire on the earth; and he added, that he desired nothing but to see this fire en kindled in our souls: And what will I but that it be kindled? And oh, what flames of love does not Jesus Christ light up in the heart of every one who receives him devoutly in this sacrament! St. Catharine of Sienna once saw the Host in a priest's hand appearing as a globe of fire; and the saint was astonished that the hearts of all men were not burned up, and, as it were, reduced to ashes by such a flame. Such brilliant rays issued from the face of St. Rose of Lima after Communion, as to dazzle the eyes of those who saw her; and the heat from her mouth was so intense, that a hand held near it was scorched. It is related of St. Wenceslaus, that by merely visiting the churches where the Blessed Sacrament was kept, he was inflamed by such an ardor, that his servant who accompanied him did not feel the cold, if when walking on the snow he trod in the footsteps of the saint.

St. John Chrysostom says that the most Holy Sacrament is a burning fire; so that when we leave the altar we breathe forth flames of love, which make us objects of terror to hell. The spouse of the Canticles says: He brought me into the cellar of wine, He set in order charity in me. St. Gregory of Nyssa says that Communion is precisely this cellar of wine, in which the soul becomes so inebriated with divine love that it forgets and loses sight of creatures; and this is that languishing with love of which the spouse again speaks: Stay me up with flowers, compass me about with apples, because I languish with love.

Affections and Prayers

God of love, O infinite lover, worthy of infinite love, tell me what more canst Thou invent to make us love Thee? It was not sufficient for Thee to become man, and to subject Thyself to all our miseries; not sufficient to shed all Thy blood for us in torments, and then to die overwhelmed with sorrow, upon a cross destined for the most shameful malefactors. Thou didst, at last, oblige Thyself to be hidden under the species of bread and wine, to become our food, and so united with each one of us. Tell me, I repeat, what more canst Thou invent to make Thyself loved by us? Ah, wretched shall we be if we do not love Thee in this life! And when we shall have entered into eternity, what remorse shall we not feel for not having loved Thee! My Jesus, I will not die without loving Thee, and loving Thee exceedingly! I am heartily sorry, and am pained for having so greatly offended Thee. But now I love Thee above all things. I love Thee more than myself, and I consecrate to Thee all my affections. Do Thou, who inspires! me with this desire, give me also grace to accomplish it. My Jesus, my Jesus, I desire nothing of Thee but Thyself. Now that Thou hast drawn me to Thy love, I leave all, I renounce all, and I bind myself to Thee Thou alone art sufficient for me.

O Mary, Mother of God, pray to Jesus for me, and make me a saint! Add this also to the many wonders thou hast done in changing sinners into saints.

III

The Great Confidence we ought to have in the Love which Jesus Christ has shown us and in all He has done for us

David placed all his hope of salvation in his future Redeemer, and said: Into Thy hands, O Lord, I commend my spirit; Thou hast redeemed me, O Lord, the God of truth.

But how much more ought we to place our confidence in Jesus Christ, now that he has come, and has accomplished the work of redemption! Hence each one of us should say, and repeat again and again with greater confidence: Into Thy hands, O Lord, I commend my spirit; Thou hast redeemed me, O Lord, the God of truth.

If we have great reason to fear everlasting death on account of our sins against God, we have, on the other hand, far greater reason to hope for everlasting life through the merits of Jesus Christ, which are infinitely more powerful for our salvation than our sins are for our damnation. We have sinned, and have deserved hell; but the Redeemer has come to take upon himself all our offences, and to make satisfaction for them by His sufferings: Surely He hath borne our infirmities, and carried our sorrows?

In the same unhappy moment in which we sinned, God had already written against us the sentence of eternal death; but what has our merciful Redeemer done? Blotting out the handwriting of the decree which was against us, the same He took out of the way, fastening it to the cross? He cancelled by his blood the decree of our condemnation, and then fastened it to the cross, in order that, when we look at the sentence of our damnation for the sins we have committed, we may at the same time see the cross on which Jesus Christ died and blotted out this sentence by his blood, and so regain hope of pardon and everlasting life.

Oh, how far more powerfully does the blood of Jesus Christ speak for us, and obtain mercy for us from God, than did the blood of Abel speak against Cain! You are come to Jesus the mediator of the New Testament, and to the sprinkling of blood, which speaketh better than that of Abel? As if the Apostle had said, "O sinners, happy are you to be able, after you have sinned, to have recourse to Jesus crucified, who has shed all his blood, in order to become the mediator of peace between sinners and God, and to obtain pardon for them! Your iniquities cry out against you, but the blood of the Redeemer pleads in your favor; and the divine justice cannot but be appeased by the voice of this precious blood."

St. Leo says, "that Jesus has brought us by his death more good than the devil has done us harm by sin." And by these words he explains what St. Paul said before him, that the gift of redemption is greater than sin grace has overcome the offence. Not as the offence, so also is the gift where sin abounded, grace hath abounded more. From this the Savior encourages us to hope for every favor and every grace through his merits. And see how he teaches us the way to obtain all we want from his Eternal Father: Amen, amen, I say to you, if you ask the Father anything in My name, He will give it you? Whatever you desire, he says, ask for it of the Father in my name, and I promise you that you shall be heard. And indeed how shall the Father be able to deny us, when he has given us his only-begotten Son, whom he loves as himself? He that spared not even His own Son, but delivered Him up for us all, how hath He not also, with Him, given us all things?" The Apostle says all things; so that no grace is excepted, neither pardon, nor perseverance, nor holy love, nor perfection, nor paradise, "all, all, he has given us." But we must pray to him. God is all liberality to those who call upon him: Rich unto all that call upon Him.

I will again quote here many other beautiful thoughts of the Venerable John of Avila, which he has left us in his letters, on the great confidence we should have in the merits of Jesus Christ:

"Do not forget that Jesus Christ is the mediator between the Eternal Father and ourselves; and that we are beloved by him, and united to him by so strong bonds of love that nothing can break them, so long as a man does not himself dissolve them by some mortal sin. The blood of Jesus cries out, and asks mercy for us; and cries out so loudly that the noise of our sins is not heard.

The death of Jesus Christ hath put to death our sins: O Death, I will be thy death! Those who are lost are not lost for want of means of satisfaction, but because they would not avail themselves of the sacraments as the means of profiting by the satisfaction made by Jesus Christ."

"Jesus has taken upon himself the affair of remedying our evils, as if it had been personally his own affair. So that he has called our sins his own, although he did not commit them, and has sought pardon for them; and with the most tender love has prayed, as if he were praying for himself, that all who should have recourse to him might become objects of love. And as he sought, so he found, because God has so ordained that Jesus and ourselves should be so united in one, that either he and we should be loved, or he and we hated: and since Jesus is not or cannot be hated, in the same way, if we remain united by love to Jesus, we shall be also loved. By his being loved by God, we are also loved, seeing that Jesus Christ can do more to make us loved than we can do to make ourselves hated; since the Eternal Father loves Jesus Christ far more than he hates sinners."

"Jesus said to his Father: Father, I will that where I am, they also whom Thou hast given Me may be with Me. Love has conquered hatred; and thus we have been pardoned and loved, and are secure of never being abandoned, so strong is the tie of love that binds us. The Lord said by Isaias: Can a woman forget her infant? And if she should forget, yet will I not forget thee. Behold, I have graven Thee in My hands. He has graven us in his hands with his own blood. Thus we should not trouble ourselves about anything, since everything is ordained by those hands which were nailed to the cross in testimony of the love he bears us."

"Nothing can so trouble us on which Jesus Christ cannot reassure us. Let the sins I have committed surround me, let the devils lay snares for me, let fears for the future accuse me, by demanding mercy of the most tender Jesus Christ, who has loved me even until death, I cannot possibly lose confidence; for I see myself so highly valued, that God gave himself for me. O my Jesus, sure haven for those who seek Thee in time of peril! O most watchful Pastor, he deceives himself who does not trust in Thee, if only he has the will to amend his life! Therefore Thou hast said: I am here, fear not; I am he who afflicts and who consoles. Some from time to time I place in desolations, which seem equal to hell itself; but after a while I bring them out and con sole them. I am thine advocate, who have made thy, cause my own. I am thy surety, who am come to pay thy debts. I am thy Lord, who have redeemed thee with my blood, not in order to abandon thee, but to enrich thee, having bought thee at a great price. How shall I fly from him who seeks me, when I went forth to meet those who sought to outrage me? I did not turn away my face from him who struck me; and shall I from him who would adore me? How can my children doubt that I love them, seeing that out of love to them I placed myself in the hands of my enemies? Whom have I ever despised that loved me? Whom have I ever abandoned that sought my aid? Even I go seeking those that do not seek me."

IV
How much we are obliged to love Jesus Christ

Jesus Christ as God has a claim on all our love; but by the love which he has shown us, he wished to put us, so to speak, under the necessity of loving him, at least in gratitude for all that he has done and suffered for us. He has greatly loved us, that we might love him greatly. "Why does God love us, but that he may be loved?" wrote St. Bernard. And Moses had said the same before him: And now, Israel, what doth the Lord thy God require of them, but that thou fear the Lord thy God and love Him? Therefore the first command which he gave us was this; Thou shalt love the Lord thy God with Thy whole heart? And St. Paul says, that love is the fulfilling of the law: Love is the fulfilling of the law. For "fulfilling" the Greek text has the "embracing of the law;" love embraces the entire law.

Who indeed, at the sight of a crucified God dying for our love can refuse to love him? Those thorns, those nails, that cross, those wounds, and that blood, call upon us, and irresistibly urge us, to love him who has loved us so much. One heart is too little wherewith to Jove this God so enamored of us. In order to requite the love of Jesus Christ, it would require another God to die for his love. "Ah, why," exclaims St. Francis de Sales, "do we not throw ourselves on Jesus Christ, to die on the cross with him who was pleased to die there for the love of us?" The Apostle clearly impresses on us that Jesus Christ died for us for this end, that we might no longer live for ourselves, but solely for that God who died for us: Christ died for all, that they also who lire may not now live to themselves, but unto Him who died for them.

O God and how is it that men do not love this God who has done so much to be loved by men! Before the Incarnation of the Word, man might have doubted whether God loved him with a true love; but after the coming of the Son of God, and after his dying for the love of men, how can we possibly doubt of his love? "O man," says St. Thomas of Villanova, "look on that cross, on those torments, and that cruel death, which Jesus Christ has suffered for thee: after so great and so many tokens of his love, thou canst no longer entertain a doubt that he loves thee, and loves thee exceedingly." And St. Bernard says, that "the cross and every wound of our Blessed Redeemer cry aloud to make us understand the love he bears us."

In this grand mystery of man s redemption, we must consider how Jesus employed all his thoughts and zeal to discover every means of making himself loved by us. Had he merely wished to die for our salvation, it would have been sufficient had he been slain by Herod with the other children; but no, he chose before dying to lead, during thirty-three years, a life of hardship and suffering; and during that time, with a view to win our love, he appeared in several different guises. First of all, as a poor child born in a stable; then as a little boy helping in the workshop; and finally, as a criminal executed on a cross. But before dying on the cross, we see him in many different states, one and all calculated to excite our compassion, and to make himself loved in agony in the garden, bathed from head to foot in a sweat of blood; afterwards, in the court of Pilate, torn with scourges; then treated as a mock-king, with a reed in his hand, a ragged garment of purple on his shoulders, and a crown of thorns on his head; then dragged publicly through the streets to death, with the cross upon his shoulders; and at length, on the hill of Calvary, suspended on the cross by three iron nails. Tell me, does he merit our love or not, this God who has vouchsafed to endure all these torments, and to use so many means in order to captivate our love? Father John Rigouleux used to say: "I would spend my life in weeping for love of a God whose love induced him to die for the salvation of men."

"Love is a great thing," says St. Bernard. A great thing, a precious thing is love. Solomon, speaking of the divine wisdom, which is holy charity, called it an infinite treasure; because he that possesses charity is made partaker of the friendship of God: For she is an infinite treasure to men, which they that use become the friends of God?

Let us hear from St. John Chrysostom what are the effects of divine love in those souls in which it reigns: "When the love of God has taken possession of a soul, it produces an insatiable desire to work for the beloved; insomuch that however many and however vast the works which she does, and however prolonged the duration of her service, all seems nothing in her eyes, and she is afflicted at doing so little for God ; and were it permitted her to die and consume herself for him, she would be most happy. Hence it is that she esteems herself an unprofitable servant in all that she does; because she is instructed by love to know what God deserves, and sees by this clear light all the defects of her actions, and finds in them motives for confusion and pain, well aware how mean is all that she can do for so great a Lord."

Let us therefore, in the present book, proceed to consider these holy practices, that we may thus see if the love which we owe to Jesus Christ truly reigns within us; as likewise that we may understand in what virtues we should chiefly exercise ourselves, in order to persevere and advance in this holy love.

Affections and Prayers

O most lovely and most loving Heart of Jesus, miserable is the heart which does not love Thee! O God, for the love of men Thou didst die on the cross, helpless and forsaken, and how then can men live so forgetful of Thee? O love of God! O ingratitude of man! O men, O men! do but cast one look on the innocent Son of God, agonizing on the cross, and dying for you, in order to satisfy the divine justice for your sins, and by this means to allure you to love him. Observe how, at the same time, he prays his eternal Father to forgive you. Behold him, and love him. Ah, my Jesus, how small is the number of those that love Thee! Wretched too am I; for I also have lived so many years unmindful of Thee, and have grievously offended Thee, my beloved Redeemer! It is not so much the punishment I have deserved that makes me weep, as the love which Thou hast borne me. O sorrows of Jesus! O ignominies of Jesus! O wounds of Jesus! O death of Jesus! O love of Jesus! rest deeply engraved in my heart, and may your sweet recollection be forever fixed there, to wound me and inflame me continually with love. I love Thee, my Jesus; I love Thee, my sovereign good; I love Thee, my love and my all; I love Thee, and I will love Thee forever. Oh, suffer me never more to forsake Thee, never more to lose Thee! Make me entirely Thine; do so by the merits of Thy death. In this I firmly trust.

And I have a great confidence also in thy intercession, O Mary, my Queen; make me love Jesus Christ and make me also love thee, my Mother and my hope.

CHAPTER I

CHARITY IS PATIENT

He that loves Jesus Christ loves Sufferings

This earth is the place for meriting, and therefore it is a place for suffering. Our true country, where God has prepared for us repose in everlasting joy, is paradise. We have but a short time to stay in this world; but in this short time we have many labors to undergo: Man born of a woman, living for a short time, is filled with many miseries. We must suffer, and all must suffer; be they just, or be they sinners, each one must carry his cross. He that carries it with patience is saved; he that carries it with impatience is lost. St. Augustine says, the same miseries send some to paradise and some to hell: "One and the same blow lifts the good to glory, and reduces the bad to ashes." The same saint observes, that by the test of suffering the chaff in the Church of God is distinguished from the wheat he that humbles himself under tribulations, and is resigned to the will of God, is wheat for paradise; he that grows haughty and is en raged, and so forsakes God, is chaff for hell.

On the day when the cause of our salvation shall be decided, our life must be found conformable to the life of Jesus Christ, if we would enjoy the happy sentence of the predestined: For whom He foreknew He also predestinated to be made conformable to the image of His Son? This was the end for which the Eternal Word descended upon earth, to teach us, by his example, to carry with patience the cross which God sends us: Christ suffered for its (wrote St. Peter), leaving you an example, that you should follow His steps? So that Jesus Christ suffered on purpose to en courage us to suffer. O God! what a life was that of Jesus Christ! A life of ignominy and pain. The Prophet calls our Redeemer despised, and the most abject of men, a man of sorrows? A man held in contempt, and treated as the lowest, the vilest among men, a man of sorrows; yes, for the life of Jesus Christ was made up of hardships and afflictions.

But patience has a perfect work? The meaning of this is, that nothing is more pleasing to God than to see a soul suffering with patience all the crosses sent her by him. The effect of love is to liken the lover to the person loved. St. Francis de Sales said, "All the wounds of Christ are so many mouths, which preach to us that we must suffer for him. The science of the saints is to suffer constantly for Jesus; and in this way we shall soon become saints." A person that loves Jesus Christ is anxious to be treated like Jesus Christ, poor, persecuted, and despised. St. John beheld all the saints clothed in white, and with palms in their hands: Clothed with white robes, and palms in their hands? The palm is the symbol of martyrs, and yet all the saints did not suffer martyrdom; why, then, do all the saints bear palms in their hands? St. Gregory replies, that all the saints have been martyrs either of the sword or of patience; so that, he adds, "we can be martyrs without the sword, if we keep patience."

The merit of a soul that loves Jesus Christ consists in loving and in suffering. Hear what our Lord said to St. Teresa: "Think you, my child, that merit consists in enjoyment? No, it consists in suffering and in loving. Look at my life, wholly embittered with afflictions. Be assured, my child, that the more my Father loves any one, the more sufferings he sends him; they are the standard of his love. Look at my wounds; your torments will never reach so far. It is absurd to suppose that my Father favors with his friendship those who are strangers to suffering." And for our consolation St. Teresa makes this remark: "God never sends a trial, but he forthwith rewards it with some favor." One day Jesus Christ appeared to the blessed Baptista Varani, and told her of three special favors which he is wont to bestow on cherished souls: the first is, not to sin; the second, which is greater, to perform good works; the third, and the greatest of all, to suffer for his love. So that St. Teresa used to say, whenever anyone does something for God, the Almighty repays him with some trial And therefore the saints, on receiving tribulations, thanked God for them. St. Louis of France, referring to his captivity in Turkey, said: "I rejoice, and thank God more for the patience which he accorded me in the time of my imprisonment, than if he had made me master of the universe." And when St. Elizabeth, princess of Thuringia, after her husband's death, was banished with her son from the kingdom, and found herself homeless and abandoned by all, she went to a convent of the Franciscans, and there had the Te Deum sung in thanks giving to God for the signal favor of being allowed to suffer for his love.

St. Joseph Calasanctius used to say, "All suffering is slight to gain heaven." And the Apostle had already said the same: The sufferings of this time are not worthy to be compared with the glory to come, that shall be revealed in us.

It would be a great gain for us to endure all the torments of all the martyrs during our whole lives, in order to enjoy one single moment of the bliss of paradise; with what readiness, then, should we embrace our crosses, when we know that the sufferings of this transitory life will gain for us an everlasting beatitude! That which is at present momentary and light of our tribulation, worketh for us above measure exceedingly an eternal weight of glory. St. Agapitus, while still a mere boy in years, was threatened by the tyrant to have his head covered with a red-hot helmet; on which he replied, "And what better fortune could possibly befall me, than to lose my head here, to have it crowned hereafter in heaven?"

But even with regard to the present life, it is certain that he who suffers with most patience enjoys the greatest peace. It was a saying of St. Philip Neri, that in this world there is no purgatory; it is either all paradise or all hell: he that patiently supports tribulations enjoys a paradise; he that does not do so, suffers a hell. Yes, for (as St. Teresa writes) he that embraces the crosses sent him by God feels them not. St. Francis de Sales, finding himself on one occasion beset on every side with tribulations, said, "For some time back the severe oppositions and secret contrarieties which have befallen me afford me so sweet a peace, that nothing can equal it; and they give me such an assurance that my soul will ere long be firmly united with God, that I can say with all truth that they are the sole ambition, the sole desire of my heart."

Let us be convinced that in this valley of tears true peace of heart cannot be found, except by him who endures and lovingly embraces sufferings to please Al mighty God this is the consequence of that corruption in which all are placed through the infection of sin. The condition of the saints on earth is to suffer and to love; the condition of the saints in heaven is to enjoy and to love. Father Paul Segneri the younger, in a letter which he wrote one of his penitents to encourage her to suffer, gave her the counsel to keep these words inscribed at the foot of her crucifix: "Tis thus one loves." It is not simply by suffering, but by desiring to suffer for the love of Jesus Christ, that a soul gives the surest signs of really loving him. And what greater acquisition (said St. Teresa) can we possibly make than to have some token of gratifying Almighty God? Alas, how ready are the greatest part of men to take alarm at the bare mention of crosses, of humiliations, and of afflictions! Nevertheless, there are many souls who find all their delight in suffering, and who would be quite disconsolate did they pass their time on this earth without suffering. The sight of Jesus crucified (said a devout person) renders the cross so lovely to me, that it seems to me I could never be happy without suffering; the love of Jesus Christ is sufficient for me for all. Listen how Jesus advises everyone who would follow him to take up and carry his cross: Let him take up his cross, and follow Me? But we must take it up and carry it, not by constraint and against our will, but with humility, patience, and love.

Oh, how acceptable to God is he that humbly and patiently embraces the crosses which he sends him! St. Ignatius of Loyola said, "There is no wood so apt to enkindle and maintain love towards God as the wood of the cross;" that is, to love him in the midst of sufferings. One day St. Gertrude asked our Lord what she could offer him most acceptable, and he replied, "My child, thou canst do nothing more gratifying to me than to submit patiently to all the tribulations that befall thee." Wherefore the great servant of God, Sister Victoria Angelini, affirmed that one day of crucifixion was worth a hundred years of all other spiritual exercises.

Let us then beseech God to make us worthy of his love; for if we did but once perfectly love him, all the goods of this earth would seem to us but as smoke and dirt, and we should relish ignominies and afflictions as delights. Let us hear what St. John Chrysostom says of a soul wholly given up to Almighty God: "He who has attained the perfect love of God seems to be alone on the earth, he no longer cares either for glory or ignominy, he scorns temptations and afflictions, he loses all relish and appetite for created things. And as nothing in this world brings him any support or repose, he goes incessantly in search of his beloved without ever feeling wearied; so that when he toils, when he eats, when he is watching, or when sleeping, in every action and word, all his thoughts and desires are fixed upon finding his beloved; because his heart is where his treasure is."

Affections and Prayers

My dear and beloved Jesus, my treasure, I have deserved by my offences never more to be allowed to love Thee; but by Thy merits, I entreat Thee, make me worthy of Thy pure love, love Thee above all things; and I repent with my whole heart, of having ever despised Thee, and driven Thee from my soul; but now I love Thee more than myself; I love Thee with all my heart, O infinite goo! I love Thee, I love Thee, I love Thee, and I have not a wish besides that of loving Thee perfectly; nor have I a fear besides that of ever seeing myself deprived of Thy love. O my most loving Redeemer, enable me to know how great a good Thou art, and how great is the love Thou hast borne me in order to oblige me to love Thee! Ah, my God, suffer me not to live any longer unmindful of so much goodness! Enough have I offended Thee, I will never leave Thee again; I wish to employ all the remainder of my days in loving Thee, and in pleasing Thee. My

Jesus, my Love, lend me Thine aid; help a sinner who wishes to love Thee and to be wholly Thine own.

O Mary my hope, thy Son hears thee; pray to him in my behalf, and obtain for me the grace of loving him perfectly!

CHAPTER II

CHARITY IS KIND
He that loves Jesus Christ loves Meekness

The spirit of meekness is peculiar to God: My spirit is sweet above honey. Hence it is that a soul that loves God loves also all those whom God loves, namely, her neighbors; so that she eagerly seeks every occasion of helping all, of consoling all, and of making all happy as far as she can. St. Francis de Sales, who was the master and model of holy meekness, says, "Humble meekness is the virtue of virtues, which God has so much recommended to us; therefore we should endeavor to practice it always and in all things." Hence the saint gives us this rule: "What you see can be done with love, do it; and what you see cannot be done without offence, leave it undone." He means, when it can be omitted without offending God; because an offence of God must always, and as quickly as possible, be prevented by him who is bound to prevent it.

This meekness should be particularly observed towards the poor, who, by reason of their poverty, are often harshly treated by men. It should likewise be especially practiced towards the sick who are suffering under infirmities, and for the most part meet with small help from others. Meekness is more especially to be observed in our behavior towards enemies Overcome evil with good. Hatred must be overcome by love, and persecution by meekness; thus the saints acted, and so they conciliated the affections of their most exasperated enemies.

"There is nothing," says St. Francis de Sales, "that gives so much edification to our neighbor as meekness of behavior." The saint, therefore, was generally seen smiling, and with a countenance beaming with charity, which gave a tone to all his words and actions. This gave occasion to St. Vincent of Paul to declare that he never knew a kinder man in his life. He said further, that it seemed to him that in his lordship of Sales was a true likeness of Jesus Christ. Even in refusing what he could not in conscience comply with, he did so with such sweetness, that all, though unsuccessful in their requests, went away satisfied and well-disposed towards him. He was gentle towards all, towards Superiors, towards equals and inferiors, at home and abroad; in contrast with some, who, as the saint used to say, "seemed angels abroad, but were devils at home." Moreover, the saint, in his conduct towards servants, never complained of their remissness; at most he would give them an admonition, but always in the gentlest terms. And this is a thing most praiseworthy in Superiors.

The Superior should use all kindness towards those under him. When telling them what they have to do, he should rather request than command. St. Vincent of Paul said: "A Superior will never find a better means of being readily obeyed than meekness." And to the same effect was the saying of St. Jane Frances of Chantal: "I have tried various methods of governing, but I have not found any better than that of meekness and forbearance."

"You know not of what spirit you are." Such were the words of Jesus Christ to his disciples James and John, when they would have brought down chastisements on the Samaritans for expelling them from their country. Ah, said the Lord to them, and what spirit is this? This is not my spirit, which is sweet and gentle; for I am come not to destroy but to save souls: The Son of Man came not to destroy souls, but to save? And would you induce me to destroy them? Oh, hush and never make the like request to me, for such is not according to my spirit. And, in fact, with what meekness did Jesus Christ treat the adulteress! Woman, said He, hath no man condemned thee? Neither will I condemn thee! Go, and now sin no more? He was satisfied with merely warning her not to sin again, and sent her away in peace. With what meekness, again, did he seek the conversion of the Samaritan woman, and so, in fact, converted her! He first asked her to give him to drink; then he said to her: If thou didst know who He is that saith to thee, Give me to drink and then he revealed to her that he was the expected Messiah. And, again, with what meekness did he strive to convert the impious Judas, admitting him to eat of the same dish with him, washing his feet and ad monishing him in the very act of his betrayal: Judas, and dost thou thus betray me with a kiss? Judas, dost thou betray the Son of -Man with a kiss? And see how he converted Peter after his denial of him! And the Lord turning, looked on Peter? On leaving the house of the high-priest, without making him a single reproach, he cast on him a look of tenderness, and thus converted him; and so effectually did he convert him, that during his whole life long Peter never ceased to bewail the injury he had done to his Master.

Oh, how much more is to be gained by meekness than by harshness! St. Francis de Sales said there was nothing more bitter than the bitter almond, but if made into a preserve, it becomes sweet and agreeable: thus corrections, though in their nature very unpleasant, are rendered pleasant by love and meekness, and so are attended with more beneficial results. St. Vincent of Paul said of himself, that in the government of his own congregation he had never corrected any one with severity, except on three occasions, when he supposed there was reason to do so, but that he regretted it ever afterwards, because he found it turned out badly; whereas he had always admirably succeeded by gentle correction.

St. Francis de Sales obtained from others whatever he wished by his meek behavior; and by this means he managed to gain the most hardened sinners to God. It was the same with St. Vincent of Paul, who taught his disciples this maxim: "Affability, love, and humility have a wonderful efficacy in winning the hearts of men, and in prevailing on them to undertake things most repugnant to nature." He once gave a great sinner to the care of one of his Fathers, to bring him to sentiments of true repentance; but that Father, in spite of all his endeavors, found his labor fruitless, so that he begged the saint to speak a word to him. The saint accordingly spoke with him, and converted him. That sinner subsequently declared that the singular sweetness of Father Vincent had worked upon his heart. Wherefore it was that the saint could not bear his missionaries to treat sinners with severity; and he told them that the infernal spirit took advantage of the strictness of some to work the greater ruin of souls.

Adversity brings out a person s real character. St. Francis de Sales very tenderly loved the Order of the Visitation, which had cost him so much labor. He saw it several times in imminent danger of dissolution on account of the persecutions it underwent; but the saint never for a moment lost his peace, and was ready, if such was the will of God, to see it entirely destroyed; and then it was that he said: "For some time back the trying oppositions and secret contrarieties which have befallen me afford me so sweet a peace, that nothing can equal it; and they give me such an earnest of the immediate union of my soul with God, that, in truth, they form the sole desire of my heart."

Whenever it happens that we have to reply to someone who insults us, let us be careful to answer with meekness: A mild answer breaketh wrath. A mild reply is enough to quench every spark of anger. And in case we feel irritated, it is best to keep silence, because then it seems only just to give vent to all that rises to our lips; but when our passion has subsided, we shall see that all our words were full of faults.

And when it happens that we ourselves commit some fault, we must also practice meekness in our own regard. To be exasperated at ourselves after a fault is not humility, but a subtle pride, as if we were anything else than the weak and miserable tilings that we are. St. Teresa said: "The humility that disturbs does not come from God, but from the devil." To be angry at ourselves after the commission of a fault is a fault worse than the one committed, and will be the occasion of many other faults; it will make us leave off our devotions, prayers, and communions; or if we do practice them, they will be done very badly. St. Aloysius Gonzaga said that we cannot see in troubled waters, and that the devil fishes in them. A soul that is troubled knows little of God and of what it ought to do. Whenever, therefore, we fall into any fault, we should turn to God with humility and confidence, and craving his forgiveness, say to him, with St. Catharine of Genoa: "O Lord, this is the produce of my own garden! I love Thee with my whole heart, and I repent of the displeasure I have given Thee! I will never do the like again: grant me Thy assistance!"

Affections and Prayers

O blessed chains that bind the soul with God, oh, enfold me still closer, and in links so firm that I may never be able to loosen myself from the love of my God! My Jesus, I love Thee; O treasure, O life of my soul, to Thee I cling, and I give myself wholly unto Thee! No, indeed, my beloved Lord, I wish never more to cease to love Thee. Thou who, to atone for my sins, didst allow Thyself to be bound as a criminal, and so bound to be led to death through the streets of Jerusalem, Thou who didst consent to be nailed to the cross, and didst not leave it until life itself had left Thee, oh, suffer me never to be separated from Thee again; I regret above every other evil, to have at one time turned my back upon Thee, and henceforth I purpose by Thy grace to die rather than to give Thee the slightest displeasure. O my Jesus, I abandon myself to Thee. I love Thee with my whole heart; I love Thee more than myself. I have offended Thee in times past; but now I bitterly repent of it, and would willingly die of grief. Oh, draw me entirely to Thyself I renounce all sensible consolations; I wish for Thee alone, and nothing more. Make me love Thee, and then do with me what Thou wilt.

O Mary, my hope, bind me to Jesus; and grant me to live and die in union with him, in order to come one day to the happy kingdom, where I shall have no more fear of ever being separated from his love!

CHAPTER III

CHARITY ENVIETH NOT
The Soul that loves Jesus Christ does not envy the Great Ones of this World, but only those who are Greater Lovers of Jesus Christ

St. Gregory explains this next characteristic of charity in saying, that as charity despises all earthly greatness, it cannot possibly provoke her envy. "She envieth not, because, as she desireth nothing in this world, she cannot envy earthly prosperity."

Hence we must distinguish two kinds of envy, one evil and the other holy. The evil kind is that which envies and repines at the worldly goods possessed by others on this earth. But holy envy, so far from wishing to be like, rather compassionates the great ones of the world, who live in the midst of honors and earthly pleasures. She seeks and desires God alone, and has no other aim besides that of loving him as much as she can; and therefore she has a pious envy of those who love him more than she does, for she would, if possible, surpass the very seraphim in loving him.

This is the sole end which pious souls have in view on earth an end which so charms and ravishes the heart of God with love, that it causes him to say: Thou hast wounded My heart, My sister; My spouse, thou hast wounded My heart with one of thy eyes. By "one of thy eyes" is meant that one end which the espoused soul has in all her devotions and thoughts, namely, to please Almighty God. Men of the world look on things with many eyes, that is, have several inordinate views in their actions; as, for instance, to please others, to become honored, to obtain riches, and if nothing else, at least to please themselves; but the saints have but a single eye, with which they keep in view, in all that they do, the sole pleasure of God; and with David they say: What have J in heaven, and besides Thee what do I desire upon earth? What do I wish, O my God, in this world or in the next, save Thee alone? Thou art my riches, Thou art the only Lord of my heart. "Let the rich," said St. Paulinus, "enjoy their riches, let the kings enjoy their kingdoms, Thou, O Christ, art my treasure and my kingdom!"

Our Lord has said, Take heed that yon do not your justice before men, to be seen by them; otherwise you shall not have a reward of your Father who is in heaven? He that works for his own gratification already receives his wages: Amen I say to you, they have received their reward. But a reward, indeed, which dwindles into a little smoke, or the pleasure of a day that quickly vanishes, and confers no benefit on the soul. The Prophet Aggeus says, that whoever labors for anything else than to please God, puts his reward in a sack full of holes, which, when he comes to open, he finds entirely empty: And he that had earned wages, put them into a bag with holes. And hence it is that such persons, in the event of their not gaining the object for which they entered on some undertaking, are thrown into great trouble. This is a sign that they had not in view the glory of God alone. He that undertakes a thing solely for the glory of God, is not troubled at all, though his undertaking may fail of success; for, in truth, by working with a pure intention, he has already gained his object, which was to please Almighty God.

The following are the signs which indicate whether we work solely for God in any spiritual undertaking, 1. If we are not disturbed at the failure of our plans, because when we see it is not God s will, neither is it any longer our will. 2. If we rejoice at the good done by others, as heartily as if we ourselves had done it. 3. If we have no preference for one charge more than for another, but willingly accept that which obedience to Superiors enjoins us. 4. If after our actions we do not seek the thanks or approbation of others, nor are in any way affected if we be found fault with or scolded, being satisfied with having pleased God. And if when the world applauds us we are not puffed up, but meet the vain glory, which might make, itself felt, with the reply of the venerable John of Avila: "Get away, thou comest too late, for all has been already given to God."

Purity of intention is called the heavenly alchemy by which iron is turned into gold; that is to say, the most trivial actions (such as to work, to take one's meals, to take recreation or repose), when done for God, become the gold of holy love. Wherefore St. Mary Magdalene of Pazzi believes for certain that those who do all with a pure intention, go straight to Paradise, without passing through purgatory. It is related (in the Spiritual Treasury) that it was the custom of a pious hermit, before set ting about any work, to pause a little, and lift his eyes to heaven; on being questioned why he did so, he replied, "I am taking my aim." By which he meant, that as the archer, before shooting his arrow, takes his aim, that he may not miss the mark, so before each action he made God his aim, in order that it might be sure of pleasing him. We should do the same; and even during the performance of our actions, it is very good for us from time to time to renew our good intention.

Those who have nothing else in view in their undertakings than the divine will, enjoy that holy liberty of spirit which belongs to the children of God; and this enables them to embrace everything that pleases Jesus Christ, however revolting it may be to their own self-love or human respect. The love of Jesus Christ establishes his lovers in a state of total indifference; so that all is the same to them, be it sweet or bitter; they desire nothing for their own pleasure, but all for the pleasure of God. With the same feelings of peace, they address themselves to small and great works; to the pleasant and the unpleasant: it is enough for them if they please God.

Many, on the other hand, are willing to serve God, but it must be in such an employment, in such a place, with such companions, or under such circumstances, or else they either quit the work, or do it with an ill-will. Such persons have not freedom of spirit, but are slaves of self love; and on that account gain very little merit by what they do; they lead a troubled life, because the yoke of Jesus Christ becomes a burden to them. The true lovers of Jesus Christ care only to do what pleases him; and for the reason that it pleases him, when he wills, and where he wills, and in the manner he wills: and whether he wishes to employ them in a state of life honored by the world, or in a life of obscurity and insignificance.

Affections and Prayers

O my Eternal God, I offer Thee my whole heart; but what sort of heart, O God, is it that I offer Thee? A heart, created, indeed, to love Thee; but which, instead of loving Thee, has so many times rebelled against Thee. But behold, my Jesus, if there was a time when my heart rebelled against Thee, now it is deeply grieved and penitent for the displeasure it has given Thee. Yes, my dear Redeemer, I am sorry for having despised Thee; and I am determined to do all to obey Thee, and to love Thee at every cost. Oh, draw me wholly to Thy love; do this for the sake of the love which made Thee die for me on the cross. I love Thee, my Jesus ; I love Thee with all my soul; I love Thee more than myself, O true and only lover of my soul; for I find none but Thee who have sacrificed their life for me. I weep to think that I have been so ungrateful to Thee. Unhappy that I am! I was already lost; but I trust that by Thy grace Thou hast restored me to life. And this shall he my life, to love Thee always, my sovereign good. Make me love Thee, O infinite love, and I ask Thee for nothing more!

O Mary my mother, accept of me for thy servant, and gain acceptance for me will. Jesus thy Son.

CHAPTER IV

CHARITY DEALETH NOT PERVERSELY
I
Lukewarmness

It must be observed that there are two kinds of tepidity or lukewarmness the one unavoidable, the other avoidable.

I. From the lukewarmness that is unavoidable, the saints themselves are not exempt; and this comprises all the failings that are committed by us without full consent, but merely from our natural frailty. Such are, for example, distractions at prayers, interior disquietudes, useless words, vain curiosity, the wish to appear, tastes in eating and drinking, the movements of concupiscence not instantly repressed, and such like. We ought to avoid these defects as much as we possibly can; but, owing to the weakness of our nature, caused by the infection of sin, it is impossible to avoid them altogether. We ought, indeed, to detest them after committing them, because they are displeasing to God; but, as we remarked in the preceding chapter, we ought to beware of making them a subject of alarm or disquietude. St. Francis de Sales writes as follows: "All such thoughts as create disquietude are not from God, who is the prince of peace; but they proceed always from the devil, or from self-love, or from the good opinion which we have of ourselves." Such thoughts, therefore, as disturb us, must be straightway rejected, and made no account of.

It was said also by the same saint, with regard to indeliberate faults, that as they were involuntarily committed, so are they cancelled involuntarily. An act of sorrow, an act of love, is sufficient to cancel them. The Venerable Sister Mary Crucified, a Benedictine nun, saw once a globe of fire, on which a number of straws were cast, and were all forthwith reduced to ashes. She was given to understand by this figure that one act of divine love, made with fervor, destroys all the defects that we may have in our soul. The same effect is produced by the holy Communion; according to what we find in the Council of Trent, where the Eucharist is called an antidote by which we are freed from daily faults. "Thus the like faults, though they are indeed faults, do not hinder perfection that is, our advancing toward perfection; because in the present life no one attains perfection before he arrives at the kingdom of the blessed."

II. The tepidity, then, that does hinder perfection is that tepidity which is avoidable when a person commits deliberate venial faults; because all these faults committed with open eyes can effectually be avoided by the divine grace, even in the present life. Wherefore St. Teresa said: "May God deliver you from deliberate sin, however small it may be." Such, for example, are willful untruths, little detractions, imprecations, expressions of anger, derisions of one's neighbor, cutting words, speeches of self-esteem, animosities nourished in the heart, inordinate attachments to persons of a different sex. "These are a sort of worm" (wrote the same saint) "which is not detected before it has eaten into the virtues." Hence, in another place, the saint gave this ad monition: "By means of small things the devil goes about making holes for great things to enter."

We should therefore tremble at such deliberate faults; since they cause God to close his hands from bestowing upon us his clearer lights and stronger helps, and they deprive us of spiritual sweetness; and the result of them is to make the soul perform all spiritual exercises with great weariness and pain; and so, in course of time, she begins to leave off prayer, Communions, visits to the Blessed Sacrament, and novenas; and, in fine, she will probably leave off all, as has not unfrequently been the case with many unhappy souls.

All the evil arises from the little love they have for Jesus Christ. Those who are puffed up with self-esteem; those who frequently take to heart occurrences that fall out contrary to their wishes; who practice great indulgence towards themselves on account of their health; who keep their heart open to external objects, and the mind always distracted, with an eagerness to listen to, and to know, so many things that have nothing to do with the service of God, but merely serve to gratify private curiosity; who are ready to resent every little inattention from others, and consequently are often troubled, and grow remiss in prayer and recollection. One moment they are all devotion and joy, the next all impatience and melancholy, just as things happen, according to or against their humor; all such persons do not love Jesus Christ, or love him very little, and cast discredit on true devotion.

But suppose any one should find himself sunk in this unhappy state of tepidity, what has he to do? Certainly it is a hard thing for a soul grown lukewarm to resume her ancient fervor; but our Lord has said, that what man cannot do, God can very well do. The things that are impossible with man, are possible with God. Whoever prays and employs the means is sure to accomplish his desire.

II
Remedies against Lukewarmness

The means to cast off tepidity, and to tread in the path of perfection, are five in number: 1. The desire of perfection; 2. The resolution to attain it; 3. Mental prayer; 4. Frequent Holy Communion; 5. Prayer.

1. Desire of Perfection

The first means, then, is the desire of perfection. Pious desires are the wings which lift us up from earth; for, as St. Laurence Justinian says, desire "supplies strength, and renders pain more light" on the one hand it gives strength to walk towards perfection, and on the other hand it lightens the fatigue of the journey. Henry has a real desire of perfection fails not to advance continually towards it; and so advancing, he must finally arrive at it. On the contrary, he who has not the desire of perfection will always go backwards, and always find himself more imperfect than before. St. Augustine says, that "not to go forward in the way of God is to go backward."

He that makes no efforts to advance will find himself carried backward by the current of his corrupt nature.

Most beautiful, indeed, are the instructions which my great patroness St. Teresa gives on this subject. She says, in one place, "Let us enlarge our thoughts; for hence we shall derive immense good." Elsewhere she says: "We must beware of having poor desires; but rather put our confidence in God, in order that, by forcing ourselves continually onwards, we may by degrees arrive where, by the divine grace, so many saints have arrived." And in confirmation of this she quoted her own experience, having known how courageous souls make considerable progress in a short period of time.

We must, therefore, have a great courage: The Lord is good to the soul that seeketh life, God is surpassingly good and liberal towards a soul that heartily seeks him. Neither can past sins prove a hindrance to our becoming saints, if we only have the sincere desire to become so. St. Teresa remarks: "The devil strives to make us think it pride to entertain lofty desires, and to wish to imitate the saints; but it is of great service to encourage ourselves with the desire of great things, because, although the soul has not all at once the necessary strength, yet she nevertheless makes a bold fight, and rapidly advances."

The Apostle writes: To than that love *God, all things work together unto good. And the gloss or ancient commentary adds "even sins" even past sins can contribute to our sanctification, inasmuch as the recollection of them keeps us more humble, and more grateful, when we witness the favors which God lavishes upon us, after all our outrages against him. I am capable of nothing (the sinner should say), nor do I deserve anything; I deserve nothing but hell; but I have to deal with a God of infinite bounty, who has promised to listen to all that pray to him.

2. Resolution

The second means of perfection is the resolution to belong wholly to God. Many are called to perfection; they are urged on towards it by grace, they conceive, a desire of it; but because they never really resolve to acquire it, they live and die in the order of their tepid and imperfect life. The desire of perfection is not enough, if it be not followed up by a stern resolve to attain it. How many souls feed themselves on desires alone, but never make withal one step in the way of God! It is of such desires that the wise man speaks when he says: Desires kill the slothful? The slothful man is ever desiring, but never resolves to take the means suitable to his state of life to become a saint. He says: "Oh, if I were but in solitude, and not in this house! I Oh, if I could but go and reside in another monastery, I would give myself entirely up to God!" And mean while he cannot support a certain companion; he cannot I put up with a word of contradiction; he is dissipated I about many useless cares; he commits a thousand faults of gluttony, of curiosity, and of pride; and yet he sighs lout to the wind: "Oh, if I had but!" or "Oh, if I could I but!" etc. Such desires do more harm than good; because some regale themselves upon them, and in the meantime go on leading a life of imperfection. It was a saying of St. Francis de Sales: "I do not approve of a person who, being engaged in some duty or vocation, stops to sigh for some other kind of life than is compatible with his actual position, or for other exercises unfitted for his present state; for it merely serves to dissipate his heart, and makes him languish in his necessary duties."

We must, therefore, desire perfection, and resolutely take the means towards it. St. Teresa says: "God only looks for one resolution on our part, and will afterwards do all the rest himself the devil has no fear of irresolute souls." For this reason mental prayer must be used, in order to take the means which lead to perfection. Some make much prayer, but never come to a practical conclusion. The same saint said: "I would rather have a short prayer, which produces great fruits, than a prayer of many years, wherein a soul never gets further than resolving to do something worthy of Almighty God." And elsewhere she says: "I have learned by experience that whoever, at the beginning, brings himself to the resolution of doing some great work, however difficult it may be, if he does so to please God, he has no reason to be afraid."

A nun of the convent of Torre de Specchi in Rome, whose name was Sister Bonaventura, led a very lukewarm sort of life. There came a religious, Father Lancicius, to give the spiritual exercises to the nuns, and Sister Bonaventura, feeling no inclination to shake off her tepidity, began to listen to the exercises with no good will. But at the very first sermon she was won by divine grace, so that she immediately went to the feet of the Father who preached, and said to him, with a tone of real determination, "Father, I wish to become a saint, and quickly a saint." And, by the assistance of God, she did so; for she lived only eight months after that event, and during that short time she lived and died a saint.

David said: And I said, now have I beguti. So likewise exclaimed St. Charles Borromeo: "Today I begin to serve God." And we should act in the same way as if we had hitherto done no good whatever; for, indeed, all that we do for God is nothing, since we are bound to do it. Let us therefore each day resolve to begin afresh to belong wholly to God. Neither let us stop to observe what or how others do. They who become truly saints are few. St. Bernard says: "One cannot be perfect without being singular." If we would imitate the common run of men, we should always remain imperfect, as for the most part they are. We must overcome all, renounce all, in order to gain all. St. Teresa said: "Because we do not come to the conclusion cf giving all our affection to God, so neither does he give all his love to us." Oh, God, how little is all that is given to Jesus Christ, who has given his blood and his life for us! "However much we give," says the same saint, "is but dirt, in comparison of one single drop of blood shed for us by our Blessed Lord." The saints know not how to spare themselves, when there is a question of pleasing a God who gave himself wholly, without reserve, on purpose to oblige us to deny him nothing.

3. Mental Prayer

The third means of becoming a saint is mental prayer. John Gerson writes: "That he who does not meditate on the eternal truths cannot, without a miracle, lead the life of a Christian. The reason is, because without mental prayer light fails us, and we walk in the dark. The truths of faith are not seen by the eyes of the body, but by the eyes of the mind, when we meditate; he that fails to meditate on them, fails to see them, and therefore walks in the dark; and being in the dark, he easily grows attached to sensible things, for the sake of which he then comes to despise the eternal." St. Teresa wrote as follows to the Bishop of Osma: "Although we seem to discover in our selves no imperfections; yet, when God opens the eyes of the soul, which he is wont to do in prayer, then they plainly appear." And St. Bernard had before said, that he who does not meditate "does not abhor himself, merely because he does not know himself." "Prayer," says the saint, "regulates the affections, directs the actions," keeps the affections of the soul in order, and directs all our actions to God; but without prayer the affections become attached to the earth, the actions conform themselves to the affections, and in this manner all runs into disorder.

We read of an awful example of this in the life of the Venerable Sister Mary Crucified of Sicily. Whilst this servant of God was praying, she heard a devil making a boast that he had succeeded in withdrawing a religious from the community-prayer; and she saw in spirit, that after this omission the devil tempted her to consent to a grievous sin, and that she was on the point of yielding. She forthwith accosted her, and by a timely admonition prevented her from falling. Abbe Diodes said, that whoever leaves off prayer "very shortly becomes either a beast or a devil."

We should not go to prayer in order to taste the sweetness of divine love; whoever prays from such a motive will lose his time, or at least derive little advantage from it. A person should begin to pray solely to please God, that is, solely to learn what the will of God is in his regard, and to beg of him the help to put it in practice. The Venerable Father Antony Torres said: "To carry the cross without consolation makes souls fly to perfection. Prayer unattended with sensible consolations confers greater fruit on the soul. But pitiable is the poor soul that leaves off prayer, because she finds no relish in it." St. Teresa said: "When a soul leaves off prayer, it is as if she cast herself into hell without any need of devils."

It results, too, from the practice of prayer, that a person constantly thinks of God. "The true lover" (says St. Teresa) "is ever mindful of the beloved one." And hence it follows that persons of prayer are always speaking of God, knowing, as they do, how pleasing it is to God that his lovers should delight in conversing about him, and on the love he bears them, and that thus they should endeavor to enkindle it in others. The same saint wrote: "Jesus Christ is always found present at the conversations of the servants of God, and he is very much gratified to be the subject of their delight."

Prayer, again, creates that desire of retiring into solitude, in order to converse alone with God, and to maintain interior recollection in the discharge of necessary external duties; I say necessary, such as the management of one's family, or of the performance of duties required of us by obedience; because a person of prayer must love solitude, and avoid dissipation in superfluous and useless affairs, otherwise he will lose the spirit of recollection, which is a great means of preserving union with God: My sister, my spouse is a garden enclosed. The soul espoused to Jesus Christ must be a garden closed against all creatures, and must not admit into her heart other thoughts, nor other business, but those of God or for God. Hearts thrown open never become saints. The saints, who have to labor in gaining souls to God, do not lose their recollection in the midst of all their labors, either of preaching, confessing, reconciling enemies, or assisting the sick. The same rule holds good with those who have to apply to study. How many from excessive study, and a desire to become learned, become neither holy nor learned, because true learning consists in the science of the saints; that is to say, in knowing how to love Jesus Christ; whereas, on the contrary, divine love brings with it knowledge and every good: All good things came to me together with her that is, with holy charity. The Venerable John Berchmans had an extraordinary love for study, but by his great virtue he never allowed study to interfere with his spiritual interests.

4. Frequent Communion

The fourth means of perfection, and even of perseverance in the grace of God, is frequently to receive the Holy Communion, of which we have already spoken in the Introduction, II, page 275, where we affirmed that a soul can do nothing more pleasing to Jesus Christ than to receive him often in the Sacrament of the Altar. St. Teresa said: "There is no better help to perfection than frequent Communion : oh, how admirably does the Lord bring such a soul to perfection!" And she adds, that, ordinarily speaking, they who communicate most frequently are found further advanced in perfection; and that there is greater spirituality in those communities where frequent Communion is the custom. For this reason it is that, as we find declared in a decree of Innocent XI, in 1679, the holy Fathers have so highly extolled, and so much promoted, the practice of frequent and even of daily Communion. Holy Communion, as the Council of Trent tells us, delivers us from daily faults, and preserves us from mortal ones. St. Bernard asserts that Communion represses the movements of anger and incontinence, which are the two passions that most frequently and most violently assail us. St. Thomas says, that Communion defeats the suggestions of the devil. And finally, St. John Chrysostom says, that Communion pours into our souls a great inclination to virtue, and a promptitude to practice it; and at the same time imparts to us a great peace, by which the path of perfection is made very sweet and easy to us. Besides, there is no sacrament so capable of kindling the divine love in souls as the Holy Sacrament of the Eucharist, in which Jesus Christ bestows on us his whole self, in order to unite us all to himself by means of holy love. Wherefore the Venerable Father John of Avila said: "Whoever deters souls from frequent Communion does the work of the devil." Yes; for the devil has a great horror of this sacrament, from which souls derive immense strength to advance in divine love.

But the proper preparation is requisite to communicate well The first preparation, or, in other terms, the remote preparation, to be able to go to Communion daily, or several times in the week, is: 1. To keep free from all deliberate affection to sin that is, to sin committed, as we say, with the eyes open. 2. The practice of much mental prayer. 3. The mortification of the senses and of the passions. St. Francis de Sales 3 teaches as follows: "Whoever has overcome the greatest part of his bad inclinations, and has arrived at a notable degree of perfection, can communicate every day." The angelic Doctor St. Thomas says, that anyone who knows by experience that his soul derives an increase of divine love from the Holy Communion may communicate daily. Hence Innocent XI, in the above-mentioned decree, said that the greater or less frequency of Holy Communion must rest on the decision of the confessor who ought to be guided in this matter by the profit which he sees accrue to the souls under his direction. In the next place, the proximate preparation for Communion is that which is made on the morning itself of Communion, for which there is need of at least half an hour of mental prayer.

To reap also more abundant fruit from Communion, we must make a long thanksgiving. Father John of Avila said that the time after communion is "a time to gain treasures of graces. "St. Mary Magdalene of Pazzi used to say that no time can be more calculated to inflame us with divine love than the time immediately after our Communion. And St. Teresa says: "After Communion let us be careful not to lose so good an opportunity of negotiating with God. His divine majesty is not accustomed to pay badly for his lodging, if he meets with a good reception."

Alas, my God, how many souls, for want of applying themselves to lead a life of greater recollection and more detachment from earthly things, care not to seek Holy Communion and this is the true cause of their not wishing to communicate more frequently. They are well aware that to be wishing always to appear, to dress with vanity, to be fond of nice eating and drinking, of bodily comforts, of conversations and amusements, does not harmonize with frequent Communion; they know that more prayer is required, more mortification, as well internal as external, more seclusion; and on this account they are ashamed to approach the altar more frequently. Without doubt, such souls are right to refrain from frequent Communion as long as they find themselves in that unhappy state of lukewarmness; but whoever is called to a more perfect life should lay aside this lukewarmness, if he would not greatly risk his eternal salvation.

It will be found likewise to contribute very much to keep fervor alive in the soul, often to make a spiritual Communion, so much recommended by the Council of Trent, which exhorts all the faithful to practice it. The spiritual Communion, as St. Thomas says, consists in an ardent desire to receive Jesus Christ in the Holy Sacrament; and therefore the saints were careful to make it several times in the day. The method of making it is this: "My Jesus, I believe that Thou art really present in the Most Holy Sacrament. I love Thee, and I desire Thee; come to my soul. I embrace Thee; and I beseech Thee never to allow me to be separated from Thee again." Or more briefly thus: "My Jesus, come to me; I desire Thee; I embrace Thee; let us remain ever united together." This spiritual Communion maybe practiced several times a day when we make our prayer, when we make our visit to the Blessed Sacrament, and especially when we attend Mass at the moment of the priest's Communion. The Dominican Sister Blessed Angela of the Cross said: "If my confessor had not taught me this method of communicating spiritually several times a day, I should not have trusted myself to live."

5. Prayer

The fifth and most necessary means for the spiritual life, and for obtaining the love of Jesus Christ, is prayer. In the first place, I say that by this means God convinces us of the great love he bears us. What greater proof of affection can a person give to a friend than to say to him, "My friend, ask anything you like of me, and I will give it you?" Now, this is precisely what our Lord says to us: Ask, and it shall be given you; seek, and you shall find? Wherefore prayer is called all-powerful with God to obtain every blessing: "Prayer, though it is one, can effect all things" as Theodoret says; whoever prays, obtains from God whatever he chooses. The words of David are beautiful: Blessed be God who had not turned away my prayer, nor his mercy from me? Commenting on this pas sage, St. Augustine says, "As long as thou seest thyself not failing in prayer, be assured that the divine mercy will not fail thee either." And St. John Chrysostom: "We always obtain, even while we are still praying." When we pray to God he grants us the grace we ask for, even before we have ended our petition. If then we are poor, let us blame only ourselves, since we are poor merely because we wish to be poor, and so we are undeserving of pity. What sympathy can there be for a beggar, who, having a very rich master, and one most desirous to provide him with everything if he will only ask for it, nevertheless chooses still to continue in his poverty sooner than ask for what he wants?

In fine, the holy Fathers say, that prayer is necessary for us, not merely as a necessity of precept (so that divines say, that he who neglects for a month to recommend to God the affair of his salvation is not exempt from mortal sin), but also as a necessity of means, which is as much as to say, that whoever does not pray cannot possibly be saved. And the reason of it is, in short, because we cannot obtain eternal salvation without the help of divine grace, and this grace Almighty God only accords to those who pray. And because temptations, and the dangers of falling into God s displeasure, continually be set us, so ought our prayers to be continual. Hence St. Thomas declares that continual prayer is necessary for a man to save himself: "Unceasing prayer is necessary to man, that he may enter heaven." And Jesus Christ himself had already said the same thing: We ought always to pray, and not to faint? And afterwards the Apostle: Pray without ceasing? During the interval in which we shall cease to pray, the devil will conquer us. And though the grace of perseverance can in no wise be merited by us, as the Council of Trent teaches us, nevertheless St. Augustine says, "that in a certain sense we can merit it by prayer." The Lord wishes to dispense his grace to us, but he will be entreated first; nay more, as St. Gregory remarks, he wills to be importuned, and in a manner constrained by our prayers: "God wishes to be prayed to, he wishes to be compelled, he wishes to be, as it were, vanquished by our importunity." St. Mary Magdalene of Pazzi said, "that when we ask graces of God, he not only hears us, but in a certain sense thanks us." Yes, because God, as the infinite goodness, in wishing to pour out himself upon others, has, so to speak, an infinite longing to distribute his gifts; but he wishes to be besought: hence it follows, that when he sees himself entreated by a soul, he receives so much pleasure, that in a certain sense he thank that soul for it.

"But," someone may say "I am a sinner, and do not deserve to be heard." But Jesus Christ says: Every one that asketh, receiveth? Every one, be he just, or be he a sinner. St. Thomas teaches us that the efficacy of prayer to obtain graces does not depend on our merits, but on the mercy of God, who has promised to hear every one who prays to him. And our Redeemer, in order to remove from us all fear when we pray, said: Amen, amen, I say to you, if you shall ask the Father anything in My name, He will give it you? As though he would say: Sinners, you have no merits of your own to obtain graces, wherefore do in this manner; when you would obtain graces, ask them of my Father in my name; that is, through my merits and through my love; and then ask as many as you choose, and they shall be granted to you. But let us mark well those words, "In My name;" which signify (as St. Thomas explains it), "in the name of the Savior;" or, in other words, that the graces which we ask must be graces which regard our eternal salvation; and consequently we must remark that the promise does not regard temporal favors; these our Lord grants, when they are profitable for our eternal welfare; if they would prove otherwise, he refuses them. So that we should always ask for temporal favors, on condition that they will benefit our soul. But should they be spiritual graces, then they require no condition; but with confidence, and a sure confidence, we should say: "Eternal Father, in the name of Jesus Christ deliver me from this temptation: grant me holy perseverance, grant me Thy love, grant me heaven." We can likewise ask these graces of Jesus Christ in his own name; that is, by his merits, since we have his promise also to this effect: If you shall ask Me anything in My name, that I will do.

Affections and Prayers

O Jesus, my love, I am determined to love Thee as much as I can, and I wish to become a saint;

and I wish to become a saint for this reason, in order to give Thee pleasure, and to love Thee exceedingly in this life and the next! I can do nothing of myself, but Thou canst do all things; and I know that Thou wishest me to become a saint. I see already that by Thy grace my soul sighs only for Thee, and seeks nothing else but Thee. I wish to live no more for myself; Thou desirest me to be wholly Thine, and I desire to be wholly Thine. Come, and unite me to

Thyself, and Thyself to me. Thou art infinite goodness; Thou art he who hast loved me so much ; Thou art, indeed, too loving and too lovely; how, then, can I love anything but Thee? I prefer Thy love before all the things of this world; Thou art the sole object, the sole end of all my affections. I leave all to be occupied solely in loving Thee, my Redeemer, my Comforter, my hope, my love, and my all. I will not despair of becoming a saint on account of the sins of my past life; for I know, my Jesus, that Thou didst die in order to pardon the truly penitent. I love Thee now with my whole heart, with my whole soul; I love Thee more than myself, and I bewail, above every other evil, ever having had the misfortune to despise Thee, my sovereign good. Now I am no longer my own, I am Thine; God of my heart, dispose of me as Thou pleasest. In order to please Thee, I accept of all the tribulations Thou mayest choose to send me sickness, sorrow, troubles, ignominies, poverty, persecution, desolation I accept all to please Thee in like manner

I accept of the death Thou hast decreed for me, with all the anguish and crosses which may accompany it: it is enough if Thou grantest me the grace to love Thee exceedingly. Lend me Thy assistance ; give me strength henceforth to compensate, by my love, for all the bitterness that I have caused Thee in past time, O only love of my soul!

O Queen of Heaven, O Mother of God, O great advocate of sinners, I trust in thee!

CHAPTER V

CHARITY IS NOT PUFFED UP

A proud person is like a balloon filled with air, which seems, indeed, great; but whose greatness, in reality, is nothing more than a little air; which, as soon as the balloon is opened, is quickly dispersed. He who loves God is humble, and is not elated at seeing any worth in himself; because he knows that whatever he possesses is the gift of God, and that of his own he has only nothingness and sin; so that this knowledge of the divine favors bestowed on him humbles him the more; whilst he is conscious of being so unworthy, and yet so favored by God.

St. Teresa says, in speaking of the especial favors she received from God: "God does with me as they do with a house, which, when about to fall, they prop up with supports." When a soul receives a loving visit from God, and feels within herself an unwonted fervor of divine love, accompanied with tears, or with a great tenderness of heart, let her beware of supposing that God so favors her, in reward for some good action; but let her then humble herself the more, concluding that God caresses her in order that she may not forsake him; otherwise, were she to make such favors the subject of vain complacency, imagining herself more privileged, because she receives greater gifts from God than others, such a fault would induce God to deprive her of his favors. Two things are chiefly requisite for the stability of a house the foundation and the roof; the foundation in us must be humility, in acknowledging ourselves good for nothing, and capable of nothing; and the roof is the divine assistance, in which alone we ought to put all our trust.

Whenever we behold ourselves unusually, favored by God, we must humble ourselves the more. When St. Teresa received any special favor, she used to strive to place before her eyes all the faults she had ever committed; and thus the Lord received her into closer union with himself: the more a soul confesses herself undeserving of any favors, the more God enriches her with his graces. Thais, who was first a sinner and then a saint, humbled herself so profoundly before God that she dared not even mention his name; so that she had not the courage to say, "My God" but she said, "My Creator, have mercy on me!" And St. Jerome writes, that in recompense for such humility, she saw a glorious throne prepared for her in heaven. In the life of St. Margaret of Cortona we read the same thing; that, when our Lord visited her one day with greater tokens of tenderness and love, she exclaimed: "But, O Lord, has Thou then forgotten what I have been? Is it possible that Thou canst repay all my outrages against Thee with so exquisite sweetness?" And God replied, that when a soul loves him, and cordially repents of having offended him, he forgets all her past infidelities; as, indeed, he formerly spoke by the mouth of Ezechiel: But if the wicked do penance… I will not remember all his iniquities? And in proof of this, he showed her a high throne, which he had prepared for her in heaven in the midst of the seraphim. Oh, that we could only well comprehend the value of humility! A single act of humility is worth more than all the riches of the universe.

It was the saying of St. Teresa, " Think not that thou has advanced far in perfection, till thou considers thyself the worst of all, and desires to be placed below all." And on this maxim the saint acted, and so have done all the. saints; St. Francis of Assisi, St. Mary Magdalene of Pazzi, and the rest, considered themselves the greatest sinners in the world, and were surprised that the earth sheltered them, and did not rather open under their feet to swallow them up alive; and they expressed themselves to this effect with the sincerest conviction, The Venerable Father John of Avila, who, from his earliest infancy had led a holy life, was on his deathbed; and the priest who came to attend him said many sublime things to him, taking him for what indeed he was, a great servant of God and a learned man; but Father Avila thus spoke to him: "Father, I pray yon to make the recommendation of my soul, as of the soul of a criminal condemned to death; for such I am." This is the opinion which saints entertain of themselves in life and death.

We, too, must act in this manner, if we would save our souls, and keep ourselves in the grace of God till death, reposing all our confidence in God alone. The proud man relies on his own strength, and falls on that account; but the humble man, by placing all his trust in God

alone, stands firm and falls not, however violent and multiplied the temptations may be; for his watchword is: I can do all things in Him that strengthens me. 1 The devil at one time tempts us to presumption, at another time to diffidence; whenever he suggests to us that we are in no danger of falling, then we should tremble the more; for were God but for ,an instant to withdraw his

grace from us, we are lost. When, again, he tempts us to diffidence, then let us turn to God, and thus address him with great confidence: Thee, O Lord, have I hoped, I shall never be confounded? My God, in Thee I have put all my hopes; I hope never to meet with confusion, nor to be bereft of Thy grace. We ought to exercise ourselves continually, even to the very last moments of our life, in these acts of diffidence in ourselves and of confidence in God, always beseeching God to grant us humility.

But it is not enough, in order to be humble, to have a lowly opinion of ourselves, and to consider ourselves the miserable beings that we really are; the man who is truly humble, says Thomas a Kempis, despises himself, and wishes also to be despised by others. This is what

Jesus Christ so earnestly recommends us to practice, after his example: Learn of Me, because I am meek and humble of heart. Whoever styles himself the greatest sinner in the world, and then is angry when others despise him, plainly shows humility of tongue, but not of heart. St. Thomas Aquinas says, that a person who resents being slighted may be certain that he is far distant from perfection, even though he should work miracles. The divine Mother sent St. Ignatius Loyola from heaven to instruct St. Mary Magdalene of Pazzi in humility; and behold the lesson which the saint gave her: "Humility is a gladness at whatever leads us to despise ourselves." Mark well, a gladness; if the feelings are stirred with resentment at the contempt we receive, at least let us be glad in spirit.

And how is it possible for a soul not to love contempt, if she loves Jesus Christ, and beholds how her God was buffeted and spit upon, and how he suffered in his Passion! Then did they spit in His face and buffeted Him; and others struck His face with the palms of their hands. For this purpose our Redeemer wishes us to keep his image exposed on our altars, not indeed representing him in glory, but nailed to the cross, that we might have his ignominies constantly before our eyes; a sight which made the saints rejoice at being vilified in this world. And such was the prayer which St. John of the Cross addressed to Jesus Christ, when he appeared to him with the cross upon his shoulders: "O Lord, let me suffer, and be despised for Thee!" My Lord, on be holding Thee so reviled for my love, I only ask of Thee to let me suffer and be despised for Thy love.

St. Francis de Sales said, "To support injuries is the touchstone of humility and of true virtue." If a person pretending to spirituality practices prayer, frequent Communion, fasts, and mortifies himself, and yet cannot put up with an affront, or a biting word, of what is it a sign? It is a sign that he is a hollow cane, without humility and without virtue. And what indeed can a soul do that loves Jesus Christ, if she is unable to endure a slight for the love of Jesus Christ, who has endured so much for her? Thomas a. Kempis, in his golden little book of the Imitation of Christ, writes as follows: "Since you have such an abhorrence of being humbled, it is a sign that you are not dead to the world, have no humility, and that you do not keep God before your eyes."

It was a saying of St. Jane of Chantal, that "a person who is truly humble takes occasion from receiving some humiliation to humble himself the more." Yes, for he who is truly humble never supposes himself humbled as much as he deserves. Those who behave in this manner are styled blessed by Jesus Christ. They are not called blessed who are esteemed by the world, who are honored and praised, as noble, as learned, as powerful; but they who are spoken ill of by the world, who are persecuted and calumniated; for it is for such that a glorious reward is prepared in heaven, if they only bear all with patience: Blessed are you when they shall revile you and persecute you, and speak all that is evil against you untruly for My sake: be glad and rejoice, for your reward is very great in heaven?

The grand occasion for practicing humility is when we receive correction for some fault from Superiors or from others. Some people resemble the hedgehog they seem all calmness and meekness as long as they remain untouched; but no sooner does a Superior or a friend touch them, by an observation on something which they have done imperfectly, than they forthwith become all prickles, and answer warmly, that so and so is not true, or that they were right in doing so, or that such a correction is quite uncalled for. In a word, to rebuke them is to become their enemy; they behave like a person who raves at the surgeon for paining them in the cure of their wounds. "He is angry with the surgeon," writes St. Bernard. "When the virtuous and humble man is corrected for a fault," says St. John Chrysostom, "he grieves for having committed it; the proud man on the other hand, on receiving correction, grieves also; but he grieves that his fault is detected; and on this account he is troubled, gives answers, and is angry with the person who corrects him." This is the golden rule given by St. Philip Neri, to be observed with regard to receiving correction: "Whoever would really become a saint must never excuse himself, although what is laid to his charge be not true."

Affections and Prayers

O Incarnate Word! I entreat Thee, by the merits of Thy holy humility, which led Thee to embrace so many ignominies and injuries for our love, deliver me from all pride, and grant me a share of Thy humility. And what right have I to complain of any affront whatever that may be offered me, after having so often deserved hell? O my Jesus, by the merit of all the scorn and affronts endured for me in Thy Passion, grant me the grace to live and die humbled on this earth, as Thou didst live and die humbled for my sake. For Thy love I would willingly be despised and forsaken by all the world ; but without Thee I can do nothing. I love Thee, O my sovereign good; I love Thee, O beloved of my soul! I love Thee; and I hope, through Thee, to fulfil my purpose of suffering all for Thee, affronts, betrayals, persecutions, afflictions, dryness, and desolation; enough is it for me if Thou dost not forsake me, O sole object of the love of my soul. Suffer me never more to estrange myself from Thee. Enkindle in me the desire to please Thee. Grant me fervor in loving Thee. Give me peace of mind in suffering for Thee. Give me resignation in all contradictions. Have mercy on me. I deserve nothing; but I fix all my hopes in Thee, who hast purchased me with Thine own blood.

And I hope all from thee, too, O my Queen and my Mother Mary, who art the refuge of sinners!

CHAPTER VI

CHARITY IS NOT AMBITIOUS
He that loves Jesus Christ desires Nothing but Jesus Christ

He that loves God does not desire to be esteemed and loved by his fellowmen: the single desire of his heart is to enjoy the favor of Almighty God, who alone forms the object of his love. St. Hilary writes, that all honor paid by the world is the business of the devil. And so it is; for the enemy traffics for hell, when he infects the soul with the desire of esteem; because, by thus laying aside humility, she runs great risks of plunging into every vice. St. James writes, that as God confers his graces with open hands upon the humble, so does he close them against the proud, whom he resists. God resists the proud, and gives His grace to the humble? He says he resists the proud, signifying that he does not even listen to their prayers. And certainly, among the acts of pride we may reckon the desire to be honored by men, and self-exaltation at receiving honors from them.

We have a frightful example of this in the history of Brother Justin the Franciscan, who had even risen to a lofty state of contemplation; but because perhaps and indeed without a perhaps he nourished within himself a desire of human esteem, behold what befell him. One day Pope Eugenius IV. sent for him; and on account of the great opinion he had of his sanctity, showed him peculiar marks of honor, embraced him, and made him sit by his side. Such high honors filled Brother Justin full of self-conceit; on which St. John Capistran said to him, "Alas, Brother Justin, thou didst leave us an angel, and thou returnest a devil!" And in fact, the hapless Brother becoming daily more and more puffed up with arrogance, and insisting on being treated according to his own estimate of himself, he at last murdered a brother with a knife; he afterwards became an apostate, and fled into the kingdom of Naples, where he perpetrated other atrocities; and there he died in prison, an apostate to the last.

Hence it is that a certain great servant of God wisely said, that when we hear or read of the fall of some towering cedars of Libanus, of a Solomon, a Tertullian, an Osius, who had all the reputation of saints, it is a sign that they were not given wholly to God; but nourished inwardly some spirit of pride and so fell away. Let us therefore tremble, when we feel arise within us an ambition to appear in public, and to be esteemed by the world; and when the world pays us some tribute of honor, let us beware of taking complacency in it, which might prove the cause of our utter ruin.

The saying of St. Francis of Assisi is most true: "What I am before God, that I am." Of what use is it to pass for great in the eyes of the world, if before God we be vile and worthless? And on the contrary, what matters it to be despised by the world, provided we be dear and acceptable in the eyes of God? St. Augustine thus writes: "The approbation of him who praises neither heals a bad conscience, nor does the reproach of one who blames wound a good conscience." As the man who praises us cannot deliver us from the chastisement of our evil doings, so neither can he who blames us rob us of the merit of our good actions. "What does it matter," says St. Teresa, "though we be condemned and reviled by creatures, if before Thee, O God! we are great and without blame?" The saints had no other desire than to live unknown, and to pass for contemptible in the estimation of all. Thus writes St. Francis de Sales: "But what wrong do we suffer when people have a bad opinion of us, since we ought to have such of ourselves? Perhaps we know that we are bad, and yet wish to pass off for good in the estimation of others."

Oh, what security is found in the hidden life for such as wish cordially to love Jesus Christ; Jesus Christ himself set us the example, by living hidden and despised for thirty years in a workshop. And with the same view of escaping the esteem of men, the saints went and hid themselves in deserts and in caves. It was said by St. Vincent of Paul, that a love of appearing in public, and of being spoken of in terms of praise, and of hearing our conduct commended, or that people should say that we succeed admirably and work wonders, is an evil which, while it makes us unmindful of God, contaminates our best actions, and proves the most fatal drawback to the spiritual life.

Whoever, therefore, would make progress in the love of Jesus Christ, must absolutely give a death-blow to the love of self-esteem. But how shall we inflict this blow? Behold how St. Mary Magdalene of Pazzi instructs us: "That which, keeps alive the appetite for self-esteem is the occupying a favorable position in the minds of all; consequently the death of self-esteem is to keep one's self hidden, so as not to be known to anyone. And till we learn to die in this manner, we shall never be true servants of God."

In order, then, to be pleasing in the sight of God, we must avoid all ambition of appearing and of making a parade in the eyes of men. And we must shun with still greater caution the ambition of governing others. Sooner than behold this accursed ambition set foot in the convent, St. Teresa declared she would prefer to have the whole convent burned, and all the nuns with it. So that she signified her wish, that if ever one of her religious should be caught aiming at the Superiorship, she should be expelled from the community, or at least undergo perpetual confinement. St. Mary Magdalene of Pazzi said, "The honor of a spiritual person consists in being put below all, and in abhorring all superiority over others."

Affections and Prayers

My Jesus, grant me the ambition of pleasing Thee, and make me forget all creatures and myself also. What will it profit me to be loved by the whole world, if I be not loved by Thee, the only love of my soul! My Jesus, Thou earnest into the world to win our hearts; if I am unable to give Thee my heart, do Thou please to take it and replenish it with Thy love, and never allow me to be separated from Thee any more. I have, alas! turned my back upon Thee in the past; but now that I am conscious of the evil I have done, I grieve over it with my whole heart, and no affliction in the world can so distress me, as the remembrance of the offences that I have so often committed against Thee. I am consoled to think that Thou art infinite goodness, that Thou dost not disdain to love a sinner who loves Thee. My beloved Redeemer, O sweetest love of my soul, I have heretofore slighted Thee; but now at least I love Thee more than myself! I offer Thee myself and all that belongs to me. I have only the one wish to love Thee, and to please Thee.

This forms all my ambition; accept of it, and be pleased to increase it, and exterminate in me all desire of earthly goods. Thou art indeed deserving of love, and great indeed are my obligations of loving Thee. Behold me then, I wish to be wholly Thine; and I will suffer whatever Thou pleasest, Thou who for love of me didst die of sorrow on the cross! Thou wishest me to be a saint; Thou canst make me a saint; in Thee I place my trust.

And I also confide in thy protection, O Mary, great Mother of God!

CHAPTER VII

CHARITY SEEKETH NOT HER OWN
He that loveth Jesus Christ seeks to detach Himself from every Creature

WHOEVER desires to love Jesus Christ with his whole heart must banish from his heart all that is not God, but is merely self-love. This is the meaning of those words, "seeketh not her own;" not to seek ourselves, but only what pleaseth God. And this is what God requires of us all, when he says: Thou shalt love the Lord tHy God with thy whole heart. Two things are needful to love God with our whole heart: 1. To clear it of earth. 2. To fill it with holy love. It follows, that a heart in which any earthly affections linger can never belong wholly to God. St. Philip Neri said, "that as much love as we bestow on the creature, is so much taken from the Creator." In the next place, how must the earth be purged away from the heart? Truly by mortification and detachment from creatures. Some souls complain that they seek God, and do not find him; let them listen to what St. Teresa says: "Wean your heart from creatures, and seek God, and you will find him."

The mistake is, that some indeed wish to become saints, but after their own fashion; they would love Jesus Christ, but in their own way, without forsaking those diversions, that vanity of dress, those delicacies in food they love God, but if they do not succeed in obtaining such or such an office, they live discontented; if, too, they happen to be touched in point of esteem, they are all on fire; if they do not recover from an illness, they lose all patience. They love God; but they refuse to let go that attachment for the riches, the honors of the world, for the vainglory of being reckoned of good family, of great learning, and better than others. Such as these practice prayer, and frequent Holy Communion; but inasmuch as they take with them hearts full of earth, they derive little profit. Our Lord does not even speak to them, for he knows that it is but a waste of words. In fact, he said as much to St. Teresa on a certain occasion: "I would speak to many souls, but the world keeps up such a noise about their ears, that my voice would never be heard by them. Oh, that they would retire a little from the world!" Whosoever, then, is full of earthly affections cannot even so much as hear the voice of God that speaks to him. But unhappy the man that continues attached to the sensible goods of this earth; he may easily become so blinded by them as one day to quit the love of Jesus Christ; and for want of forsaking these transitory goods he may lose God, the infinite good, forever. St. Teresa said: "It is a reasonable consequence, that he who runs after perishable goods should himself perish."

David longed to have wings free from all lime of worldly affections, in order to fly away and repose in God: Who will give me wings like a dove, and I will fly and be at rest? & Many souls would wish to see themselves released from every earthly trammel to fly to God, and would in reality make lofty flights in the way of sanctity, if they would but detach themselves from everything in this world; but whereas they retain some little inordinate affection, and will not use violence with themselves to get rid of it, they remain always languishing on in their misery, without ever so much as lifting a foot from the ground. St. John of the Cross said: "The soul that remains with her affections attached to anything, however small, will, notwithstanding many virtues which she may possess, never arrive at divine union; for it signifies little whether the bird be tied by a slight thread or a thick one; since, however slight it may be, provided she does not break it, she remains always bound, and unable to fly. Oh, what a pitiful thing it is to see certain souls, rich in spiritual exercises, in virtues and divine favors; yet, because they are not bold enough to break off some trifling attachment, they cannot attain to divine union, for which it only needed one strong and resolute flight to break effectually that fatal thread! Since, when once the soul is emptied of all affection to creatures, God cannot help communicating himself wholly to her."

He who would possess God entirely must give himself up entirely to God: My beloved to me and I to him says the Sacred Spouse. My beloved has given himself entirely to me, and I give myself entirely to him. The love which Jesus Christ bears us causes him to desire all our love; and without all he is not satisfied. On this account we find St. Teresa thus writing to the Prioress of one of her convents: "Endeavor to train souls to a total detachment from everything created, because they are to be trained for the spouses of a king so jealous, that he would have them even forget themselves." St. Mary Magdalene of Pazzi took a little book of devotion from one of her novices, merely because she observed that she was too much attached to it. Many souls acquit themselves of the duty of prayer, of visiting the Blessed Sacrament, of frequenting Holy Communion; but nevertheless they make little or no progress in perfection, and all because they keep some fondness for something in their heart; and if they persist in living thus, they will not only be always miserable, but run the risk of losing all.

We must, therefore, beseech Almighty God, with David, to rid our heart of all earthly attachments: Create a clean heart in me, O God. Otherwise we can never be wholly his. He has given us to understand very plainly, that whoever will not renounce everything in this world, cannot be his disciple: Every one of you that doth not renounce all that he possesseth cannot be my disciple? For this reason the ancient Fathers of the desert were accustomed first to put this question to any youth who desired to associate himself with them: "Dost thou bring an empty heart, that the Holy Spirit may fill it?" Our Lord said the same thing to St. Gertrude, when she besought him to signify what he wished of her: "I wish nothing else, he said, but to find a heart devoid of creatures." We must therefore say to God with great resolution and courage: O Lord, I prefer Thee to all; to health, to riches, to honors and dignities, to applause, to learning, to consolations, to high hopes, to desires, and even to the very graces and gifts which I may receive of Thee! In short, I prefer Thee to every created good which is not Thee, O my God. Whatever benefit Thou grantest me, O my God, nothing besides Thyself will satisfy me. I desire Thee alone, and nothing else.

The Prophet Jeremias says, that the Lord is all goodness towards him who seeks him: The Lord is good to the soul that seeketh him? But he understands it of a soul that seeks God alone. O blessed loss! O blessed gain! to lose worldly goods, which cannot satisfy the heart and are soon gone, in order to obtain the sovereign and eternal good, which is God! It is related that a pious hermit, one day while the king was hunting through the wood, began to run to and fro as if in search of something ; the king, observing him thus occupied, inquired of him who he was and what he was doing; the hermit replied: "And may I ask your majesty what you are engaged about in this desert?" The king made answer: "I am going in pursuit of game." And the hermit replied: "I, too, am going in pursuit of God." With these words he continued his road and went away. During the present life this must likewise be our only thought, our only purpose, to go in search of God in order to love him, and in search of his will in order to fulfil it, ridding our heart of all love of creatures. And whenever some worldly good would present itself to our imaginations to solicit our love, let us be ready prepared with this answer: "I have despised the kingdom of this world, and all the charms of this life, for the sake of the love of my Lord Jesus Christ." And what else are all the dignities and grandeurs of this world but smoke, filth, and vanity, which all disappear at death? Blessed he who can say: "My Jesus, I have left all for Thy love; Thou art my only love; Thou alone art sufficient for me."

Ah, when once the love of God takes full possession of a soul, she of her own accord (supposing always, of course, the assistance of divine grace) strives to divest herself of everything that could prove a hindrance to her belonging wholly to God. St. Francis de Sales remarks that when a house catches fire, all the furniture is thrown out of the window; meaning thereby, that when a person gives himself entirely to God, he needs no persuasion of preachers or confessors, but of his own accord seeks to get rid of every earthly affection. Father Segneri the younger called divine love a robber, which happily despoils us of all, that we may come into possession of God alone. A certain man, of respectable position in life, having renounced everything in order to become poor for the love of Jesus Christ, was questioned by a friend how he fell into such a state of poverty; he took from his pocket a small volume of the Gospels, and said: "Behold, this is what has stripped me of all." The Holy Spirit says: If a man shall give all the substance of his house for love, he shall despise it as nothing. And when a soulness her whole love in God, she despises all, wealth, pleasures, dignities, territories, kingdoms, and all her longing is after God alone; she says, again and again: "My God, I wish for Thee only, and nothing more." St. Francis de Sales writes: "The pure love of God consumes everything which is not God, to convert all into itself; for whatever we do for the love of God is love."

The Sacred Spouse said: He brought me into the cellar of wine, he set in order charity in me. This cellar of wine, writes St. Teresa, is divine love, which, on taking possession of a soul, so perfectly inebriates it as to make it forgetful of everything created. A person intoxicated is, as it were, dead in his senses; he does not see, nor hear, nor speak; and so it happens to the soul inebriated with divine love. She has no longer any sense of the things of the world; she wishes to think only of God, to speak only of God; she recognizes no other motive in all her actions but to love and to please God. In the sacred Canticles the Lord forbids them to awake his beloved, who sleeps: Stir not up, nor make the beloved to awake, till she please?

Wherefore, to arrive at perfect union with God, a total detachment from creatures is of absolute necessity. And to come to particulars, we must divest ourselves of all in ordinate affection towards relatives. Jesus Christ says: If any man come to Me and hate not his father and mother, and wife and children, and brethren and sisters, yea, and his own life also, he cannot be My disciple? And wherefore this hatred to relatives because generally, as regards the interests of the soul, we cannot have greater enemies than our own kindred. And a man's enemies shall be those of his own household. St. Charles Borromeo declared that he never went to pay a visit to his family without returning cooled in fervor. And when Father Antony Mendoza was asked why he refused to enter the house of his parents, he replied, "Because I know, by experience, that nowhere is the devotion of religious so dissipated as in the house of parents."

When, moreover, the choice of a state of life is concerned, it is certain that we are not obliged to obey our parents, according to the doctrine of St. Thomas Aquinas. Should a young man be called to the religious life, and find opposition from his parents, he is bound to obey

God, and not his parents, who, as the same St. Thomas says, with a view to their own interests and private ends, stand in the way of our spiritual welfare. "Friends of flesh and blood are oftentimes opposed to our spiritual profit." And they are content, says St. Bernard, to have their children go to eternal perdition, rather than leave home. It is surprising, in this matter, to see some fathers and mothers, even though fearing God, yet so blinded by mistaken fondness, that they use every effort, and exhaust every means, to hinder the vocation of a child who wishes to become a religious. This conduct, however (except in very rare cases), cannot be excused from grievous sin.

But someone may say: What, then, and if such a youth does not become a religious, can he not be saved? Are, then, all who remain in the world castaway? I answer: Those whom God does not call into religion may be saved in the world by fulfilling the duties of their state; but those who are called from the world, and do not obey God, may, indeed, possibly be saved; but they will be saved with difficulty, because they will be deprived of those helps which God had destined for them in religion, and for want of which they will not accomplish their salvation. The theologian Habert writes, that he who disobeys his vocation remains in the Church like a member out of joint, and cannot discharge his duty without the greatest pain; and so will hardly effect his salvation.

But to return to our subject. St. Thomas advises those who are called to a more perfect life not to take their parents advice, because they would be their enemies in such a case. And if children are not bound to take the advice of their parents on their vocation, they are under less obligation of asking or waiting for their permission, particularly when they have reason to fear that they would unjustly refuse their consent, or prevent them from fulfilling their designs. St. Thomas of Aquinas, St. Peter of Alcantara, St. Francis Xavier, St. Louis Bertrand, and many others, embraced a religious state without even acquainting their parents.

Sanctity required to enter Holy Orders

Again, it must be observed that as we are very much exposed to be lost when to please our relatives we do not follow the divine vocation, so we also endanger our salvation when not to displease them we embrace the ecclesiastical state without being called to it by God. Now, a true vocation to this sublime dignity is distinguished by three signs, namely the requisite knowledge, the intention of applying one's self only to God's service, and positive goodness of life. We shall here speak only of this last condition.

The Council of Trent has prescribed to bishops to raise to Holy Orders only those whose irreproachable conduct has been proved. This is a rule that Canon Law had already established. Although this is directly understood of the external proof that the bishop should have in regard to the irreproachable conduct of the aspirants to the priesthood, yet one cannot doubt that the Council requires not only external irreproachableness, but even with greater reason, interior irreproachableness, without which the former would be illusory. The Council also adds that those only are to be admitted to Holy Orders who show themselves worthy by a wise maturity. We, moreover, know that the Council prescribes for this end the keeping of the interstices, that is, of an interval of time between the different degrees of Holy Orders.

St. Thomas gives a reason for such a regulation it is this, that in receiving Holy Orders one is destined to the most sublime ministry, that of serving Jesus Christ in the Sacrament of the Altar. Hence the angelic Doctor adds that the sanctity of ecclesiastics ought to surpass that of the religious. He elsewhere explains that sanctity is required not only in those who are ordained, but also in the subject who presents himself to be admitted to Holy Orders, and he shows the difference that exists in this respect between the religious and the ecclesiastical state. For in religion one purifies one's self of one's vices, whilst to receive Holy Orders it is necessary that one has already led a pure and holy life. The holy Doctor also says in another place that the candidates for Holy Orders ought to be raised above the simple faithful by their virtue as well as by the dignity of their functions. And this merit he requires before ordination, for he calls it necessary not only in order to exercise well the ecclesiastical functions, but also to be worthily admitted among the number of the ministers of Jesus Christ.

In my Moral Theology, I have given on this point a long dissertation to establish that those cannot be excused from mortal sin who without having been sufficiently tried by a holy life receive a Holy Order; since they raise themselves to this sublime state without a divine vocation; for one cannot regard those as having been called by God who have not yet succeeded in overcoming a bad habit, especially the habit of offending against chastity. And whenever among those one might be found who is disposed by repentance to receive the Sacrament of Penance, he would nevertheless not be in a condition to receive Holy Orders, for in his case there must be more holiness of life manifested during a long trial. Otherwise the candidate would not be exempt from mortal sin on account of the grave presumption that he wished to intrude into the holy ministry without a vocation. Hence St. Anselm says: "Those who thus thrust themselves into Holy Orders and have in view only their own interests are robbers who arrogate to themselves the grace of God; instead of benediction they would receive God's malediction." As Bishop Abelly remarks they would expose themselves to the great danger of being lost forever: "Whoever deliberately and without troubling himself whether or not he had a vocation would thrust himself into the priesthood, would without doubt plainly expose himself to eternal perdition." Soto holds the same opinion when he asserts, in speaking of the Sacrament of Holy Orders, that positive sanctity in the candidate is of divine precept: "As surely," he says, "this sanctity is not essential to the sacrament, though it is altogether necessary by a divine precept. Now, the sanctity that should characterize the candidates to Holy Orders does not consist in the general disposition required for the reception of the other sacraments, and sufficient in order that the sacrament may not be impeded. For, in the Sacrament of Holy Orders, one receives not only grace, but one is raised to a much more sublime state. Hence in the candidates there must be great purity of life and perfect virtue." Thomas Sanchez, Holzmann, the school of Salamanca, are also of the same opinion. Thus, what I have advanced is not only the opinion of one theologian, but it is the common teaching based upon what is taught by St. Thomas.

Detachment from Human Respect and from Self-will. Moreover, any one that would belong wholly to God must be free of all human respect. Oh, how many souls does this accursed respect keep aloof from God, and even separate them from him forever! For instance, if they hear mention made of some or other of their failings, oh, what do they not do to justify themselves, and to convince the world that it is a calumny! If they perform some good work, how industrious are they to circulate it everywhere! They would have it known to the whole world, in order to be universally applauded. The saints behave in a very different way they would rather publish their defects to the whole world, in order to pass in the eyes of all for the miserable creatures which they really are in their own eyes; and, on the contrary, in practicing any act of virtue, they prefer to have God alone know of it; for their only care is to be acceptable to him. It is on this account that so many of them were enchanted with solitude, mindful, as they were, of the words of Jesus Christ: But when thou dost alms, let not thy left hand know what thy right hand doth. And again: But thou, when thou shalt pray, enter into thy chamber; and having shut the door, pray to thy Father in secret?

Unhappy the man that lives the slave of self-will for he shall have a yearning for many things, and shall not possess them; while, on the other hand, he will be forced to undergo many things distasteful and bitter to his inclinations: From whence are wars and contentions among you? Are they not hence? From your concupiscences, which war in your members? You covet, and have not. The first war springs from the appetite for sensual delights. Let us take away the occasion; let us mortify the eyes; let us recommend ourselves to God, and the war will be over. The second war arises from the covetousness of riches: let us cultivate a love of poverty, and this war will cease. The third war has its source in ambitiously seeking after honors let us love humility and the hidden life, and this war too will be no more. The fourth war, and the most

ruinous of all, comes from self-will let us practice resignation in all things which happen by the will of God, and the war will cease. St. Bernard tells us that whenever we see a person troubled, the origin of his trouble is nothing else but his inability to gratify self will. "Whence comes disquiet," says the saint, "except that we follow self-will?" Our Blessed Lord once complained of this to St. Mary Magdalene of Pazzi, in these words: "Certain souls desire my Spirit, but after their own fancy; and so they become incapable of receiving it."

In a word, he that truly loves Jesus Christ loses all affection for things of earth, and seeks to strip himself of all, in order to keep himself united with Jesus Christ alone. Jesus is the object of all his desires, Jesus the subject of all his thoughts; for Jesus lie continually sighs; in every place, at every time, on every occasion, his sole aim is to give pleasure to Jesus. But to reach this point, we must study unceasingly to rid the heart of every affection which is not for God. And, I ask, what is meant by giving the soul entirely to God? It means, first, to shun whatever may be displeasing to God, and to do what is most pleasing to him; secondly, it means to accept unreservedly all that comes from his hands, how hard or disagreeable so ever it may be; it means, thirdly, to give the preference in all things to the will of God over our own: this is what is meant by belonging wholly to God.

Affections and Prayers

Ah, my God and my all! I cannot help feeling that, in spite of all my ingratitude and remissness in Thy service, Thou still invitest me to love Thee. Behold me, then; I will resist Thee no longer. I will leave all to be wholly Thine. I will no more live for myself: Thy claims on my love are too strong. My soul is enamored of Thee; my Jesus, it sighs after Thee. And how can I possibly love anything else, after seeing Thee die of sufferings on a cross in order to save me! how could I behold Thee dead, and exhausted with torments, and not love Thee with my whole heart? Yes, I love Thee indeed with all my soul; and I have no other desire but to love Thee in this life and for all eternity. My love, my hope, my courage, and my consolation, give me strength to be faithful to Thee; grant me light, and make known to me from what I ought to detach myself; supply me too with a strong will to obey Thee in all things. love of my soul! I offer myself, and deliver myself up entirely, to satisfy the desire which Thou hast to unite Thyself to me, that I may be wholly united with Thee, my God and my all. Oh, come then, my Jesus; come and take possession of my whole self, and occupy all my thoughts and all my affections. I renounce all my appetites, all my comforts, and all created things; Thou alone art sufficient for me. Grant me the grace to think only of Thee, to desire only Thee, to seek only Thee, my beloved and my only good!

O Mary, Mother of God, obtain for me holy perseverance!

CHAPTER VIII

CHARITY IS NOT PROVOKED TO ANGER
He that loves Jesus Christ is never angry with his Neighbor

The virtue not to be angry at the contrarieties that happen to us is the daughter of meekness. We have already spoken at length of the acts which belong to meekness in preceding chapters; but since this is a virtue which requires to be constantly practiced by everyone living among his fellow-men, we will here make some remarks on the same subject more in particular, and more adapted for practice.

Humility and meekness were the favorite virtues of Jesus Christ; so that he bade his disciples learn of him to be meek and humble: Learn of Me, for I am meek and humble of heart? Our Redeemer was called the Lamb, Behold the Lamb of God? as well in consideration of his having to be offered in sacrifice on the cross for our sins, as in consideration of the meekness exhibited by him during his entire life, but more especially at the time of his Passion. When in the house of Caiphas he received a blow from that servant, who at the same time upbraided him with presumption in those words: Answerest thou the high-priest so? Jesus only answered: If I have spoken evil, give testimony of the evil; but if well, why strikest thou me?

Oh, how dear to Jesus Christ are those meek souls who, in suffering affronts, derisions, calumnies, persecutions, and even chastisement and blows, are not irritated against the person that thus injures or strikes them: The prayer of the meek hath always pleased thee? God is always pleased with the prayers of the meek; that is to say, their prayers are always heard. Heaven is expressly promised to the meek: Blessed are the meek, for they shall possess the land. Father Alvarez said that paradise is the country of those who are despised and persecuted and trodden under foot, Yes, for it is for them that the possession of the eternal kingdom is reserved, and not for the haughty, who are honored and esteemed by the world. David declares that the meek shall not only inherit eternal happiness, but shall likewise enjoy great peace in the present life: The meek shall inherit the land, and shall delight in abundance of peace. It is so, because the saints

harbor no malice against those who ill-treat them, but rather love them the more; and the Lord, in reward for their patience, gives them an increase of interior peace. St. Teresa said: "I seem to experience a renewed love towards those persons who speak ill of me." This gave occasion to the Sacred Congregation to say of the saint, that "even affronts themselves supplied her with the food of charity."

Blessed are the dead who die in the Lord. We must, in deed, die in the Lord to be blessed, and to enjoy that blessedness even in the present life: we mean, such happiness as can be had before entering heaven, which, though certainly much below that of heaven, yet far surpasses all the pleasures of sense in this world: And the peace of God, which surpasseth all understanding, keep your hearts? so wrote the Apostle to his disciples. But to gain this peace, even in the midst of affronts and calumnies, we must be dead in the Lord: a dead person, how much so ever he may be ill-treated and trampled on by others, resents it not; in like manner, he who is meek, like a dead body, which no longer sees or feels, should endure all the outrages committed against him. Whoever loves Jesus Christ from his heart easily attains to this; because, as he is conformed in all things to his will, he accepts with equal composure and peace of mind prosperous and adverse occurrences, consolations and afflictions, injuries and courtesies. Such was the conduct of the Apostle; and he says, therefore: I exceedingly abound with joy in all our tribulation. Oh, happy the man who reaches this point of virtue! he enjoys a continual peace, which is a treasure precious beyond all other goods of this world. St. Francis de Sales said: "Of what value is the whole universe in comparison with peace of heart?"

In short, in order to remain constantly united with Jesus Christ, we must do all with tranquility, and not be troubled at any contradiction that we may encounter. The Lord is not in the earthquake. The Lord does not abide in troubled hearts. Let us listen to the beautiful lessons given on this subject by that master of meekness St. Francis de Sales: "Never put yourself in a passion, nor open the door to anger on any pretext whatever; because, when once it has gained an entrance, it is no longer in our power to banish it, or moderate it, when we wish to do so. The remedies against it are: 1. To check it immediately, by diverting the mind to some other object, and not to speak a word. 2. To imitate the Apostles when they beheld the tempest at sea, and to have recourse to God, to whom it belongs to restore peace to the soul. 3. If you feel that, owing to your weakness, anger has already got footing in your breast, in that case do yourself violence to regain your composure, and then try to make acts of humility and of sweetness towards the person against whom you are irritated; but all this must be done with sweetness and without violence, for it is of the utmost importance not to irritate the wounds." The saint said that he himself was obliged to labor much during his life to overcome two passions which predominated in him, namely, anger and love: to subdue the passion of anger, he avowed it had cost him twenty-two years hard struggle,

Someone may say: But why should I use courtesy and gentleness towards an impertinent fellow, that insults me without cause? But St. Francis de Sales replies: "We must practice meekness, not only with reason, but against reason."

We must therefore endeavor, on such occasions, to make a kind answer; and in this way we shall allay the fire: A mild answer breaketh wrath? But when the mind is troubled, the best expedient will be to keep silence. St. Bernard writes: "The eye troubled by anger sees not straight." When the eye is dimmed with passion, it no longer distinguishes between what is and what is not unjust; anger is like a veil drawn over the eyes, so that we can no longer discern betwixt right and wrong; where fore we must, like St. Francis de Sales, make a compact with our tongue: "I have made a covenant with my tongue," he wrote, "never to speak while my heart is disturbed."

But there are moments when it seems absolutely necessary to check insolence with severe words. David said: Be angry, and sin not. Occasions do exist, therefore, when we may be lawfully angry, provided it be without sin. But here is just the matter: speculatively speaking,

it seems expedient at times to speak and reply to some people in terms of severity, in order to make an impression on them; but in practice it is very difficult to do this without some fault on our part; so that the sure way is always to admonish, or to reply, with gentleness, and to scrupulously guard against all resentment. St. Francis de Sales said: "I have never been angry without afterwards repenting of it." And when, for some reason or other, we still feel warm, the safest way, as I said before, is to keep silence, and reserve the remonstrance till a more convenient moment, when the heart is cooled down.

We ought particularly to observe this meekness when we are corrected by our Superiors or friends. St. Francis de Sales again writes: "To receive a reprimand willingly, shows that we love the virtue opposed to the fault for which we are corrected; and consequently this is a great sign of progress in perfection."

Meekness is also more especially necessary when we have to correct others. Corrections made with a bitter zeal often do more harm than good, especially when he who must be corrected is himself excited: in such cases the correction should be put off, and we must wait until he is cool. And we ourselves ought no less to refrain from correcting while we are under the influence of ill temper; for then our admonition will always be accompanied with harshness; and the person in fault, when he sees that he is corrected in such a way, will take no heed of the admonition, considering it the mere effect of passion. This has good as far as concerns the good of our neighbor; as concerns our personal advantage, let us show how dearly we love Jesus Christ, by patiently and gladly supporting every sort of ill-treatment, injury, and contempt.

Affections and Prayers

O my despised Jesus, O love, O joy of my soul, Thou hast by Thy example made contempt most acceptable to Thy lovers! I promise Thee, from this day forward, to submit to every affront for the love of Thee, who for love of me didst submit on earth to every species of revilement from men. Do Thou grant me strength to keep this promise. Enable me to know and to perform whatever Thou desirest at my hands. My God and my all, I crave no other good than Thyself, who art infinite good! O Thou who takest my interests so much too heart, grant that my only care may be to gratify Thee! Grant that all my thoughts may be occupied in avoiding whatever may offend Thee, and in promoting whatever may contribute to Thy good pleasure. Ward off every occasion that may draw me from Thy love. I strip myself of my liberty, and consecrate it entirely to Thy good will. I love Thee, O infinite goodness! I love Thee, O my delight! O Word incarnate, I love Thee more than myself! Take pity on me, and heal whatever wounds remain in my poor soul from its past disloyalties towards Thee. I resign myself wholly into Thy arms, O my Jesus; I will be wholly Thine; I will suffer everything for love of Thee; and I ask of Thee nothing but Thyself!

O Holy Virgin and my Mother Mary, I love thee, and I rely on thee; succor we by thy powerful intercession!

CHAPTER IX

CHARITY THINKETH NO EVIL, REJOICETH NOT IN INEQUITY BUT REJOICETH WITH THE TRUTH

He that loves Jesus Christ only wishes what Jesus Christ wishes

Charity and truth always go together; so that charity, conscious that God is the only and the true good, detests iniquity, which is directly opposed to the divine will, and takes no satisfaction but in what pleases Almighty God. Hence the soul that loves God is heedless of what people say of it, and only aims at pleasing God. The Blessed Henry Suso said: "That man stands well with God who strives to conform himself to the truth, and for the rest is utterly indifferent to the opinion or treatment of mankind."

As we have already more than once asserted, the sanctity and perfection of a soul consists in renouncement of self and in submission to the will of God; but now it will be well to enter more into detail.

The necessity of conforming to the Will of God

If, then, we would become saints our whole endeavor must be, never to follow our own will, but always the will of God; the substance of all the precepts and divine counsels is comprised in doing and suffering what God wills, and in the manner he wills it. Let us, therefore, entreat the Lord to bestow on us a holy liberty of spirit; liberty of spirit leads us to embrace whatever is pleasing to Jesus Christ, regardless of all feelings of repugnance arising from self-love and human respect. The love of Jesus Christ makes those who love him utterly indifferent; so that all things are alike to them, whether bitter or sweet: they do not wish for anything that pleases themselves, but only for that which is pleasing to God; they employ themselves in little and great things, be they pleasant or unpleasant, with the same peace of mind; it is enough for them if they please God.

St. Augustine says: "Love, and do what you like." Whoever really yes God seeks only to please him; and in this is all his pleasure. St. Teresa says: "He that seeks but the gratification of one he loves, is gratified with all that pleases that person. Love in its perfection produces this result; it makes a person heedless of all private interests and self-satisfaction, and concentrates all his thoughts on endeavoring to please the person be loved, and to do all he can to honor him himself, and to make him honored by others. O Lord, all our ills come from not keeping our eyes fixed on Thee! Were we solely intent on advancing, we should soon come to the end of our journey; but we fall and stumble a thousand times, and we even lose our way, for want of looking attentively to the right path." Here we may see what should be the single aim of all our thoughts, actions, desires, and of all our prayers, namely, the pleasure of God; our way to perfection must be this, to walk according to the will of God.

But our conformity to the divine will must be entire, without any reserve, and constant without withdrawal. In this consists the height of perfection; and to this (I repeat) all our works, all our desires, and all our prayers ought to tend. Some souls given to prayer, on reading of the ecstasies and raptures of St. Teresa and St. Philip Neri, come to wish to enjoy themselves these super natural unions. Such wishes must be banished as contrary to humility; if we really desire to be saints, we must aspire after true union with God, which is to unite our will entirely to the will of God. St. Teresa said, "Those persons are deceived who fancy that union with God consists in ecstasies, raptures, and sensible enjoyments of him. It consists in nothing else than in submitting our will to the will of God; and this submission is perfect when our will is detached from everything, and so completely united with that of God, that all its movements depend solely on the will of God. This is the real and essential union which I have always sought after, and continually beg of the Lord." And then she adds: "Oh, how many of us say this, and seem to ourselves to desire nothing besides this; but, miserable creatures that we are, how few of us attain to it!" Such, indeed, is the undeniable truth; many of us say: O Lord! I give Thee my will, I desire nothing but what Thou desirest; but, in the event of some trying occurrence, we are at a loss how to yield calmly to the divine will. And this is the source of our continually complaining that we are unfortunate in the world, and that we are the butt of every misfortune; and so of our dragging on an unhappy life.

Thus we, too, shall be happy when we receive from God all the dispositions of his Providence in the spirit of perfect conformity to his divine will, utterly regardless whether or not they coincide with our private inclinations. The saintly Mother de Chantal said: "When shall we come to relish the divine will in every event that happens, without paying attention to anything else but the good pleasure of God, from whom it is certain that prosperity and adversity proceed alike from motives of love and for our best interests? When shall we resign ourselves unreservedly into the arms of our most loving heavenly Father, entrusting him with the care of our persons and our affairs, and reserving nothing for ourselves but the sole desire of pleasing God?" The friends of St. Vincent of Paul said of him while he was still on earth: "Vincent is always Vincent." By which they meant to say, that the saint was ever to be seen with the same smiling face, whether in prosperity or in adversity; and was always himself, because, as he lived in the total abandonment of himself to God, he feared nothing and desired nothing but what was pleasing to God. St. Teresa said: "By this holy abandonment that admirable liberty of spirit is generated, which those who are perfect possess, wherein they find all the happiness in this life which they can possibly desire; inasmuch as, fearful of nothing, and desirous or wanting for nothing in the things of this world, they possess all."

Many, on the other hand, fabricate a sort of sanctity according to their own inclinations; some, inclined to melancholy, make sanctity consist in living in seclusion; others, of a busy temperament, in preaching and in making up quarrels; some, of an austere nature, in penitential inflictions and macerations; others, who are naturally generous, in distributing alms; some in saying many vocal prayers; others in visiting sanctuaries; and all their sanctity consists in such or the like practices. External acts are the fruit of the love of Jesus Christ; but true love itself consists in a complete conformity to the will of God; and as a consequence of this, in denying ourselves and in preferring what is most pleasing to God, and solely because he deserves it.

Jesus Christ said: Many shall say: Lord, we have cast out devils and done great wonders in Thy name: Lord, have we not prophesied in Thy name, and cast out devils in Thy name, and done many miracles in Thy name? But the Lord will answer them: I never knew you; depart from Me, you that work iniquity. Depart from me; I never acknowledged you for my disciples, because you preferred to follow your own inclinations rather than my will. And this is especially applicable to those priests who labor much for the salvation or perfection of others, while they themselves continue to live on in the mire of their imperfections. Perfection consists: First, in a true contempt of one's self. Secondly, in a thorough mortification of our own appetites. Thirdly, in a perfect conformity to the will of God: whosoever is wanting in one of these virtues is out of the way of perfection. On this account a great servant of God said, it was better for us in our actions to have the will of God rather than his glory as their sole end; for in doing the will of God, we at the same time promote his glory; whereas in proposing to ourselves the glory of God, we frequently deceive ourselves, and follow our own will under pretext of glorifying God. St. Francis de Sales said: "There are many who say to the Lord: I give myself wholly to Thee without reserve; but few indeed, in point of fact, practically embrace this abandonment. It consists in a certain indifference in accepting all kinds of events, just as they fall out according to the order of divine Providence, afflictions as well as consolations, slights and injuries as well as honor and glory."

Wherefore St. Mary Magdalene of Pazzi said, that all our prayers should have for their end to obtain from God the grace to follow his holy will in all things. Certain souls; greedy of spiritual dainties in prayer, go in search only of these banquets of sweet and tender feelings; but courageous souls that seek sincerely to belong wholly to God, ask him only for light to understand his will, and for strength to put it in execution. In order to attain to purity of love, it is necessary to submit our will in all things to the will of God: Never consider yourselves, said St. Francis de Sales, "to have arrived at the purity which you ought to have, as long as your will is not cheerfully obedient, even in things the most repulsive, to the will of God." "Because," as St. Teresa remarks, "the giving up of our will to God draws him to unite himself to our lowliness." But this can never be obtained, except by means of mental prayer and of continual petitions addressed to the divine majesty, nor without a cordial desire to belong entirely to Jesus Christ without reserve.

O most amiable Heart of my divine Savior, Heart enamored of mankind, since Thou lovest us with such a depth of tenderness; O Heart, in fine, worthy to rule over and possess all our hearts, would that I could make all men comprehend the love Thou bearest them, and the tender caresses Thou dost lavish on those who love Thee without reserve! O Jesus my love, be pleased to accept the offering and the sacrifice which I this day make to Thee of my entire will! Acquaint me with what Thou wouldst have me to do; for I am determined to do all by the help of Thy grace.

I
Obedience

Now what is the surest way to know and ascertain what God requires of us? There is no surer way than to practice obedience to our Superiors and directors. St. Vincent of Paul said: "The will of God is never better complied with than when we obey our Superiors." The Holy Ghost says:

Much better is obedience than the victims of fools? God is more pleased with the sacrifice which we make to him of our own will, by submitting it to obedience, than with all other sacrifices which we can offer him; because in other things, as in alms-deeds, fastings, mortifications, and the like, we give of what is ours to God, but in giving him our will we present him ourselves: when we give him our goods, our mortifications, we give him part; but when we give him our will, we give him everything. So that when we say to God, O Lord, make me know by means of obedience what Thou requires! of me, for I wish to comply with all, we have nothing more to offer him.

For obedience to be perfect, we must obey with the will and with the judgment. To obey with the will signifies to obey willingly, and not by constraint, after the fashion of slaves; to obey with the judgment means to conform our judgment to that of the Superior, without examining what is commanded. St. Mary Magdalene of Pazzi remarks on this: "Perfect obedience demands a soul without judgment." To the like purpose, St. Philip Neri said that, in order to obey with perfection, it was not enough to execute the thing commanded, but it must be done without reasoning on it; taking it for certain that what is commanded us is for us the most perfect thing we can do, although the opposite might be better before God.

This holds good not merely for religious, but likewise for seculars living under obedience to their spiritual directors. Let them request their director to prescribe them rules for the guidance of their affairs, both spiritual and temporal; and so they will make sure of doing what is best. St. Philip Neri said: "Let those who are desirous of progressing in the way of God submit themselves to a prudent confessor, whom they should obey as in God's place. By so doing, we are certain of not having to render an account to God of the actions we perform."

Among the maxims of St. Francis de Sales are the two following, most consolatory for scrupulous souls: "First, a truly obedient soul was never yet lost; secondly, we ought to be satisfied on being told by our spiritual director that we are going on well, without seeking to be convinced of it ourselves." It is the teaching of many Doctors, as of Gerson, St. Antoninus, Cajetanus, Navarrus, Sanchez, Bonacina, Cordovius, Castropalao, and the Doctors of Salamanca, with others, that the scrupulous person is bound, under strict obligation, to act in opposition to scruples, when from such scruples there is reason to apprehend grievous harm happening to soul or body, such as the loss of health, or of intellect; wherefore scrupulous persons ought to have greater scruple at not obeying the confessor than at acting in opposition to their scruples.

To sum up, therefore, all that has been said in this chapter, our salvation and perfection consist: 1. In denying ourselves; 2. In following the will of God; 3. In praying him always to give us strength to do both one and the other.

Affections and Prayers

What have I in heaven and besides Thee what do I desire upon earth ? Thou art the God of my heart, and the God that is my portion forever? My beloved Redeemer, infinitely amiable, since Thou hast come down from heaven to give Thyself wholly to me, what else shall I seek for on earth or in heaven besides Thee, who art the sovereign good, the only good worthy to be loved? Be Thou, then, the sole Lord of my heart, do Thou possess it entirely may my soul love Thee alone, obey Thee alone, and seek to please no other than Thee. Let others enjoy the riches of this world, I wish only for Thee: Thou art and shalt ever be my treasure in this life and in eternity Wherefore I give Thee, O my Jesus, my whole heart and all my will. It was at one time, alas! a rebel against Thee; but now I dedicate it wholly to Thee. Lord, what wilt Thou have me to do?" Tell me what Thou requirest of me, and lend me Thy assistance; for I will leave nothing undone. Dispose of me, and of all that concerns me, as Thou pleasest; I accept of all, and resign myself to all. O Love deserving of infinite love, Thou hast loved me so as even to die for me; I love Thee with my whole heart, I love Thee more "than myself, and into Thy hands I abandon my soul. On this very day I bid farewell to every worldly affection, I take leave of everything created, and I give myself without reserve to Thee; Through the merits of Thy Passion receive me, and make me faithful unto death. My Jesus, my Jesus, from this day forward I will live only for Thee, I will love none but Thee, I will seek nothing else than to do Thy blessed will.

Aid me by Thy grace, and aid me, too, by thy protection, O Mary my hope.

CHAPTER X

CHARITY BEARETH ALL THINGS
I
Patience in Sickness

In the first place, let us speak of bodily infirmities, which, when borne with patience, merit for us a beautiful crown.

St. Vincent de Paul said: "Did we but know how precious a treasure is contained in infirmities, we should accept of them with joy as the greatest possible blessings." Hence the saint himself, though constantly afflicted with ailments, that often left him no rest day or night, bore them with so much peace and such serenity of countenance that no one could guess that anything ailed him at all. Oh, how edifying is it to see a sick person bear his illness with a peaceful countenance, as did St. Francis de Sales! When he was ill, he simply explained his complaint to the physician, obeyed him exactly by taking the prescribed medicines, however nauseous; and for the rest he remained at peace, never uttering a single complaint in all his sufferings. What a contrast to this is the conduct of those who do nothing but complain even for the most trifling indisposition, and who would like to have around them all their relatives and friends to sympathize with them! Far different was the instruction of St. Teresa to her nuns: "My sisters, learn to suffer something for the love of Jesus Christ, without letting all the world know of it." One Good Friday Jesus Christ favored the Venerable Father Louis da Ponte with so much bodily suffering, that no part of him was exempt from its particular pain: he mentioned his severe sufferings to a friend; but he was afterwards so sorry at having done so, that he made a vow never again to reveal to anybody whatever he might afterwards suffer. I say "he was favored;" for, to the saints, the illnesses and pains which God sends them are real favors. One day St. Francis of Assisi lay on his bed in excruciating torments; a companion said to him: "Father, beg God to ease your pains, and not to lay so heavy a hand upon you." On hearing this, the saint instantly leaped from his bed, and going on his knees, thanked God for his sufferings; then, turning to his companion, he said: "Listen, did I not know that you so spoke from simplicity, I would refuse ever to see you again."

There was a certain pious lady lying bedridden with many disorders; and on the servant putting the crucifix into her hand, and telling her to pray to God to deliver her from her miseries, she made answer: "But how can you desire me to seek to descend from the cross, whilst I hold in my hand a God crucified? God forbid chat I should do so. I will suffer for him who chose to suffer torments for me incomparably greater than mine." This was, indeed, precisely what Jesus Christ said to St. Teresa when she was laboring under serious illness; he appeared to her all covered with wounds, and then said to her: "Behold, my daughter, the bitterness of my sufferings, and consider if yours equal mine." Hence the saint was accustomed to say, in the midst of her infirmities: "When I remember in how many ways my Savior suffered, though he was innocence itself, I know not how it could enter my head to complain of my sufferings." During a period of thirty-eight years, St. Lidwine was afflicted with numberless evils fevers, gout in the feet and hands, and sores, all her lifetime; nevertheless, from never losing sight of the sufferings of Jesus Christ, she maintained an unbroken cheerfulness and joy. In like manner, St. Joseph of Leonessa, a Capuchin, when the surgeon was about to amputate his arm, and his brethren would have bound him, to prevent him from stirring through vehemence of pain, seized hold of the crucifix and exclaimed: "Wherefore bind me? Where fore bind me behold who it is that binds me to support every suffering patiently for love of him;" and so he bore the operation without a murmur. St. Jonas the Martyr, after passing the entire night immersed in ice by order of the tyrant, declared next morning that he had never spent a happier night, because he had pictured to himself Jesus hanging on the cross; and thus, compared with the torments of Jesus, his own had seemed rather caresses than torments.

Oh, what abundance of merits may be accumulated by patiently enduring illnesses! Almighty God revealed to Father Balthazar Alvarez the great glory he had in store for a certain nun, who had borne a painful sickness with resignation; and told him that she had acquired greater merit in those eight months of her illness than some other religious in many years. It is by the patient endurance of ill-health that we weave a great part, and perhaps the greater part, of the crown that God destines for us in heaven. St. Lidwine had a revelation to this effect. After sustaining many and most cruel disorders, as we mentioned above, she prayed to die a martyr for the love of Jesus Christ; now as she was one day sighing after this martyrdom, she suddenly saw a beautiful crown, but still incomplete, and she understood that it was destined for herself; whereupon the saint, longing to behold it completed, entreated the Lord to increase her sufferings. Her prayer was heard, for some soldiers came shortly after, and ill-treated her, not only with injurious words, but with blows and outrages. An angel then appeared to her with the crown completed, and informed her that those last injuries had added to it the gems that were wanting; and shortly afterwards she expired.

Above all, in time of sickness we should be ready to accept of death, and of that death which God pleases. We must die, and our life must finish in our last illness; nor do we know which will be our last illness. Where fore in every illness we must be prepared to accept that death which God has appointed for us. A sick person says: "Yes; but I have committed many sins, and have done no penance. I should like to live, not for the sake of living, but to make some satisfaction to God before my death." But tell me, my brother, how do you know that if you live longer you will do penance, and not rather do worse than before? At present you can well cherish the hope that God has pardoned you; what penance can be more satisfactory than to accept of death with resignation, if God so wills it? St. Aloysius Gonzaga, at the age of twenty-three, gladly embraced death with this reflection: "At present," he said, "I am, as I hope, in the grace of God. Hereafter, I know not what may befall me; so that I now die contentedly, if God calls me to the next life." It was the opinion of Father John of Avila that every one, provided he be in good dispositions, though only moderately good, should desire death, to escape the danger, which always surrounds us in this world, of possibly sinning and losing the grace of God.

Besides, owing to our natural frailty, we cannot live in this world without committing at least venial sins; this should be a motive for us to embrace death willingly, that we may never offend

God any more. Further, if we truly love God, we should ardently long to go to see him, and love him with all our strength in Paradise, which no one can do perfectly in this present life; but unless death open us the door, we cannot enter that blessed region of love. This caused St. Augustine, that loving soul, to cry out: "Oh, let me die, Lord, that I may behold Thee!" O Lord, let me die, otherwise I cannot behold and love Thee face to face.

II
Patience in Poverty

In the second place, we must practice patience in the endurance of poverty. Our patience is certainly very much tried when we are in need of temporal goods. St. Augustine said: "He that has not God, has nothing; he that has God, has all." He who possesses God, and remains united to his blessed will, finds every good. Witness St. Francis, barefooted, clad in sackcloth, and deprived of all things, yet happier than all the monarchs of the world, by simply repeating, "My God and my all." A poor man is properly he that has not what he desires; but he that desires nothing, and is contented with his poverty, is in fact very rich. Of such St. Paul says: Having nothing, yet possessing all things? The true lovers of God have nothing, and yet have everything; since, when temporal goods fail them, they exclaim: "My Jesus, Thou alone art sufficient for me;" and with this they rest satisfied. Not only did the saints maintain patience in poverty, but sought to be despoiled of all, in order to live detached from all, and united with God alone. If we have not courage enough to renounce all worldly goods, at all events let us be contented with that state of life in which God has placed us; let our solicitude be not for earthly goods, but for those of Paradise, which are immeasurably greater, and last forever; and let us be fully persuaded of what St. Teresa says: "The less we have here, the more we shall have there."

One day Jesus Christ thus spoke to the Blessed Angela of Foligno: "If poverty were not of great excellence, I would not have chosen it for myself, nor have bequeathed it to my elect." And, in fact, the saints, seeing Jesus poor, had therefore a great affection for poverty. St. Paul says, that the desire of growing rich is a snare of Satan, by which he has wrought the ruin of innumerable souls: They that will become rich, fall into temptation, and into the snare of the devil, and into many unprofitable and hurtful desires, which drown men into destruction and perdition. Unhappy beings who, for the sake of vile creatures of earth, forfeit an infinite good, which is God! St. Basil the Martyr was quite in the right, when the Emperor Licinius proposed to make him the chief among his priests, if he would renounce Jesus Christ; he was right, I say, to reply: "Tell the emperor, that were he to give me his whole kingdom, he would not give me as much as he would rob me of, by depriving me of God." Let us be content then with God, and with those things which he gives us, rejoicing in our poverty, when we stand in need of something we desire, and have it not; for herein consists our merit. "Not poverty," says St. Bernard, "but the love of poverty, is reckoned a virtue." Many are poor, but from not loving their poverty, they merit nothing; therefore St. Bernard says, that the virtue of poverty consists not in being poor, but in the love of poverty.

To such persons is applicable the saying of the Blessed Salomea, a nun of St. Clare: "That religious shall be a laughing-stock to angels and to men, who pretends to be poor, and yet murmurs when she is in want of something." Good religious act differently; they love their poverty above all riches. The daughter of the Emperor Maximilian II, a discalced nun of St. Clare, called Sister Margaret of the Cross, appeared on occasion before her brother, the Archduke Albert, in a patched-up habit, who evinced some astonishment, as if it were unbecoming her noble birth; but she made him this answer: "My brother, I am more content with this torn garment than all monarchs with their purple robes."

The bereavement of relatives and friends by death belongs also, in some measure, to holy poverty; and in this we must especially practice patience. Some people, at the loss of a parent or friend, can find no rest; they shut themselves up to weep in their chamber, and giving free vent to their sorrow, become insupportable to all around them, by their want of patience. I would ask these persons, for whose gratification they thus lament and shed tears? For that of God? Certainly not for God's will is, that they should be resigned to his dispensations. For that of the soul departed? By no means: if the soul be lost, she abhors both you and your tears; if she be saved, and already in heaven, she would have you thank God on her part; if still in purgatory, she craves the help of your prayers, and wishes you to bow with resignation to the divine will, and to become a saint, in order that she may one day enjoy your society in paradise. Of what use, then, is all this weeping? On one occasion, the Venerable Father Joseph Caracciolo, the Theatine, was surrounded by his relatives, who were all bitterly lamenting the death of his brother, whereupon he said to them: "Come, come! let us keep these tears for a better purpose, to weep over the death of Jesus Christ, who has been to us a father, a brother, and spouse, and who died for love of us." On such occasions we must imitate Job, who, on hearing the news of the death of his sons, exclaimed, with full resignation to the Divine will, The Lord gave, and the Lord hath taken away God gave me my sons, and God hath taken them away. As it hath pleased the Lord, so is it done blessed be the name of the Lord; it hath pleased God that such things should hap pen, and so it pleaseth me; wherefore may he be blessed by me forever.

III
Patience under Contempt

In the third place, we must practice patience, and show our love to God, by tranquilly submitting to contempt.

As soon as a soul delivers herself up to God, he sends her from himself, or through others, insults and persecution. One day an angel appeared to the Blessed Henry Suso and said to him, "Henry, thou hast hitherto mortified thyself in thy own way; henceforth thou shalt be mortified after the pleasure of others." On the day following, as he was looking from a window on the street, he saw a dog shaking and tearing a rag which it held in its mouth; at the same moment a voice said to him, "So hast thou to be torn in the mouths of men." Forth with the Blessed Henry descended into the street and secured the rag, putting it by to encourage him in his coming trials.

Let us now draw this chapter to a conclusion. That we may be able to practice patience to advantage in all our tribulations, we must be fully persuaded that every trial comes from the hands of God, either directly, or indirectly through men; we must therefore render God thanks whenever we are beset with sorrows, and accept, with gladness of heart, of every event, prosperous or adverse, that proceeds from him, knowing that all happens by his disposition for our welfare: To them that love God all things work together unto good. In addition to this, it is well in our tribulations to glance a moment at that hell which we have formerly deserved for assuredly all the pains of this life are incomparably smaller than the awful pains of hell. But above all, prayer, by which we gain the divine assistance, is the great means to suffer patiently all affliction, scorn, and contradictions; and is that which will furnish us with the strength which we have not of ourselves. The saints were persuaded of this; they recommended themselves to God, and so overcame every kind of torments and persecutions.

Affections and Prayers

O Lord, I am fully persuaded that without suffering, and suffering with patience, I cannot win the crown of Paradise. David said: From Him is my patience? And I say the same; my patience in suffering must come from Thee. I make many purposes to accept in peace of all tribulations; but no sooner are they at hand than I grow sad and alarmed; and if I suffer, I suffer without merit and without love, because I know not how to suffer them so as to please Thee. O my Jesus, through the merits of Thy patience in bearing so many afflictions for love of me, grant me the grace to bear crosses for the love of Thee! I love Thee with my whole heart, O my dear Redeemer! I love Thee, my sovereign good! I love Thee, my own love, worthy of infinite love. I am grieved at any displeasure I have ever caused Thee, more than for any evil whatever. I promise Thee to receive with patience all the trials Thou mayest send me; but I look to Thee for help to be faithful to my promise, and especially to be enabled to bear in peace the throes of my last agony and death.

O Mary, my Queen, vouchsafe to obtain for me a true resignation in all the anguish and trials that await me in life and death.

CHAPTER XI

CHARITY BELIEVETH ALL THINGS
He that loves Jesus Christ believes all His Words

Whoever loves a person, believes all that proceeds from the lips of that person; consequently, the more a soul loves Jesus Christ, the more lively and unshaken is her faith. When the good thief beheld our Redeemer, though he had done no ill, suffering death upon the cross with such patience, he began at once to love him; under the influence of this love, and of the divine light which then broke upon his soul, he believed that this was truly the Son of God, and begged not to be forgotten by him when he should have passed into his kingdom.

Faith is the foundation of charity; but faith afterwards receives its perfection from charity. His faith is most perfect whose love of God is most perfect. Charity produces in man not merely the faith of the understanding, but the faith of the will also: those who believe only with the understanding, but not with the will, as is the case with sinners who are perfectly convinced of the truths of the faith, but do not choose to live according to the divine commandments, such as these have a very weak faith; for had they a more lively belief that the grace of God is a priceless treasure, and that sin, because it robs us of this grace, is the worst of evils, they would assuredly change their lives. If, then, they prefer the miserable creatures of this earth to God, it is because they either do not believe, or because their faith is very weak. On the contrary, he who believes not only with the understanding, but also with the will, so that he not only believes, but has the will to believe in God, the revealer of truth, from the love he has for him, and rejoices in so believing, such a one has a perfect faith, and consequently seeks to make his life conformable to the truths that he believes.

Weakness of faith, however, in those who live in sin, does not spring from the obscurity of faith; for though God, in order to make our faith more meritorious, has veiled the objects of faith in darkness and secrecy, he has at the same time given us so clear and convincing evidence of their truth, that not to believe them would argue not merely a lack of sense, but sheer madness and impiety. The weakness of the faith of many persons is to be traced to their wickedness of living. He who, rather than forego the enjoyment of forbidden pleasures, scorns the divine friendship, would wish there were no law to forbid, and no chastisement to punish, his sin; on this account he strives to blind himself to the eternal truths of death, judgment, and hell, and of divine justice; and because such subjects strike too much terror into his heart, and are too apt to mix bitterness in his cup of pleasure, he sets his brain to work to discover proofs, which have at least the look of plausibility; and by which he allows himself to be flattered into the persuasion that there is no soul, no God, no hell, in order that he may live and die like the brute beasts, without laws and without reason.

The true lover of Jesus Christ keeps the eternal truths constantly in view, and orders all his actions according to them. Oh, how thoroughly does he who loves Jesus Christ understand the force of that saying of the Wise Man, Vanity of vanities, and all is vanity that all earthly greatness is mere smoke, dirt, and delusion; that the soul's only welfare and happiness consists in loving its Creator, and in doing his blessed will; that we are, in reality, no more than what we are before God; that it is of no use to gain the whole world, if the soul be lost; that all the goods in the world can never satisfy the human heart, but only God himself; and, in fine, that we must leave all in order to gain all.

Charity believeth all things

There are other Christians, though not so perverse as the class we have mentioned, who would fain believe in nothing, that they may give full scope to their unruly passions, and live on undisturbed by the stings of remorse, there are others, I say, who believe, indeed, but their faith is languid; they believe the most holy mysteries of religion, the truths of Revelation contained in the Gospel, the Trinity, the Redemption, the holy Sacraments, and the rest; still they do not believe all. Jesus Christ has said: Blessed are the poor; blessed are the sorrowful; blessed are the mortified; blessed are those whom men persecute, calumniate and curse. Blessed are the poor; blessed are they that hunger; blessed are they that suffer persecution; blessed are you when men shall revile you, and shall say all manner of evil against you? This is the teaching of Jesus Christ in the Gospel. How, then, can it be said, that those believe in the Gospel who say: "Blessed are those who have money; blessed are those who suffer nothing; blessed are those who can take their amusements; pitiable is the man that suffers persecution and ill-treatment from others?" We must certainly say of such as these, that either they do not believe the Gospel, or that they believe only a part of it. He who believes it all esteems it his highest fortune, and a mark of the divine favor in this world, to be poor, to be sick, to be mortified, to be despised and ill-treated by men. Such is the belief, and such the language, of one who believes all that is said in the Gospel, and has a real love for Jesus Christ.

Affections and Prayers

My beloved Redeemer, O life of my soul, I firmly believe that Thou art the only good worthy of being loved. I believe that Thou art the greatest lover of my soul, since through love alone Thou didst Mie, overwhelmed with sorrows for love of me. I believe there is no greater blessing in this world, or in the next, than to love Thee, and to do Thy adorable will. All this I believe most firmly; so that I renounce all things, that I may belong wholly to Thee, and that I may possess Thee alone. Help me, through the merits of Thy sacred Passion, and make me such as Thou wouldst have me to be. I believe in Thee, O infallible truth! I trust in Thee, O infinite mercy! I love Thee, O infinite goodness! O infinite love, I give myself wholly to Thee, who hast wholly given Thyself to me in Thy Passion, and in the holy Sacrament of the Altar.

And I recommend myself to Thee, O Mary, refuge of sinners, and Mother of God.

CHAPTER XII

CHARITY HOPE ALL THINGS
He that loves Jesus Christ hopes for all Things from Him

Hope increases charity, and charity increases hope.

Hope in the divine goodness undoubtedly gives an increase to our love of Jesus Christ. St. Thomas says, that in the very moment when we hope to receive some benefit from a person, we begin also to love him. On this account, the Lord forbids us to put our trust in creatures:

Put not your trust in princes? Further, he pronounces a curse on those who do so: Cursed be the man that trusteth in man? God does not wish us to trust in creatures, because he does not wish us to fix our love upon them. Hence St. Vincent of Paul said: "Let us beware of reposing too much confidence in men; for when God beholds us thus leaning on them for support, he himself withdraws from us." On the other hand, the more we trust in God, the more we shall advance in his holy love: I have run the way of Thy commandments, when Thou didst enlarge my heart? Oh, how rapidly does that soul advance in perfection that has her heart dilated with confidence in God! She flies rather than runs; for by making God the foundation of all her hope, she flings aside her own weakness, and borrows the strength of God himself, which is communicated to all who place their confidence in him: They that hope in the Lord shall renew their strength, they shall take wings as eagles, they shall run and not be weary, they shall walk and not faint? The eagle is the bird that soars nearest the sun; in like manner, the soul that has God for her trust becomes detached from the earth, and more and more united to God by love.

The primary object of Christian hope is God, whom the soul enjoys in the kingdom of heaven. But we must not suppose that the hope of enjoying God in Paradise is any obstacle to charity; since the hope of Paradise is inseparably connected with charity, which there receives its full and complete perfection. Charity is that infinite treasure, spoken of by the Wise Man, which makes us the friends of God: An infinite treasure to men, which they that use become the friends of God. The angelic Doctor St. Thomas says, that friendship is founded on the mutual communication of goods; for as friendship is nothing more than a mutual love between friends, it follows that there must be a reciprocal interchange of the good which each possesses. Hence the saint says: "If there be no communication, there is no friendship." On this account Jesus Christ says to his disciples: I have called you friends, because all things whatsoever I have heard of My Father I have made known to you? Since he had made them his friends, he had communicated all his secrets to them.

St. Francis de Sales says: "If, by a supposition of what is impossible, there could be an infinite good (that is a God) to whom we belonged in no way whatever, and with whom we could have no union or communication, we should certainly esteem him more than ourselves; so that we might feel great desire of being able to love him; but we should not actually love him, because love is built upon union; for love is a friendship, and the foundation of friendship is to have things in common; and its end is union." Thus St. Thomas teaches us that charity does not exclude the desire of the reward prepared for us in heaven by Almighty God; on the contrary, it makes us look to it as the chief object of our love, for such is God, who constitutes the bliss of paradise; for friendship implies, that friends rejoice with one another.

The Spouse in the Canticles refers to this reciprocal interchange of goods, when she says: My Beloved to me and I to Him? In heaven the soul belongs wholly to God and God belongs wholly to the soul, according to the measure of her capacity and of her merits. But from the persuasion which the soul has of her own nothingness in comparison with the infinite attractions of Almighty God, and aware consequently that the claims of God on her love are beyond measure greater than her own can be on the love of God, she is therefore more anxious to procure the divine pleasure than her own enjoyment; so that she is more gratified by the pleasure which she affords Almighty God by giving herself entirely to him, than by God s giving himself entirely to her; but at the same time she is delighted when God thus gives himself to her, inasmuch as she is thereby animated to give herself up to God with a greater intensity, of love. She indeed rejoices at the glory which God imparts to her, but for the sole purpose of referring it back to God himself, and of thus doing her utmost to increase the divine glory. At the sight of God in heaven the soul cannot help loving him with all her strength on the other hand, God cannot hate any one that loves him but if (supposing what is impossible) God could hate a soul that loves him, and if a beatified soul could exist without loving God, she would much rather endure all the pains of hell, on condition of being allowed to love God as much as he should hate her, than to live without loving God. even though she could enjoy all the other delights of Paradise. So it is; for that conviction which the soul has of God's boundless claims upon her love gives her a greater desire to love God than to be loved by him.

Charity hopeth all things. St. Thomas, with the Master of the Sentences, defines Christian hope to be a "sure expectation of eternal happiness." Its certainty arises from the infallible promise of God to give eternal life to his faithful servants. Now charity, by taking away sin, at the same time takes ways all obstacles to our obtaining the happiness of the blessed; hence the greater our charity, the greater also and firmer is our hope on the other hand, can in no way interfere with the purity of love, because, according to the observation of St. Dionysius the Areopagite, love tends naturally to union with the object beloved; or, as St. Augustine asserts in stronger terms, love itself is like a chain of gold that links together the hearts of the lover and the loved. "Love is as it were a kind of bond uniting two together." And as this union can never be effected at a distance, the person that loves always longs for the presence of the object of his love. The sacred spouse languished in the absence of her beloved, and entreated her companions to acquaint him with her sorrow, that he might come and console her with his presence I adjure you, O daughters of Jerusalem, if you find my Beloved, that you tell Him that I languish with love. A soul that loves Jesus Christ exceedingly cannot but desire and hope, as long as she remains on earth, to go without delay and be united to her beloved Lord in heaven.

Behold, then, the scope of all our desires and aspirations, of all our thoughts and ardent hopes; to go and enjoy God in heaven, in order to love him with all our strength, and to rejoice in the enjoyment of God. The blessed certainly rejoice in their own felicity in that kingdom of delights;

but the chief source of their happiness, and that which absorbs all the rest, is to know

that their beloved Lord possesses an infinite happiness; for they love God incomparably more than themselves. Each one of the blessed has such a love for him, that he would willingly forfeit all happiness, and undergo the most cruel torments, rather than that God should lose (if it were possible for him to lose) one, even the least particle of his happiness. Hence the sight of God's in

finite happiness, and the knowledge that it can never suffer diminution for all eternity, constitutes his paradise. This is the meaning of what our Lord says to every soul on whom he bestows the possession of eternal glory: Enter into the joy of thy Lord. It is not the joy that enters into the blessed soul, but the soul that enters into the joy of God, since the joy of God is the object of the joy of the blessed. Thus the good of God will be the good of the blessed; the riches of God will

be their riches, and the happiness of God will be their happiness.

On the instant that a soul enters heaven, and sees by the light of glory the infinite beauty of God face to face, she is at once seized and all consumed with love. The happy soul is then as it were lost and immersed in that boundless ocean of the goodness of God. Then it is that she quite forgets herself, and inebriated with divine love, thinks only of loving her God: They shall be inebriated with the plenty of Thy House? As an intoxicated person no longer thinks of himself, so a soul in bliss can only think of loving and affording delight to her beloved Lord; she desires to possess him entirely, and she does in fact possess him, without fear of losing him anymore;

she desires to give herself wholly to him, at every moment, and she does indeed possess him for every moment she offers herself to God without reserve, and God receives her in his loving embraces, and so holds her, and shall hold her in the same fond embraces for all eternity.

In this manner the soul is wholly united to God in heaven, and loves him with all her strength; her love is most perfect and complete, and though necessarily finite, since a creature is not capable of infinite love, it nevertheless renders her perfectly happy and contented, so that she desires nothing more. On the other hand, Almighty God communicates himself, and unites himself wholly to the soul, filling her with himself proportionately to her merits; and this union is not merely by means only of his gifts, lights, and loving attractions, as is the case during the present life, but by his own very essence. As fire penetrates iron, and seems to change it into itself, so does God penetrate the soul and fill her with himself; and though she never loses her own being, yet she becomes so penetrated and absorbed by that immense ocean of the divine substance, that she remains, as it were, annihilated, and as if she ceased to exist. The Apostle prayed for this happy lot for his disciples when he said: That you may be filled unto all the fullness of God.

The holy souls in purgatory feel no pain more acutely than that of their yearning to possess God, from whom they remain still at a distance. And this sort of pain will afflict those especially who in their lifetime had but little desire of paradise. Cardinal Bellarmine also says,

that there is a certain place in purgatory called, prison of honor, where certain souls are not tormented with any pain of sense, but merely with the pain of privation of the sight of God; examples of this are related by St. Gregory, Venerable Bede, St. Vincent Ferrer, and St. Bridget;

and this punishment is not for the commission of sin, but for coldness in desiring heaven. Many souls aspire to perfection; but for the rest, they are too indifferent whether they go to enjoy the sight of God, or continue on earth. But eternal life is an inestimable good, that has been purchased by the death of Jesus Christ; and God punishes such souls as have been during life in their desires to obtain it.

Affections and Prayers

O God, my Creator and my Redeemer, Thou hast created me for heaven; Thou hast redeemed me from hell to bring me into heaven; and I have so many times, in Thy very face, renounced my claim to heaven by my sins, and have remained contented in seeing myself doomed to hell! But blessed forever be Thy infinite mercy, which, I would fain hope, has pardoned me, and many a time rescued me from perdition. Ah, my Jesus, would that I had never offended Thee! would that I had always loved Thee! I am glad that at least I have still time to do so. I love Thee! O love of my soul, I love Thee with my whole heart; I love Thee more than myself! I see plainly that Thou wishest to save me, that I may be able to love Thee for all eternity in that kingdom of love. I thank Thee, and beseech Thee to help me for the remainder of my life, in which I wish to love Thee most ardently, that I may ardently love Thee in eternity. Ah, my Jesus, when will the day arrive that shall free me from all danger of losing Thee, that, shall consume me with love, by unveiling before my eyes Thy infinite beauty, so that I shall be under the necessity of loving Thee? Oh, sweet necessity! oh, happy and dear and most desired necessity, which shall relieve me from all fear of evermore displeasing Thee, and shall oblige me to love Thee with all my strength ! My conscience alarms me, and says: "How canst Thou presume to enter heaven?" But, my dearest Redeemer, Thy merits are all my hope.

O Mary, Queen of Heaven, thy intercession is all-powerful with God, in thee I put my trust!

CHAPTER XIII

CHARITY BEARETH ALL THINGS
He that loves Jesus Christ with a Strong Love does not cease to love Him in the midst of all Sorts of Temptations and Desolations

It is not the pains of poverty, of sickness, of dishonor and persecution, which in this life most afflict the souls that love God, but temptations and desolations of spirit. Whilst a soul is in the enjoyment of the loving presence of God, she is so far from grieving at all the afflictions and ignominies and outrages of men, that she is rather comforted by them, as they afford her an opportunity of showing God a token of her love; they serve, in short, as fuel to enkindle her love more and more. But to find herself solicited by temptations to forfeit the divine grace, or in the hour of desolation to apprehend having already lost it, oh, these are torments too cruel to bear for one who loves Jesus Christ with all her heart! However, the same love supplies her with strength to endure all patiently, and to pursue the way of perfection, on which she has entered. And, oh, what progress do those souls make by means of these trials, which God is pleased to send them in order to prove their love!

Temptations

Temptations are the most grievous trials that can happen to a soul that loves Jesus Christ; she accepts with resignation of every other evil, as calculated only to bind her in closer union with God; but temptations to commit sin would drive her, as we said above, to a separation from Jesus Christ; and on this account they are more intolerable to her than all other afflictions.

Why God permits Temptations

We must know, however, that although no temptation to evil can ever come from God, but only from the devil or our own corrupt inclinations: for God is not a tempter of evils, end he tempteth no man nevertheless, God does at times permit his most cherished souls to be the most grievously tempted.

In the first place, in order that from temptations the soul may better learn her own weakness, and the need she has of the divine assistance not to fall. Whilst a soul is favored with heavenly consolations, she feels as if she were able to vanquish every assault of the enemy, and to achieve every undertaking for the glory of God. But when she is strongly tempted, and is almost reeling on the edge of the precipice, and just ready to fall, then she becomes better acquainted with her own misery and with her inability to resist, if God did not come to her rescue. So it fared with St. Paul, who tells us that God had suffered him to be troubled with a temptation to sensual pleasure, in order to keep him humble after the revelations with which God had favored him: And lest the greatness of the revelations should exalt me, there was given me a sting of my flesh an angel of Satan to buffet me.

Besides, God permits temptations with a view to detach us more thoroughly from this life; and to kindle in us the desire to go and behold him in heaven. Hence pious souls, finding themselves attacked day and night by so many enemies, come at length to feel a loathing for life, and exclaim: Wo is me, that my sojourning is prolonged. And they sigh for the moment when they can say: The snare is broken and we are delivered. The soul would willingly wing her flight to God; but as long as she lives upon this earth she is bound by a snare which detains her here below, where she is continually assailed with temptations; this snare is only broken by death so that the souls that love God sigh for death, which will deliver them from all danger of losing him.

Almighty God, moreover, allows us to be tempted, to make us richer in merits; as it was said to Tobias: And because thou was acceptable to God, it was necessary that temptations should prove thee? Thus a soul need not imagine herself out of God's favor because she is tempted, but should make it rather a motive of hope that God loves her. It is a delusion of the devil to lead some pusillanimous persons to suppose that temptations are sins that contaminate the soul. It is not bad thoughts that make us lose God, but the consenting to them; let the suggestions of the devil be ever so violent, let those filthy imaginations which overload our minds be ever so lively, they cannot cast the least stain on our souls, provided only we yield no consent to them; on the contrary, they make the soul purer, stronger, and dearer to Almighty God. St. Bernard says, that every time we overcome a temptation we win a fresh crown in heaven: "As often as we conquer, so often are we crowned." An angel once appeared to a Cistercian monk, and put a crown into his hands, with orders that he should carry it to one of his fellow-religious, as a reward for the temptation that he had lately overcome.

Remedies against Temptations

Let us come now to the means which we have to employ in order to vanquish temptations. Spiritual masters prescribe a variety of means; but the most necessary, and the safest (of which only I will here speak), is to have immediate recourse to God with all humility and confidence, saying: Incline unto my aid, O God; O Lord, make haste to help me! This short prayer will enable us to overcome the assaults of all the devils of hell; for God is infinitely more powerful than all of them. Almighty God knows well that of ourselves we are unable to resist the temptations of the infernal powers; and on this account the most learned Cardinal Gotti remarks,

"that whenever we are assailed, and in danger of being overcome, God is obliged to give us strength enough to resist as often as we call upon him for it."

And how can we doubt of receiving help from Jesus Christ, after all the promises that he has made us in the Holy Scriptures? Come to Me, all you that labor and are heavy laden, and I will refresh you? Come to me, ye who are wearied in fighting against temptations, and I will restore your strength. Call upon Me in the day of trouble: I will deliver thee, and thou shalt honor Me. When thou seest thyself troubled by thine enemies, call upon me, and I will bring thee out of the danger, and thou shalt praise me. Then shalt thou call, and the Lord shall hear: thou shalt cry, and He shall say, Here I am. Then shalt thou call upon the Lord for help, and he will hear thee: thou shalt cry out, Quick, O Lord, help me! and he will say to thee, Behold, here I am; I am present to help thee. Who hath called upon Him, and He despised him? And who, says the prophet, has ever called upon God, and God has despised him without giving him help? David felt sure of never falling a prey to his enemies, whilst he could have recourse to prayer; he says: Praising, I will call upon the Lord: and I shall be saved from my enemies? For he well knew that God is close to all who invoke his aid: The Lord is nigh unto all them that call upon Him?

Should the temptation, however, obstinately persist in attacking us, let us beware of becoming troubled or angry at it; for this might put it in the power of our enemy to overcome us. We must, on such occasions, make an act of humble resignation to the will of God, who thinks fit to allow us to be tormented by these abominable temptations; and we must say: O Lord, I deserve to be molested with these filthy suggestions, in punishment of my past sins; but Thou must help to free me. And as long as the temptation lasts, let us never cease calling on Jesus and Mary. It is also very profitable, in the like importunity of temptations, to renew our firm purpose to God of suffering every torment, and a thousand deaths, rather than offend him; and at the same time we must invoke his divine assistance. And even should the temptation be of such violence as to put us in imminent risk of consenting to it, we must then redouble our prayers, hasten into the presence of the Blessed Sacrament, cast ourselves at the feet of the crucifix, or of some image of our Blessed Lady, and there pray with increased fervor, and cry out for help with groans and tears. God is certainly ready to hear all who pray to him; and it is from him alone, and not from our own exertions, that we must look for strength to resist; but sometimes Almighty God wills these struggles of us, and then he makes up for our weakness, and grants us the victory. It is an excellent practice also, in the moment of temptation, to make the sign of the cross on the forehead and breast. It is also of great service to discover the temptation to our spiritual director. St. Philip Neri used to say, that a temptation disclosed is half overcome.

Wherefore, with regard to certain souls of delicate conscience, and solidly rooted in virtue, but at the same time timid and molested with temptations (especially if they be against faith or chastity), the director will find it sometimes expedient to forbid them to discover them or make any mention of them; because, if they have to mention them they are led to consider how such thoughts got entrance into their minds, and whether they paused to dispute with them, or took any complacency in them, or gave any consent to them; and so, by this too great reflection, those evil imaginations make a still deeper impression on their minds, and disturb them the more. Whenever the confessor is morally certain that the penitent has not consented to these suggestions, the best way is to forbid him to speak any more about them. And I find that St. Jane Frances de Chantal acted precisely in this manner. She relates of herself, that she was for several years assailed by the most violent storms of temptation, but had never spoken of them in confession, since she was not conscious of having ever yielded to them; and in this she had only followed faithfully the rule received from her director. She says, "I never had a full conviction of having consented." These words give us to understand that the temptations did produce in her some agitation from scruples; but in spite of these, she resumed her tranquility on the strength of the obedience imposed by her confessor, not to confess similar doubts. With this exception, it will be generally found an admirable means of quelling the violence of temptations to lay them open to our director, as we have said above.

But I repeat, the most efficacious and the most necessary all remedies against temptations, is that remedy of all remedies, namely, to pray to God for help, and to continue praying as long as the temptation continues. Almighty God will frequently have decreed success, not to the first prayer, but to the second, third, or fourth. In short, we must be thoroughly persuaded that all our welfare depends on prayer: our amendment of life depends on prayer; our victory over temptations depends on prayer; on prayer depends our obtaining divine love, together with perfection, perseverance, and eternal salvation.

Affections and Prayers

O Jesus, My Redeemer, I trust in Thy blood, that Thou hast forgiven me all my offences against Thee; and I fondly hope to come one day to bless Thee for it eternally in heaven: The mercies of the Lord I will sing forever? I plainly see now that I have over and over again fallen in times past, from the want of entreating Thee for holy perseverance. I earnestly beg Thee at this present moment to grant me perseverance: "Never suffer me to be separated from Thee." And I purpose to make this prayer to Thee always; but especially when I am tempted to offend Thee. I indeed make this resolution and promise; but what will it profit me thus to resolve and promise, if Thou dost not give me the grace to run and cast myself at Thy feet? By the merits, then, of Thy sacred Passion, oh, grant me this grace, in all my necessities to have recourse to Thee.

O Mary, my Queen, and my Mother, I beseech thee, by thy tender love for Jesus Christ, to procure me the grace of always fleeing for succor, as long as I live, to thy blessed Son and to thee.

II
Desolations

St. Francis de Sales says: "It is a mistake to estimate devotions by the consolations which we feel. True devotion in the way of God consists in having a determined will to execute all that is pleasing to God." Almighty God is wont to make use of aridities in order to draw closer to him his most cherished souls. Attachment to our own inordinate inclinations is the greatest obstacle to true union with God; and when, therefore, God intends to draw a soul to his perfect love, he endeavors to detach her from all affection to created goods. Thus his first care is to deprive her of temporal goods, of worldly pleasures, of property, honors, friends, relatives, and bodily health; by the like means of losses, troubles, neglects, bereavements, and infirmities, he extirpates by degrees all earthly attachment, in order that the affections may beset on him alone.

With a view to produce a fondness for spiritual things, God regales the soul at first with great consolations, with an abundance of tears and tenderness; she is thus easily weaned from the gratifications of sense, and seeks further to mortify herself with works of penance, fasts, hair cloths, and disciplines; at this stage the director must keep a check on her, and not allow her to practice mortifications at least not all those for which she asks permission because, under the spur of this sensible devotions, a soul might easily ruin her health by indiscretion. It is a subtle artifice of the devil, when he beholds a person giving himself up to God, and receiving the consolations and caresses which God generally gives to beginners, to do his utmost to plunge him into the performance of immoderate penances, so as utterly to destroy his health; so that afterwards, by reason of bodily weakness, he not only gives up the mortifications, but prayer, Communion, and all exercises of devotion, and eventually sinks back into his old way of living.

But to come back to our point. The soul then, in the commencement of her conversion to God, tastes the sweetness of those sensible consolations with which God seeks to allure her, and by them to wean her from earthly pleasures; she breaks off her attachment to creatures, and becomes attached to God. Still, her attachment is imperfect, inasmuch as it is fostered more

by that sensibility of spiritual consolations than by the real wish to do what is pleasing to God; and she deceives herself by believing that the greater the pleasure she feels in her devotions, the more she loves Almighty God. The consequence of this is, that if this food of spiritual consolations is stopped, by her being taken from her ordinary exercises of devotion, and employed in other works of obedience, charity, or duties of her state, she is disturbed, and takes it greatly to heart and this is a universal defect in our miserable human nature, to seek our own satisfaction in all that we do. Or again, when she no longer finds this sweet relish of devotion in her exercises, she either forsakes them, or lessens them; and continuing to lessen them from day to day, she at length omits them entirely. And this misfortune befalls many souls who, when called by Almighty God to love him, enter upon the way of perfection, and as long as spiritual sweetness lasts, make a certain progress; but alas! when this is no longer tasted, they leave off all, and resume their former ways. But it is of the highest importance to be fully persuaded that the love of God and perfection do not consist in feelings of tenderness and consolation, but in overcoming self-love, and in following the divine will. St. Francis de Sales says: "God is as worthy of our love when he afflicts us as when he consoles us."

Amid these consolations, it requires no remarkable degree of virtue to forego sensual delights, and to endure affronts and contradictions. The soul in the midst of these sweetnesses can endure all things; but this endurance comes far more frequently from those sensible consolations than from the strength of true love of God. On this account the Lord, with a view to give her a solid foundation in virtue, retires from her, and deprives her of that sensible devotion, that he may rid her of all attachment to self-love, which was fed by such consolations. And hence it happens, that whereas formerly she felt a joy in making acts of offering, of confidence, and of love, now that the vein of consolations is dried up, she makes these acts with coldness and painful effort; and finds a weariness in the most pious exercises, in her prayers, spiritual readings, and Communions; she even finds in them nothing but darkness and fears, and all seems lost to her. She prays and prays again, and is overwhelmed with sadness, because God seems to have abandoned her.

When a soul that loves God finds herself in this state, she must not lose courage; and neither must he who directs her become alarmed. Those sensual movements, those temptations against faith, those feelings of distrust, and those attacks which urge her to hate Almighty God, are fears, are tortures of the soul, are efforts of the enemy; but they are not voluntary, and therefore they are not sins. The sincere lover of Jesus Christ resists valiantly on such occasions, and withholds all consent to such suggestions; but because of the darkness which envelops her, she knows not how to distinguish, her soul is thrown into confusion, and the privation of the presence of divine grace makes her fearful and sad. But it can be soon discovered that in these souls, thus tried by God, all is dread and apprehension, but not truth only ask them, even in their state of desolation, whether they would willingly commit one single deliberate venial sin; they will answer, that they are ready to suffer not one, but a thousand deaths, rather than be guilty of such displeasure to Almighty God.

It is necessary, therefore, to make this distinction, that it is one thing to perform an act of virtue, such as to repel a temptation, to trust in God, to love God, and to will what he wills; and it is another thing to have the consciousness of really making these good acts. This consciousness of doing good contributes to our pleasure; but the profit consists in the first point, that is, in actually doing good. With the first God is satisfied, and deprives the soul of the latter that is, of the consciousness of doing good, in order thus to remove from her all self-satisfaction, which adds nothing to the merit of the action; for our Lord seeks more our real advantage than our own satisfaction.

Wherefore, in this state of desolation the soul must not heed the devil, when he suggests that God has abandoned her; nor must she leave off prayer. This is the object at which the devil is aiming, in order afterwards to drag her down some precipice. St. Teresa writes: "The Lord proves his true lovers by dryness and temptations. What though the dryness should be of life long duration, let the soul never relax in prayer; the time will arrive when all will be abundantly repaid." In such a state of suffering, a person should humble himself by the reflection that his offences against God are undeserving of any milder treatment he should humble himself, and be fully resigned to the divine will, saying: O my Lord, behold me at Thy feet; if it be Thy will that I should remain thus desolate and afflicted for my whole life, and even for all eternity, only grant me Thy grace and the gift of Thy love, and do with me whatever Thou wilt.

It will be useless then, and perhaps a source of greater disquiet, to wish to assure yourself that you are in the grace of God, and that what you experience is only a trial, and not abandonment on the part of God. At such times it is not the will of God that you should have this assurance; and he so wills it for your greater advantage, in order that you may humble yourself the more, and increase your prayers and acts of confidence in his mercy. You desire to see, and God wills that you should not see. For the rest, St. Francis de Sales says: "The resolution not to consent to any sin, however small, is a sure sign that we are in God's grace." But a soul in profound desolation cannot even clearly discern this resolution; nevertheless, in such a state she must not aim at feeling what she wills; it is enough to will with the point of the will. In this manner she should entirely abandon herself into the arms of the divine goodness. Oh, how do such acts of confidence and resignation ravish the heart of God, when made in the midst of the darkness of desolation! Ah, let us simply trust in a God, who (as St. Teresa says) loves us far better than we love ourselves.

Let these souls, then, so dear to God, and who are resolutely determined to belong entirely to him, take comfort, although at the same time they see themselves deprived of every consolation. Their desolation is a sign of their being very acceptable to God, and that he has for them a place prepared in his heavenly kingdom, which overflows with consolations as full as they are lasting. And let them hold for certain, that the more they are afflicted in the present life, so much the more they shall be consoled in eternity: According to the solitude of my sorrows in my heart. Thy comforts have given joy to my soul.

Example

For the encouragement of souls in desolation, I will here mention what is related in the life of St. Jane Frances de Chantal.

For the space of forty years she was tormented by the most fearful interior trials, by temptations, by fears of being in enmity with God, and of being even quite forsaken by him. Her afflictions were so excruciating and unremitting, that she declared her sole ray of comfort came from the thought of death. Moreover she said: "I am so furiously assaulted, that I know not where to hide my poor soul. I seem at times on the point of losing all patience, and of giving up all as utterly lost." "The tyrant of temptation is so relentless," she says, "that any hour of the day I would gladly barter it with the loss of my life; and sometimes it happens that I can neither eat nor sleep."

During the last eight or nine years of her life, her temptations became still more violent. Mother de Chatel said that her saintly Mother de Chantal suffered a continual interior martyrdom night and day, at prayer, at work, and even during sleep; so that she felt the deepest compassion for her. The saint endured assaults against every virtue (except chastity), and had likewise to contend with doubts, darkness, and disgusts. Sometimes God would withdraw all lights from her, and seem indignant with her, and just on the point of expelling her from him; so that terror drove her to look in some other direction for relief but failing to find any, she was obliged to return to look on God, and to abandon herself to his mercy. She seemed each moment ready to yield to the violence of her temptations. The divine assistance did not indeed forsake her; but it seemed to her to have done so, since, instead of finding satisfaction in anything, she found only weariness and anguish in prayer, in reading spiritual books, in Communion, and in all other exercises of piety. Her sole resource in this state of dereliction was to look upon God, and to let him do his will.

Affections and Prayers

O Jesus, my hope, my love and only love of my soul, I deserve not Thy consolations and sweet visitations; keep them for those innocent souls that have always loved Thee; sinner that I am, I do not deserve them, nor do I ask for them this only do I ask, give me grace to love Thee, to accomplish Thy adorable will during my whole life; and then dispose of me as Thou pleasest! Unhappy me! far other darkness, other terrors, other abandonments would be due to the outrages which I have done Thee hell were my just award, where, separated from Thee for ever, and totally abandoned by Thee, I should shed tears eternally, without ever being able to love Thee more. But no, my Jesus, I accept of every punishment; only spare me this. Thou art deserving of an infinite love; Thou hast placed me under an excessive obligation of loving Thee; oh, no, I cannot trust myself to live and not love Thee! I do love Thee, my sovereign good; I love Thee with my whole heart; I love Thee more than myself; I love Thee, and have no other desire than to love Thee. I own that this my good-will is the pure effect of Thy grace; but do Thou, O my Lord, perfect Thy own work; with draw not Thy helping hand till death! Oh, never fora moment leave me in my own hands; give me strength to vanquish temptations and to overcome myself; and for this end give me grace always to have recourse to Thee! I wish to belong wholly to Thee; I give

Thee my body, my soul, my will, and my liberty; I will no longer live for myself, but for Thee alone, my Creator, my Redeemer, my love, and my all : my God and my all. I desire to become a saint, and I hope this of Thee. Afflict me as Thou wilt, deprive me of all; only deprive me not of Thy grace and of Thy love.

O Mary, the hope of sinners, great is thy power with God; I confide fully in thy intercession: I entreat thee by thy love of Jesus Christ, help me, and make me a saint!

NOVENA TO THE HOLY SPIRIT

The Novena to the Holy Spirit is the chief of all the Novenas, because it was the first that was ever celebrated, and that by the holy Apostles and the most holy Mary in the supper-room, and distinguished by so many remarkable wonders and gifts; principally by the gift of the same Holy Spirit, a gift merited for us by the Passion of Jesus Christ himself. Jesus himself made this known to us, when he said to his disciples, that if he did not die, he could not send us the Holy Ghost: If I go not, the Paraclete will not come to you; but if I go, I will send Him to you. We know well by faith that the Holy Ghost is the love that the Father and the Eternal Word bear one to the other; and therefore the gift of love, which the Lord infuses into our souls, and which is the greatest of all gifts, is particularly attributed to the Holy Ghost, as St. Paul says: The charity of God is poured forth in our hearts by the Holy Ghost, who is given to us? In this Novena, therefore, we must consider, above all, the great value of divine love, in order that we may desire to obtain it, and endeavor, by devout exercises, and specially by prayer, to be made partakers of it, since God has promised it to him who asks for it with humility.

MEDITATION I
Love is a Fire that inflames the Heart

God had ordered, in the ancient law, that there should be a fire kept continually burning on his altar: The fire on the altar shall always burn. St. Gregory says, that the altars of God are our hearts, where he desires that the fire of his divine love should always be burning; and therefore the Eternal Father, not satisfied with having given us his Son Jesus Christ, to save us by his death, would also give us the Holy Ghost, that he might dwell in our souls, and keep them constantly on fire with love.

And Jesus himself declared, that he had come into the world on purpose to inflame our hearts with this holy fire, and that he desired nothing more than to see it kindled: I am come to cast fire upon the earth; and what will I but that it be kindled? Forgetting, therefore, the injuries and ingratitude he received from men on this earth, when he had ascended into heaven he sent down upon us the Holy Spirit. O most loving Redeemer, Thou dost, then, love us as well in Thy sufferings and ignominies as in Thy kingdom of glory! Hence it was that the Holy Ghost chose to appear in the supper-room under the form of tongues of fire: And there appeared to them parted tongues, as it were of fire. And hence the Church teaches us to pray: "May the Holy Ghost, we beseech Thee, O Lord, inflame us with that fire which our Lord Jesus Christ came to cast upon the earth, and which he ardently desired should be enkindled."

This was the holy fire which has inflamed the saints to do so great things for God, to love their enemies, to desire contempt, to deprive themselves of all earthly goods, and to embrace with delight even torments and death. Love cannot remain idle, and never says, "It is enough." The soul that loves God, the more she does for her beloved, the more she desires to do, in order to please him, and to attract to herself his affections the more.

This holy fire is enkindled by mental prayer: In my meditation a fire shall flame out? If, therefore, we desire to burn with love towards God, let us love prayer; this is the blessed furnace in which this divine ardor is enkindled.

Affections and Prayers

O my God, hitherto I have done nothing for Thee, who has done such great things for me! Alas! my coldness deserves that Thou shouldst "vomit me out of Thy mouth." O Holy Spirit, I beseech Thee, "warm what is cold," deliver me from this coldness, and enkindle within me an earnest desire of pleasing Thee. I now renounce all my worldly gratifications; and I will rather die than give Thee the least displeasure. Thou didst appear in the shape of fiery tongues; I consecrate my tongue to Thee, that it may never offend Thee more. Thou didst give it me, O my God, to praise Thee with; and I have made use of it to offend Thee, and to draw others also into sinning against Thee. I repent of this with my whole soul. Oh, for the love of Jesus Christ, who, during his life on earth honored Thee so much with his tongue, grant that I also may from this day forth honor Thee constantly, by celebrating Thy praises, by frequently invoking Thy aid, and by speaking of Thy goodness and the infinite love which Thou deservest! I love Thee, my sovereign good, I love Thee, O God of love! O Mary, thou art the most dear spouse of the Holy Ghost, obtain for me this holy fire!

MEDITATION II
Love is a Light that Enlightens the Soul

One of the greatest evils that the sin of Adam has produced in us, is that darkening of our reason by means of the passions which cloud our mind. Oh, how miserable is that soul that allows itself to be ruled by any passion ! Passion, is as it were, a vapor, a veil which prevents us from seeing the truth. How can he fly from evil, who does not know what is evil? Besides, this obscurity increases in proportion as our sins increase, But the Holy Spirit, who is called "most blessed light," is he who not only inflames our hearts to love him, through his divine splendor, but also dispels our darkness, and shows us the vanity of earthly things, the value of eternal goods, the importance of salvation the price of grace, the goodness of God, the infinite love which he deserves, and the immense love which he bears us. The sensual man perceiveth not those things that are of the Spirit of God? A man who is absorbed in the pleasures of earth knows little of these truths, and therefore, unfortunate that he is, he loves what he ought to hate, and hates what he ought to love. St. Mary Magdalene of Pazzi exclaimed: "O love not known! O love not loved!" And therefore St. Teresa said that God is not loved because he is not known.

Affections and Prayers

O holy and divine Spirit, I believe that Thou art really God, but one only God with the Father and the Son. I adore Thee, and acknowledge Thee as the giver of all those lights by which Thou hast made known to me the evil which I have committed in offending Thee, and the obligation which I am under of loving Thee. I thank Thee for them, and I repent with my whole heart of having offended Thee. I have deserved that Thou shouldst abandon me in my darkness; but I see that Thou hast not yet forsaken me. Continue, O eternal Spirit, to enlighten me, and to make me know more and more Thy infinite goodness; and give me strength to love Thee for the future with my whole heart. Add grace to grace; so that I may be sweetly overcome, and constrained to love none other but Thee. I implore this of Thee, through the merits of Jesus Christ. I love Thee, my sovereign good; I love Thee more than myself. I desire to be entirely Thine; do Thou accept me, and suffer me not to be separated from Thee any more. O Mary, my Mother, do thou always assist me by thy intercession!

MEDITATION III
Love is a Fountain that Satisfies

Love is also called a living fountain: "a living fountain, fire, and charity." Our Blessed Redeemer said to the Samaritan woman: "But he that shall drink of the water that I will give him shall not thirst for ever." Love is the water which satisfies our thirst; he who loves God really with his whole heart neither seeks nor desires anything else; because in God he finds every good. Wherefore, satisfied with God, he often joyfully ex claims, "My God and my all!" My God, Thou art my whole good.

But the Almighty complains that man's souls go about seeking for fleeting and miserable pleasures from creatures, and leave him, who is the infinite good and fountain of all joy: They have forsaken Me, the fountain of living water, and have digged to themselves cisterns, broken cisterns, that bean hold no water. Wherefore God, who loves us, and desires to see us happy, cries out and makes known to all: If any thirst, let them come to me? He who desires to be happy, let him come to me; and I will give him the Holy Ghost, who will make him blessed both in this life and the next. He that believeth in Me (he goes on to say), as the Scripture saith, Out of his belly shall flow rivers of living water? He therefore, that believes in Jesus Christ, and loves him, shall be enriched with so much grace, that from his heart (the heart, that is, the will), shall flow many fountains of holy virtues, which shall not only serve to preserve his own life, but also to give life to others.

Affections and Prayers

Lord, give me this water? O my Jesus, with the Samaritan woman, I beseech Thee, give me this water of Thy love, which may make me forget the earth, to live only for Thee, O amiable, infinite one. "Water that which is dry." My soul is a barren soil, which produces nothing but the weeds and thorns of sin; oh, do Thou water it with Thy grace, so that it may bring forth some fruits to Thy glory, before death takes me out of this world. O fountain of living water, O sovereign good, how many times have I left Thee for the puddles of this earth, which have deprived me of Thy love! Oh, would that I had died before I offended Thee! But for the future I will seek after nothing but Thee, O my God. Do Thou assist me, and enable me to be faithful to Thee. Mary, my hope, do thou keep me always under thy protection!

MEDITATION IV
Love is a Dew which fertilizes

Thus does Holy Church teach us to pray: "May the infusion of the Holy Ghost cleanse our hearts, and fertilize them by the interior sprinkling of his dew." Love fertilizes the good desires, the holy purposes, and the good works of our souls: these are the flowers and fruits which the grace of the Holy Spirit produces. Love is also called dew, because it cools the heart of bad passions and of temptations. Therefore the Holy Ghost is also called refreshment and cooling in the heat: "In heat refreshment and pleasing coolness." This dew descends into our hearts in the time of prayer. A quarter of an hour s prayer is sufficient to appease every passion of hatred or of inordinate love, however ardent it may be: He brought me into the cellar of wine, He set in order charity in me? Holy meditation is this cellar where love is set in order, so that we love our neighbor as ourselves, and God above everything. He who loves God loves prayer; and he that loves not prayer will find it morally impossible to overcome his passions.

Affections and Prayers

O holy and divine Spirit, I will no longer live to myself; but I will spend all the days that remain for me in this lire in loving Thee and pleasing Thee. Therefore I beseech Thee to grant me the gift of prayer. Do Thou descend into my heart, and teach me to pray as I ought. Give me strength not to leave it off through weariness in times of aridity; and give me the spirit of prayer, that is to say, the grace constantly to pray to Thee, and to use those prayers which are clearest to Thy Sacred Heart. I was once lost through my sins; but I see, from all the kind nesses I have received from Thee, that Thou wiliest that I should be saved and become a saint; and I desire to become a saint to give Thee pleasure, and that I may love Thy infinite goodness more and more. I love Thee, O my sovereign good, my love, my all; and because I love Thee I give myself entirely to Thee. O Mary, my hope, do thou protect me!

MEDITATION V
Love is a Repose that refreshes

Love is also called, "in labor rest, in mourning comfort." Love is repose that refreshes; because the principal office of love is to unite the will of the lover to that of the beloved one. To a soul that loves God, in every affront that it receives, in every sorrow that it endures, in every loss that happens to it, the knowledge that it is the will of its beloved that it should suffer these trials is enough to comfort it. It finds peace and contentment in all tribulations by merely saying, This is the will of my God. This is that peace which surpasses all the pleasure of sense: The peace of God which surpasseth all understanding? St. Mary Magdalene of Pazzi, by merely saying, "The will of God," was always filled with joy.

In this life everyone must carry his cross; but St. Teresa says, that the cross is heavy for him that drags it, not for him that embraces it. Thus our Lord knows well how to strike and how to heal: He woundeth and cureth, says Job. The Holy Spirit, by his sweet unction, renders even ignominies and torments sweet and pleasant: Yea, Lord; for so hath it seemed good in Thy sight. Thus ought we to say in all adversities that happen to us: So be it done. Lord, because so hath it pleased Thea. And when the fear of any temporal evil that may befall us alarms us, let us always say: "Do what Thou wilt, my God; whatever Thou doest, I accept it all, hence forth."

Affections and Prayers

O my God, how often, for the sake of doing my own will, have I opposed myself to Thy will and despised it! I regret this evil more than every other evil. O Lord, from this day forward I will love Thee with my whole heart: Speak, Lord; for Thy servant heareth. Tell me what Thou wouldst have me to do, I will do it all. Thy will shall be my only desire, my only love. O Holy Spirit, help my weakness. Thou art goodness itself; how can I love any other but Thee? Oh, do Thou draw all my affections to Thyself by the sweetness of Thy holy love. I renounce everything, to give myself entirely to Thee. Do Thou accept me and help me. O Mary, my Mother, I trust in thee!

MEDITATION VI
Love is the Virtue which gives us Strength

Love is strong as death. As there is no created strength that can resist death, so there is no difficulty for a loving soul that love cannot overcome. When there is question of pleasing its beloved, love conquers all, losses, contempt, and sorrow: "Nothing is so hard, but that the fire of love can conquer it."

This is the most certain mark whereby to know if a soul really loves God, if it is as faithful in love when things are adverse as when they are prosperous. St. Francis de Sales said, that "God is quite as amiable when he chastises as when he consoles us, because he does all for love." Indeed, when he strikes us most in this life, then it is that he loves us most. St. John Chrysostom& esteemed St. Paul in chains more fortunate than St. Paul rapt up into the third heaven.

Affections and Prayers

O God of my soul, I say that I love Thee; and yet what do I do for Thy love? Nothing. This shows, therefore, that either I do not love Thee, or I love Thee too little. Send me there fore, O my Jesus, Thy Holy Spirit, that he may come and give me strength to suffer for Thy love, and to do something for the love of Thee before death overtakes me. O my beloved Redeemer, let me not die cold and ungrateful as I have hitherto been to Thee. Grant me strength to love suffering, after so many sins whereby I have deserved hell. O my God, who art all goodness and love, Thou desirest to dwell in my heart from which I have so often expelled Thee; come, then, dwell within it, take possession of it, and make it entirely Thine. I love Thee, O my Lord; and if I love Thee, Thou art already with me, as St. John assures me: He that abideth in charity abideth in God, and God in him? Since, therefore, Thou art with me, increase the flames, increase the chains, so that I may neither seek nor love anything else but Thee; and thus bound, may never be separated from Thy love. I desire to be Thine, O my Jesus, and entirely Thine. O Mary, my Queen and Advocate, obtain for me love and perseverance!

MEDITATION VII
Love causes God to dwell in our Souls

The Holy Ghost is called "Sweet guest of the soul." This was the great promise made by Jesus Christ to those who love him, when he said: If you love Me, I will pray My Father, and He will send you the Holy Spirit, that He may always dwell in you. If you love Me, keep My commandments. And I will ask the Father, and He shall give you another Paraclete, that He may abide with you forever. For the Holy Spirit never forsakes a soul, says the Council of Trent, if he is not driven away from it: "He does not forsake, unless he be first forsaken."

Affections and Prayers

O my God, I see that Thou desirest to have me entirely for Thine own. I have oftentimes driven Thee from my soul, and yet Thou hast not disdained to return to me and reunite Thy self to me again. Oh, do Thou now take possession of my whole self. I give myself this day entirely to Thee; accept of me, O my Jesus, and let me never for the future live one moment deprived of Thy love. Thou seekest me, and I seek none other but Thee. Thou desirest my soul, and my soul desires none but Thee. Thou lovest me, and I love Thee; and since Thou lovest me, bind me to Thyself, so that I may never more be separated from Thee. O Queen of heaven, I trust in thee!

MEDITATION VIII
Love is a Bond which binds

As the Holy Spirit, who is uncreated love, is the in dissoluble bond which binds the Father to the Eternal Word, so he also unites the soul to God. "Charity is a virtue," says St. Augustine, "uniting us to God." Hence, full of joy, St. Laurence Justinian exclaims: O love, thy bond has such strength, that it is able to bind even God, and unite him to our souls: "O love, how strong is thy bond, which could bind God!"

The bonds of the world are bonds of death; but the bonds of God are bonds of life and salvation: Her bonds are a healthful binding? Yes, because the bonds of God by means of love unite us to God, who is our true and only life.

Before the coming of Jesus Christ men fled away from God, and being attached to the earth, refused to unite themselves to their Creator; but the loving God has drawn them to himself by the bonds of love, as he promised by the prophet O see: I will draw them with the cords of Adam, with the bands of love? These bands are the benefits, the lights, the calls to his love, the promises of paradise, which he makes to us; but above all, the gift which he has bestowed upon us of Jesus Christ in the Sacrifice of the Cross and in the Sacrament of the Altar, and finally, the gift of his Holy Spirit. Therefore the prophet exclaims: Loose the bonds from off thy neck, O captive daughter of Zion? O my soul, thou who art created for heaven, loose thyself from the bonds of earth, and unite thyself to God by the bonds of holy love: Have charity, which is the bond of perfection. Love is a bond which unites to herself all other virtues, and makes the soul

perfect. "Love, and do what you will," said St. Augustine. Love God, and do what thou wilt; because he who loves God tries to avoid causing any displeasure to his beloved, and seeks in all things to please him.

Affections and Prayers

My dearest Jesus, how much hast Thou not done to oblige me to love Thee, and how much hath it cost Thee to gain to Thy self my love! Ah, I should be too ungrateful if I loved Thee little, or divided my heart between Thy creatures and Thyself, after Thou hast given me Thy blood and Thy life. I will detach myself from everything, and in Thee alone will I place all my affections. But I am weak in carrying out this my desire ; O Thou who hast inspired me with it, do Thou give me strength to execute it. Pierce my poor soul, O dearest Jesus, with the sweet dart of Thy love, so that I may ever languish with desire of Thee, and be dissolved with the love of Thee; that I may seek Thee alone, desire only Thee, and find none but Thee. My Jesus, I desire Thee, and Thee alone. Make me repeat continually in this life, and especially at the hour of my death, "Thee alone do I desire, and nothing else." O Mary, my Mother, obtain for me that henceforth I may desire nothing but God.

MEDITATION IX
Love is a Treasure containing every Good

Love is that treasure of which the Gospel says that we must leave all to obtain it; yes, because love makes us partakers of the friendship of God: An infinite treasure to men, which they that use become the friends of God. O man, says St. Augustine, wherefore, then, goest thou about seeking for good things seek that one good alone in which all other good things are contained. But we cannot find God, who is this sovereign good, if we do not forsake the things of the earth. St. Teresa writes, "Detach thy heart from creatures, and thou shalt find God."

He that finds God finds all that he can desire: Delight in the Lord, and He will give thee the requests of thy heart? The human heart is constantly seeking after good things that may render it happy; but if it seeks them from creatures, how much so ever it may acquire, it will never be satisfied with them; but if it seeks God alone, God will satisfy all its desires.

Affections and Prayers

O my God, hitherto I have not sought Thee, but myself and my own pleasures; and for the sake of these I have turned my back upon Thee, my sovereign good. But I am comforted by these words of Jeremias, The Lord is good to the soul that seeketh Him? They tell me that Thou art all goodness towards him who seeks Thee. My beloved Savior, I know the evil that I have committed in forsaking Thee, and I repent of it with my whole heart. I know that Thou art an infinite treasure. I will not abuse this light; I will forsake all, and choose Thee for my only love. My God, my love, my all, I love Thee, I desire Thee, I sigh after Thee. Come, O Holy Spirit, and destroy in me by Thy sacred fire every affection which has not Thee for its object. Grant that I may be all Thine, and that I may conquer everything to please Thee. O Mary, my advocate and Mother, do thou help me by thy prayers!

MEDITATION X
The Means of loving God and of becoming a Saint

The more we love God, the more holy do we become. St. Francis Borgia says that it is prayer that introduces divine love into the human heart; and it is mortification that withdraws the heart from the earth, and renders it capable of receiving this holy fire. The more there is of the earth in the heart, the less room there is for holy love: Wisdom is not to be found in the land of them that live in delights. Hence the saints have always sought to mortify as much as possible their self-love and their senses. The saints are few; but we must live with the few, if we will be saved with the few: "Live with the few," writes St. John Climacus, "if you would reign with the few." And St. Bernard says, "That cannot be perfect which is not singular." He who would lead a perfect life must lead a singular life.

We must therefore be of good courage, make strong resolutions, and begin. Prayer can do everything. What we cannot do by our own strength, we shall do easily with the help of God, who has promised to give us whatever we ask of him: You shall ask whatever you will, and it shall be done unto you?

Affections and Prayers

My dearest Redeemer, Thou desirest my love, and commandest me to love Thee with my whole heart. Yes, my Jesus, I desire to love Thee with my whole heart. O my God, I will say to Thee, trusting in Thy mercy, my past sins do not make me fear, because I now hate them and detest them above every other evil; and I know that Thou dost forget the offences of a soul that is penitent and loves Thee. Indeed, because I have offended Thee more than others, I will also love Thee more than others, with the help that I hope to obtain from Thee. O my Lord, Thou desirest that I should be a saint; and I desire to become a saint to please Thee. I love Thee, O infinite goodness. To Thee do I give myself entirely. Thou art my only good, my only love. Accept of me, O my beloved, and make me entirely Thine, and suffer me not to offend Thee any more. Grant that I may be wholly consumed for Thee, as Thou hast wholly consumed Thyself for me, O Mary, the most loving and most beloved spouse of the Holy Spirit, obtain for me love and fidelity!

Manufactured by Amazon.ca
Bolton, ON